ARVO PÄRT

Oxford Studies of Composers

Arvo Pärt

PAUL HILLIER

Oxford New York

OXFORD UNIVERSITY PRESS

·1997

Oxford University Press, Great Clarendon Street, Oxford OX2 6DP

Oxford New York
Athens Auckland Bangkok Bombay Bogota
Buenos Aires Calcutta Cape Town Dar es Salaam
Delhi Florence Hong Kong Istanbul Karachi
Kuala Lumpur Madras Madrid Melbourne
Mexico City Nairobi Paris Singapore
Taipei Tokyo Toronto

and associated companies in
Berlin Ibadan

Oxford is a trade mark of Oxford University Press

Published in the United States
by Oxford University Press Inc., New York

British Library Cataloguing in Publication Data
Data available

Library of Congress Cataloging in Publication Data
Hillier, Paul.
The music of Arvo Pärt / Paul Hillier.
p. cm. — (Oxford studies of composers)
'List of works by Arvo Pärt': p.
Discography: p.
Includes bibliographical references and index.
1. Pärt, Arvo—Criticism and interpretation.   I. Title.
II. Series.
ML410.P1755H55   1997   780'.92–dc20   96-26035
ISBN 0-19-816550-1 (cloth)
ISBN 0-19-816616-8 (pbk.)

1 3 5 7 9 10 8 6 4 2

Typeset by Best-set Typesetter Ltd., Hong Kong
Printed in Great Britain
on acid-free paper by
Biddles Ltd
Guildford & Kings Lynn

This book is
for
Lena, Clara, and Kaia

PREFACE

It was in London's Victoria Station that I first met Arvo Pärt, on a rainy January day in 1984. He was travelling back to Germany with his young son after visiting friends who lived in Essex. On the train to Gatwick I plied him with questions about various works, my wife, who speaks Estonian, translating. This meeting led eventually to a BBC Radio programme, which in turn led directly to the Arbos recording, and then on to many, many performances, and to the recordings of *Passio*, *Miserere*, and other works.

I had first encountered Pärt's music a couple of years earlier. The initial attraction was essentially visual: the notation had the appearance of having been refracted through medieval music, though there was also something else that fascinated me. The scores I saw then (small, oblong productions that had been published in Tallinn) seemed primarily to consist of just a few dots on the page and some sustained, drone-like square shapes. There was almost nothing there . . . but from my experiences with medieval music, I knew that therefore *everything* might be there. I felt like one of those English travellers of an earlier epoch, confronting a foreign desert and discovering that something powerful and joyful was offered by its luminous emptiness. I must confess that I still cling to that vision, and I remain drawn above all to the early tintinnabuli works, which reach their apotheosis in *Passio*.

Although at that time and for a few years longer Pärt would remain relatively unknown in the West, the forces that would help bring his name to prominence were already at work. In retrospect, I have the sense of a network spreading across from the East, with important centres in Germany, and reaching out to touch England and even, briefly, New York. It was a relatively small network—had we known each other, we might conceivably have constituted a large dinner party in someone's house.

Since then, things have certainly changed, and Pärt's following has grown beyond all expectations. From being the almost hidden object of obscure enthusiasms, his music has come to be recognized and celebrated around the world to a degree rivalled in recent times only by that of the American 'minimalists'. From one moment to the next this progress has had the appearance of inevitability. As the music's sphere of influence widened, one had the sense of watching a natural unfolding of events, as logical and recognizable as the tintinnabuli style itself. But any form of popularity carries with it certain risks. The media soon homed in on what they were quick to term 'holy minimalism', and what had been an essentially musical activity has become commodified, appropriated for purposes of publicity and selling, packaged and distributed in ways and to a degree which we in the West are all too familiar with, but which bear little resemblance to the composer's previous experience of music either as art object or cultural activity. Surrounded by the noise of its public esteem, the music's own signals are threatened with distortion, filtered as they now are through the preconceived attitudes and sloganizing reflexes of certain members of the musical press, who merely seek to identify the latest musical development in order to reduce it to a size they can feel comfortable with.

In some ways Pärt himself indirectly contributed to this situation. His unwillingness to give interviews has given rise to the idea that he is a recluse. This is simply not true. He is certainly a private person with a distaste for the vapid excess of 'communication' that so readily pours itself into the interstices of daily life (and in this hardly untypical of many composers). None the less, Pärt's ability to interact with people, as individuals or in groups, is always at first surprising. He has what is commonly described as 'presence'. In Pärt this is accentuated by his striking appearance, but ultimately resides in the strength of his personality, which is as uncluttered yet powerfully focused as his music.

With some notable exceptions, the critics have been hesitant to welcome Pärt with open arms, concerned perhaps that they were somehow being cheated of substance, that the music was simply too easy. But for the majority of listeners this delicacy of feeling was beside the point. The very idea that new music should, and indeed could, engage the hearts and ears of a general public (in addition to their minds) is something we have grown unaccustomed to. The drift towards greater and greater complexity which has indelibly marked twentieth-century music has encouraged the unconscious assumption that music should provide food for thought. Yet, throughout the century there has also been a persistent alternative current that may be traced back via Cage to Satie. It is sometimes described as *musique pauvre*, sometimes simply as 'experimental'. Pärt's music taps into this same current, although it brings with it a much more incisive sense of expression and purpose. Its essential qualities—directness of feeling, transparency of form, austerity of mood, economy of gesture—together with the timeliness of its appearance, have joined Pärt to a stylistic phenomenon that reaches out beyond polemic, just as Satie and Cage did, but with a force and intensity that neither of them would have envisaged or indeed desired. These qualities are to be found not only in Pärt's music. They can be found also in the work of Gorecki and Tavener, to name just two other composers with whom Pärt is invariably, though at times excessively, linked.[1] The recent and quite sudden popularity of chant is connected to that same phenomenon. Whatever one may think of such bandwagon effects, and however natural may be the instinct to recoil from such 'vulgar' recognition (treating that adjective in its etymological sense), Pärt's music is no more to blame, and should be no more demeaned as a result, than should the anonymous composers of chant in all their secure innocence, blissfully remote in time from designer-stubble record labels and sceptical journalists alike.

This book is primarily devoted to the music itself, and ultimately that means to the style which Pärt has called 'tintinnabuli'. The first three chapters may be regarded as a preliminary text, leading to the three central chapters which focus on the 1970s and describe Pärt's search for a new style, the basic principles of that style, and a discussion of the early tintinnabuli works. The next three chapters examine the later works, especially *Passio*, up to the 1994 *Litany*, and thus loosely speaking cover the years since Pärt's emigration to the West. The final chapter is addressed primarily to performers.

Four topics in particular form a useful background to this subject. Three of them—music and spirituality (with special reference to Russian Orthodoxy), the sound of bells, and minimalism—are treated in Chapter 1, where, I believe, they can appropriately set the tone for a reading of tintinnabuli aesthetics. The fourth—early music—is considered in the more specific context of Pärt's development during the 1970s, and is located in Chapter 4.

In addressing the subject of Russian Orthodoxy from 'outside', what I have sought to indicate is a particular mode of spiritual thought which, as I discern it, can help define the kind of music Pärt composes, or can at least illuminate our approach to it. It would, after all, be

---

[1] Some record companies are attempting to add the names of Giya Kancheli and Peteris Vasks to the canon.

ix

churlish to pretend that the almost exclusively sacred nature of the texts which Pärt has chosen to set since 1968 is somehow irrelevant to our understanding of the music. There is a difference between the composer who 'sets' a religious text, but uses a style which is essentially unaltered by the nature of the words and their theological or liturgical context, and a composer for whom these texts are the very breath of life, and who probably cannot imagine himself working with any other kind. There are many composers who set religious texts with skilled attention to the poetical imagery and to the rhetoric and drama contained in the words. Pärt's approach is quite different, and works outwards from the structure of the text and, simultaneously, inwards from the significance of the text as a whole (historically, spiritually, and liturgically).

Some people may consider this approach to be an anomaly in today's predominantly secular society. But a concentration on religious texts represents not so much a rejection of the world and 'contemporary problems' (which is how some critics seem to view it), but rather a profound recognition of what is most important and enduring. Of course, the music should be able to stand by itself—but what does that mean? In almost every culture except our own, the spiritual nature of music, its sacred power, is taken for granted. Even to raise the issue already presumes a specific position on the relationship between music and spirituality—one that sees them, falsely, as intrinsically separate entities. We are reminded of the difficulty facing certain ethnomusicologists studying a people whose daily lives were so permeated with music that they did not have an actual word to describe it.

I recognize that the topic of spirituality in music is like quicksand! Pärt's music has an effect on people that may be described, cautiously, as inspirational. There seems to be a general awareness of a special quality, already alluded to, which touches people in ways they had forgotten to expect from new music. Many critics have likewise sensed the unusual power of this outwardly simple music, and have been moved to celebrate it in prose which yearns to become poetry. Hitherto perfectly rational commentators find themselves talking about timelessness, ritual, and mysticism, testing the limits of their points of reference and sometimes, it is whispered, overstepping them. The problem is that, in most cases, contact with the more abstruse areas of spirituality has been cursory; it is unfamiliar territory, and the vocabulary it summons up is untried and remains superficial, decorative at best.

The problem is compounded by the fact that in discussing any music, words can render only a limited account of what is significant; the music either overwhelms the words, or the words take on their own meaning and, however unintentionally, leave the music behind, and set off on some errand of their own. In this way too Pärt's music is inspirational; we breathe it in and, if we are not careful, out come—words.

Pärt's earliest extant music, from his student years, is neoclassical in style. But he soon adopted a more abrasive idiom, and throughout the 1960s explored serialism and collage techniques, in which glimpses of tonality sometimes appeared like a bitter-sweet premonition. Eventually, with *Credo* (1968) he reached a creative impasse. After some years of studying early music (and composing a transitional third symphony), he discovered the reductive, tonal style which he calls 'tintinnabuli', and which enabled him to compose fluently once again. This is the music, immediately recognizable and unique, that has made his name famous, and which is ultimately the reason for this book. However, it was always my intention to discuss the earlier music as well. That music has its own merit, but, more important, is essential for an understanding of Pärt's later evolution. There is, moreover, both an underlying continuity of musical *value* between works in the two idioms and a striking similarity in certain compositional processes. Indeed, there are times when it seems that the earlier music holds up a mirror to the later works—though the glass is not without flaw.

I have been fortunate in my capacity as singer and conductor to have performed numerous works by Pärt under the composer's guidance (including several first performances): this has undoubtedly given me an insider's privilege, which I trust I have not abused. While I have attempted to be as accurate as possible in all aspects of 'translation'—both of the composer's words to me and my own accumulated sense over the years of what the composer and his music stand for—there remains the inevitable possibility of error, whether of fact, tone, or interpretation. Therefore I must make it clear that responsibility for the contents of the book rests with me, and that I should not be interpreted as speaking on behalf of the composer. For any errors that may have persisted, I offer my apologies both to the composer and to the reader.

ACKNOWLEDGEMENTS

IN preparation for this book I engaged the composer in several lengthy conversations (during 1993 and 1994) during which I either took copious notes or used a tape recorder. These conversations (held in a mixture of German and English, and even in Estonian and Russian, on two occasions with interpreters present) are to be understood as the source on all the (relatively few) occasions in this book when the composer is quoted or his speech reported without further reference or acknowledgement. More substantially, these same conversations are also the source for much incidental information regarding the composer's life and work which has duly informed and been worked into the text at different levels and in different ways.

It is a pleasure also to record my gratitude for the help and encouragement I received in numerous ways from Christopher Bowers-Broadbent, Susan Bradshaw, Richard Clark, Ave Hirvesoo, Aili Jõeleht, Tõnu Kaljuste, Ilmar Kiesel, Ulle Laido, Alex Lingas, Ingram Marshall, Taivo Niitvägi, Pablo Ortiz, Arthur Quinn, Rein Rannap, Seymour Simmons, Heljo Tauk, and Liza Wilson. Music examples were drawn by Michael Malone.

Pitch indications follow the Helmholtz system, which may be found in Grove Vol. XIV, p. 788.

Acknowledgement is made for permission to quote from the following copyright sources:

Nekrolog © 1990 by M.P. Belaieff. Reproduced by permission of M.P. Belaieff, Frankfurt/M; *Symphony No. 3* © 1978 by Edition Peters, Leipzig. Reproduced by permission of C.F. Peters, Frankfurt/M, Leipzig, London and New York; *Symphony No. 1* © 1967 Hans Sikorski, Hamburg; *Pro et Contra* © 1973 Hans Sikorski, Hamburg.

The following works published by Universal Edition A.G., Wien, all rights reserved; and used by permission of European American Music Distributors Corporation, sole U.S. and Canadian agent for Universal Edition A.G., Wien:

Perpetuum Mobile © copyright 1968 by Universal Edition A.G., Wien. Copyright renewed; *Credo* © copyright 1982; *When Sarah Was 90* © copyright 1984; *Für Altna* © copyright 1980, 1990; *Missa Sillabica* © copyright 1977; *Tabula Rasa* © copyright 1980; *An den Wassern* © copyright 1984, 1991; *Arbos* © copyright 1981; *Cantus In memory of Benjamin Britten* © copyright 1981; *Fratres* © copyright 1982; *Summa* © copyright 1980, 1990; *Passio* © copyright 1982, 1985; *Te Deum* © copyright 1984; *Stabat Mater* © copyright 1985; *Miserere* © copyright 1989; *7 Magnificat Antiphons* © copyright 1990; *Silouans Song* © copyright 1991; *2 Slavonic Psalms* © copyright 1984; *The Beatitudes* © copyright 1990; *De Profundis* © copyright 1981; *Magnificat* © copyright 1989; *Berlin Mass* © copyright 1990, 1991; *Beatus Petronius* © copyright 1990; *Litany* © copyright 1994.

CONTENTS

SOUNDING ICONS

Nothing is outside, nothing is inside; for what is outside, is inside.

Music and Spirituality

ALL music emerges from silence, to which sooner or later it must return. At its simplest we may conceive of music as the relationship between sounds and the silence that surrounds them. Yet silence is an imaginary state in which all sounds are absent, akin perhaps to the infinity of time and space that surrounds us. We cannot ever hear utter silence, nor can we fully imagine such concepts as infinity and eternity. When we create music, we express life. But the source of music is silence, which is the ground of our musical being, the fundamental note of life. How we live depends on our relationship with death; how we make music depends on our relationship with silence.

Arvo Pärt's music seems to me to testify to this concept in which silence and death are creatively linked, and thereby to reaffirm the spiritual basis of our existence, in all its frailty and potential beauty. Pärt uses the simplest of means—a single note, a triad, words—and with them creates an intense, vibrant music that stands apart from the world, and beckons us to an inner quietness and an inner exaltation.

This inwardly flowering sense of reverence cannot be ignored in any lengthy account of Pärt's music, and although the music does not insist upon ontological discussion (it does, after all, manifest itself powerfully as 'pure' music), it is pointless to pretend that the forces that have motivated Pärt are somehow exterior to a proper understanding of the composer and his work. We could draw our own veil of silence across this issue, allowing only that a kind of humanistic generosity is at work, allied to a historical perspective which dutifully cultivates the fruitful garden of the 'objective', creating a chant-inspired musical utterance of special intensity, unique in character if not in force. Such a backdrop will be all too apparent to many, but it hardly provides the sustained engagement with substantive issues that the music itself conjures forth and seems to require.

In its spiritual posture, just as in some degree in its technical organization, Pärt's music reveals a kinship with the likes of Ockeghem and Josquin Desprez, while it is also loosely aligned with the finest outcrop of minimalist[1] and post-minimalist work. In doing so, it functions within the contemporary musical world (whether or not it wishes to) as one of the forces displacing the hitherto central language of serialism.

Minimalism itself can already be seen to have deposited a rich legacy, in which the use of non-narrative process structures and a general sense of harmonic stasis are now taken for granted; it is currently in the use of repetitive, though often asymmetric, rhythms, complexly interwoven, that a younger generation of composers is establishing a more settled vision of a shared musical language.[2]

Pärt's earlier compositions offer a direct allegory of recent musical history, not just in the stylistic evolution they represent, but in the growing frequency with which, in a single work, tonality and dissonance are placed in direct opposition. This opposition duly becomes the thematic 'subject' of the music. At length, by unfolding the triadic stasis of tintinnabuli, Pärt eschewed the agonistic world of dialectic and incident, of narrative or linear time, preferring instead to seek the world of revelation, of circular or mythic time. This came about not 'merely' from musical necessity, but as a direct reflection of his own spiritual odyssey, in which the identity of music, its place in society, could not be sustained without directly reflecting the meanings and the modes of thought which his journey had uncovered. Alan Merriam expressed a similar realization at the beginning of his study of the Flathead Indians:

All people, in no matter what culture, must be able to place their music firmly in the context of the totality of their beliefs, experiences and activities, for without such ties, music cannot exist. This means that there must be a body of theory connected with any music system—not necessarily a theory of the structure of music sound, although that may be present as well, but rather a

---

[1] The implications of this word are discussed later in the chapter.

[2] Pärt's own example has helped liberate many composers from a sense of duty towards gestural dissonance, and there has been a proliferation of scores (especially in the choral world) featuring slow tempos and diatonic absolutism to show this! Even though it must be admitted, and without surprise, that many of these lack Pärt's precision and imaginative intensity, one can at the very least welcome the lack of pretension, and indeed the practicality of such music, often representing the only kind of new music that amateur choirs can dream of attempting. This is a far from unimportant contribution to contemporary music's biggest task: to rebuild its constituency through the re-establishment of a common musical language, or rather a plurality of mutually intelligible languages!

theory of what music is, what it does, and how it is coordinated with the total environment, both natural and cultural, in which man moves.[3]

For Pärt this totality derives from the Russian Orthodox Church. Although Pärt has not composed any liturgical music as such (with the possible exception of the two Mass settings), and has more often set Latin than Church Slavonic, his aesthetic sensibility has been deeply marked by the spiritual values of the Russian Orthodox Church and its particular estimation of tradition and focus on verbal expression. More than in Western Christian liturgy, Orthodox liturgy eschews the everyday mode of speech so that some manner of singing is used for all types of utterance (except sermons). These may range by degrees from solo monotonal recitation to full choral polyphony, but there is no boundary separating portions of what is basically heightened speech from the more conventional harmonic kinds of singing. Instead, the whole service is a flux of different gradations of musical complexity, at the heart of which is the word, its meanings duly balanced according to content and liturgical significance by appropriate musical formulation.

There are two quite specific aspects of Russian Orthodoxy, strongly relevant to Pärt's tintinnabuli music, to which I wish to draw attention: its mystical or contemplative tradition, which both surrounds and permeates the air from which Pärt draws his deepest breaths, and the art of icon painting, which can help illuminate the nature of Pärt's music, even though it is composed, in a practical sense, as concert music.

Icon and Music

To understand the meaning and function of sacred icons, it is necessary to distinguish between the idea of merely creating an image, which dramatically or aesthetically affords us a glimpse of the subject, and the formulation of a picture which participates directly in the subject, rendering it present by venerating the prototype. This type of art will be discussed briefly here, not as an 'explanation' of Pärt's music, but as a potentially useful corollary of it.

An icon asserts the interpenetration of God and the world. During the eighth century, iconoclasts attacked the very validity of seeking to depict an image of Christ whose divine nature (in the apophatic tradition) was beyond description, arguing that only the human na-

[3] Merriam, p. 3.

ture of Christ could be represented. But this was precisely the point on which the arguments in favour of icons turned: through the Incarnation, God had provided a fleshly image of himself, so that now it was possible to draw an image of that image—which was something quite different from (idolatrously) drawing an image of the transcendent God. The authenticity of the image, however, could only be upheld by adherence to a continuous tradition. The strongly stylized elements that characterize icon painting are the result of accepting and working within such a tradition; this in turn sanctions the work that is done as having been guided by divine authority. The stylization thus becomes a way of maintaining God's transcendence while depicting the Incarnation as something real and substantial, not as something imaginary or abstract.

More than one writer has observed the strong correspondence that exists between medieval Russian chant (and polyphony) and the spiritually charged Russian icon. Both have an exalted severity, devoid of external effect.

The task of the musician and painter was not self-expression . . . but the comprehension and reproduction of heavenly songs, the recreation of divine images that were transmitted by means of ancient religious archetypes. . . . In icon painting, as in religious chant, there existed collections of patterns called *podlinniki*—prototypes. These prototypes and the pattern melodies served to preserve the artistic canon, a collective creation. . . . The work of the medieval icon painter and the composer-musician-chanter began with the solving of identical problems: The painter 'designs' his panel, tracing and outlining the canonic forms of the future icon, while the singer-musician broke up his text . . . into the required number of fragments to correspond to the number of musical lines in the model . . . [applying] the musical formula of the pattern melodies as clichés to the new text, varying details where necessary.[4]

Despite the suggestiveness of this description, it is not the precise manner of working which I would draw attention to here (though it does remarkably foreshadow some of Pärt's preoccupations in tintinnabuli music), but the sense of conforming to a tradition, of working with given elements, the content and disposition of which lie beyond the particular whim and character of the artist-composer. Moreover, this objective approach does not eliminate the need for talent; indeed, it requires a very special degree and quality of talent—

[4] Tatiana Vladyshevskaia, 'On the Links between Music and Icon Painting in Medieval Russia', in Brumfield and Velimirovic, pp. 14–29.

painting and composing *in* numbers rather than merely by numbers. Furthermore, the spiritual cast of the icon painter and composer had to be calm and prayerful, for their work is a 'visible [audible] testimony of eternity'.[5]

Sacred art (as opposed to art using or illustrating sacred themes) cannot be identified with the idea of progress. Ouspensky argues that the true significance of icons has been falsified: 'Scholarship disconnected from dogma has inserted the icon into the general trend of art as such, and defined its creation as belonging to the domain of general culture, thereby separating it from the church.'[6] The tradition of icon painting may be likened somewhat to Gregorian chant; both existed for a thousand years, and did not fully enter the historical purview until the the end of the Middle Ages (which happened later in Russia than in Western Europe). Changes took place, of course, but these occurred 'within' the canonized style, rather than as a passage from one style to another. 'The historical course of this artistic language is epitomized by periods of greater precision and purity or, by contrast, of decay and deviation.'[7]

The modern discovery of icons, where it is not merely aesthetic, is better described as a return *to* icons; and it is in a similar spirit, I believe, that Pärt regards the example of chant and early music. The timelessness of such music overrides the question of contemporaneity. He has not sought to imitate the external appearance of chant or early music, but rather to incorporate its manner of operation[8] (as an approach to sound, and as an expression of all-encompassing purpose), into his own. Pärt is strongly aware that the initial development of Christian chant predated the separation of Eastern and Western churches in 1054. Although, strictly speaking, his music is not created for liturgical use, it none the less seems to have absorbed the same criteria which direct composers of sacred music away from exclusively aesthetic or subjective goals, towards the continuation and preservation of a tradition. This can only be achieved, to paraphrase Ouspensky, by an existential entry into the living texture of that tradition, not simply treating it as a subject of external study.[9]

---

[5] P. A. Florensky, quoted in ibid. p. 20.

[6] Ouspensky, p. 468.

[7] Ibid. p. 470.

[8] Cf. 'We shall find that Asiatic art is ideal in the mathematical sense: like Nature . . . not in appearance . . . , but in operation' (Coomaraswamy, p. 11)—a quotation with which John Cage was very familiar.

[9] Cf. Ouspensky, p. 450, where he is discussing the debasement of iconographical themes under the influence of 19th-century German Romanticism.

'The word *God*, in or outside of quotation marks, has become the last taboo in the postmodern era.'[10] It is hardly surprising, then, that words such as 'mysticism' and 'contemplation' have become similarly compromised, imperilled by misuse. This should not keep us from addressing the things they stand for, though we are obliged, perhaps, to examine the origins of these terms before proceeding.

Whole volumes might be consulted in an attempt to define and explain what 'mysticism' is about, though in the short term it is best to borrow from St Augustine and describe it as the effort of the mind to know God. In his famous study of Western mysticism,[11] Dom Butler also observes that this word is widely misused, being loosely applied to theosophy, spiritualism, demonology, occultism, psychical experiences, visions, other-worldliness, seeing God in nature, and 'poetry and painting and music of which the motif is unobvious and vague', and so on. By contrast, he proposes a clear traditional meaning, drawing on the older Latin term *contemplatio*, which remained in force well into the Middle Ages. Although the late fifth-century treatise by Pseudo-Dionysius entitled *Mystical Theology* had introduced the word 'mystic' early on, it being connected originally with the Eleusinian Greek mysteries, it was only much later, in comparatively modern times, that the word 'mysticism' itself came to have any currency. 'A direct and objective intellectual intuition of Transcendental Reality' is perhaps the best of the definitions offered by Butler himself.

From this we learn that 'contemplation' is not a mere meditating upon things, but grasping them, dwelling in them. Some passages from a paper delivered by the Italian scholar Elémire Zolla (at a 1973 colloquium in the Rothko Chapel in Houston) will help define this word:

In the ancient worlds one was trained in the various complex patterns of holy gesticulation which acknowledged and praised the manifestation of other worldly powers. . . . One knew the convenient ritual, one felt thankful, at home in the cosmos. . . . A ritual is thus born, separating a space from space, a moment from time. The holy spot should be cut off from the everyday time of ordinary space: set apart, sacrificed, tabooed. . . . Man still feels attracted by such regular patterns; their proportions soothe his soul . . . tradition in the highest sense is the handing down of a method of contemplation . . . the

---

[10] Meltzer and Tracy, p. 569.
[11] This and the following references in this paragraph are drawn from Butler, pp. 3 and 4.

act of looking upon visible things as signs of what lies beyond them. . . . Contemplation seeks the hidden workings, the formal and the material, the final and the efficient causes behind things. In this light, things are seen as though they were in the act of emerging out of their cause, in the process of being created. . . . Order is made of interconnected proportions which acoustically respond to rhythms.

Contemplation feels the rhythmic molds of all forms. The primitive drummer is a master of precise contemplation; he seizes the rhythmic essence of each reality.

But deep contemplation goes beyond the realm of archetypes or ideas, beyond the patterns of order. It goes to the source of all rhythms, the fundamental beat one-two, male-female throbbing against the final, ultimate silence, the source of everything. It relates everything to its archetype and archetypes to God: multiplicity to Oneness.[12]

The rich suggestiveness that this account holds for anyone interested in Pärt's music is hard to ignore, and it is in this light that we might proceed to consider the mysticism of the Russian Orthodox Church: not for its own sake, it must be admitted, but for the possibly deeper understanding it may give us of the 'totality' (recalling Merriam) that has moved Pärt to compose as he does.

The hesychast tradition, which forms the contemplative core of Eastern Christian spirituality, emanated from the eastern Mediterranean regions where the roots of early Christianity first took hold. The Orthodox Church—of which Pärt is a member—grew out of this background, and was not at first to be distinguished from Western Christianity. Just as the Latin culture centred on Rome characterized the West, so the Greek-speaking Byzantine culture centred on Constantinople dominated the East. By the ninth century a degree of mutual estrangement could be discerned, which grew in proportion as doctrinal differences[13] acquired ever greater significance (inevitably exacerbated by cultural, political, and economic factors as well), and this led to a formal schism in 1054, which was given tragic finality when Western Crusaders sacked the city of Constantinople in the year 1204. Eventually, after the fall of Constantinople to the Turks in 1453, the Orthodox hegemony was sustained in Greece and the Slavic countries northwards to Russia. Thus the two branches, West and East, stem from a single tree, but have different histories. Unlike the Western Church, the Orthodox Church did not undergo a humanist Refor-

---

[12] E. Zolla, 'Traditional Methods of Contemplation and Action', in Ibish, pp. 105–35.

[13] One of the more important doctrinal differences between Eastern and Western Christianity hinges upon the use of the word *filioque* in the Creed.

mation, and, while changes have occurred, it has nevertheless retained a direct sense of its source in the Patristic tradition. This yields a very special attitude towards time and the presence (or, rather, continuity) of the past; it also reinforces the perceived strength of tradition, all of which closely concerns the aesthetic properties we find in Pärt's music.[14]

The ritual repetition of the name of Jesus has long been at the heart of Orthodox worship, most commonly in the form of the Jesus Prayer: 'Lord Jesus Christ, Son of God, have mercy on me, a sinner.' The repetition of this simple prayer, with its steady reminder of the Incarnation, is central to Orthodox practice—so quietly central in fact that it is easy for outsiders to miss its significance amidst the revelation of more overtly impressive features. None the less, this dwelling upon the mystery of Christ should not be over-looked, and in the study of Pärt's music it first comes forcefully before us in the text of his Credo. The centrality of Christ also underpins what we will have to say below about icons, and in turn suffuses the entire study of Orthodox art and music and its imprint on Pärt's music.[15]

'The hesychast tradition took different forms down through the centuries, but it remained unified in its fundamental inspiration: in Christ . . . man recovers his original destiny, re-adapts his existence to the divine model.'[16] The term 'hesychasm' implies stillness, silence, tranquillity, and also stability, being seated, fixed in concentration. As early as the fourth century it was used to designate the state of inner peace and freedom from bodily or mental passion from which point only one might proceed to actual contemplation. Leonid Ouspensky defines hesychia as 'impassibility', a dispassionate sobriety of spirit, in which the heart and mind are each in control of the other. 'Anchored in the tradition of the Fathers, the hesychast spiritual renewal, which received its dogmatic expression in the writings of St Gregory Palamas and in the fourteenth-century councils . . . exercised an enor-mous influence on the entire Orthodox world, as much in the realm of spiritual life as in that of sacred art.'[17]

[14] It has also affected the history of Russian church music, which retained what we might call medieval features well into the 17th century, and then made a fairly rapid transition into the baroque.

[15] See also John Tavener's *Ultimos Ritos* (1969–72), which makes extensive, and even dra-matic, use of the name of Jesus in various languages.

[16] Meyendorff 1975, p. 128.

[17] Ouspensky, pp. 235–7.

The ideal of tranquillity should not be viewed as an invitation to inaction. The hesychast way calls for the practice of pure prayer and a constant watchfulness over heart and mind. The condition it espouses is not simply silence, but an attitude of listening to God. By 'dispassionate' is implied that degree of spiritual freedom in which the passions are absorbed or reintegrated into a purity of being, and although this correctly suggests a measure of impartiality and detachment, it does not mean indifference: 'for if a dispassionate man does not suffer on his own account, he suffers for his fellow creatures. [Dispassion] consists, not in ceasing to feel the attacks of the demons, but in no longer yielding. It is positive, not negative.'[18]

One primary question absorbs all others: if God exists and is immaterial and transcendent, how can he be known to us? How can a mystery be understood, if it always remains, and can only remain ultimately, a mystery? How can something which is beyond human intelligence be grasped by that intelligence? In attempting to answer this, the Church Fathers argued that God can only be known by what He is *not*—an approach known as apophatic, or negative, theology.

By the *via negativa* famously expounded by an anonymous writer now referred to as Pseudo-Dionysius, we understand that the intellect, through a process of gradual purification, perceives that

by plunging into the darkness of unknowing . . . [one] is enwrapped in that which is altogether intangible and noumenal . . . and through the inactivity of all his reasoning powers is united by his highest faculty to Him who is wholly unknowable; thus by knowing nothing to know that which is beyond knowledge . . . the higher we soar in contemplation the more limited become our expressions of that which is purely intelligible. . . . He who is the preeminent cause of all things sensibly or intelligently perceived is not Himself any of those things.[19]

The Dionysian tradition was sustained and further developed by important theologians such as Maximus the Confessor (d. 662) and St John of Damascus (d. 749), while the hesychast way of prayer continued to bear witness to a direct apprehension of the eternal light of God. However, there was a growing debate, which came to a head in the fourteenth century, about how to reconcile this claim with the negative theology of God as transcendent.

[18] Palmer, i. 359 (the glossary, from which much information in this paragraph is condensed).

[19] Abstracted from *The Mystical Theology* as translated and reprinted in Happold, pp. 212–17.

It was St Gregory Palamas (1296–1359) who achieved a doctrinal solution to this problem. Orthodox spirituality had long distinguished between God's 'essence' (unknowable, inexpressible, transcendent) and the 'energies' by which in the world of phenomena we may encounter him. Gregory advanced these concepts further to show that the negative way to God was not sufficient in itself. 'Elevation by negation is actually only an intellection of that which appears different from God; it does not bring the image of inexpressible contemplation; it is not by itself that fulfilment.'[20] Thus, according to Meyendorff, Gregory asserts that 'Revelation always remains a free and sovereign act of God, by which the Transcendent comes down from his transcendence and the Unknowable makes himself known; therefore the knowledge we have of him is always the knowledge "through grace", subject to his will, and dependent on an *act* of condescension of Almighty God.'[21] The 'energies' are not to be thought of as separate or incomplete manifestations of God, however: ' "They do not compose," Palamas writes, "the being of God," for that is not a composite entity, and "it is he who gives them their existence, without taking his existence from them; indeed it is not the realities which surround God which are the essence of God, but he is their essence." '[22]

God's transcendence is thus preserved, but his continual presence in the world is also allowed for, centred above all in the Incarnation. The specific act of God appearing in the flesh, as well as in the spirit, of Jesus Christ not only sustains the Christocentric theme of Orthodox prayer, but also encourages the depiction of Jesus in icons.

The Existential Ritual

Any encounter with 'silence' brings us not only to the mystical tradition, in which silence is at once profound and positive, but close also to the modern fear of silence as absence: the silence of a God who is otherwise engaged, or simply not there. From the one point of view, silence is filled with an apprehension of presence and compassion, while from the other it presents us with a sense of utter aloneness. It is probably true to say that few experience the one without also having experienced the other.

[20] From Gregory's 'The Triads', quoted in translation in Meyendorff 1974, p. 206.

[21] Ibid. p. 209.

[22] Ibid. p. 214. For further information on the hesychastic way of thought and prayer, see *The Philokalia*, a collection of writings that date from a period of over a thousand years from the 4th to the 14th centuries, published (in Greek) in Venice in 1782, and subsequently translated into Russian and (only as recently as the 1960s) into English. See Palmer.

It is a peculiarly Western tragedy that forces a rational distinction between fullness and presence on the one hand and absence and loneliness on the other. A sense of the human spirit in its sublime aloneness, without reference to the question of 'God', is expressed powerfully in certain Chinese and Japanese works of art, and with particular precision by the poet Basho. In his haiku we encounter the littlest of actions or observations at the point of merging suddenly, yet perpetually, into the infinity of time and space that surrounds them. In his study of Basho, Ueda writes: 'To realise that all living things are evanescent is sad, but when one sees a tiny creature enduring that sadness and fulfilling its destiny one is struck with a sublime feeling.'[23] He defines one of the underlying concepts of Basho's poetry—*sabi*— as the idea 'that one attains spiritual serenity by immersing oneself in the egoless, impersonal life of nature.

> The sound is clear
> And reaches the Big Dipper—
> Someone pounding cloth.

How does one explain the relationship . . . between the eternal Big Dipper and the brief sound of cloth being pounded?'[24] The explanation, if there is one, is less important than the experience. A sense of individual insignificance is humbling, but also cleansing. Many writers have sought to express the view that if existence is understood to be linear in form, if every life and action is merely unique, then indeed our insignificance is bitter and tragic; but if the pattern of being is understood to be cyclic, then our moment of life becomes meaningful in all its brevity and aloneness.

During the post-World War II decades, so many currents of thought and belief flowed into and out of one another that it is tempting to sit back and view the whole period as a quintessential sampling of Heraclitean flux. Nowhere is the bewildered sense of spiritual abandonment and sterility so profoundly communicated than in the writings of Samuel Beckett, which often seem to prefigure the purer, abstract minimalism that was to follow. It is finally this abstraction, this repudiation, horror even of personal emotion that marks the passage from modernism to what follows it. Auschwitz and the atomic bomb, twin evils of numbing proportion, finally force us to push free of the immediate past and to seek our future salvation in remote quarters of time and place. It is not enough for art simply to register the horror or re-enact the details of our fall. In our aesthetic imagina-

---

[23] Ueda, p. 52.   [24] Ibid. pp. 30 and 53.

11

tion we have become like wounded beings crawling among the remains of our broken civilization—which Ezra Pound early in the century described as 'botched'—clutching perhaps a single token of beauty, a line or two of poetry, a Bach Prelude, a white canvas, which must now symbolize everything.

In and out of history, like the Tartar invasion portrayed in Tarkovsky's film *Andrei Rublev*, waves of barbarians have come riding across the tundra to rape and destroy the tender fruits of culture, defiling the holy places and trampling crops into the ground. Finally, pressed ever closer together on our tiny planet, we are coming to the realization that the barbarians are within, that 'them' is in fact 'us'. Like an ancient monastic order, we carry within us the seeds of renewal—the grain of hope—which we plant again and again after each fresh disaster, digging ever deeper into the past to re-establish only what is essential, that which alone can endure across time. In such times (and therefore at all times) the role of the artist is the preservation of spiritual values, a role which demands exploration and sacrifice, quite as much as conservation.

Minimalism in Music

Labels in music are like clichés in conversation. They are not entirely empty of meaning, but the information they convey depends as much on the context in which they are uttered as on the ideas they denote. Twentieth-century art and music are liberally sprinkled with '-isms' (indeed, most of the musical ones are borrowed from art), testifying to the deeply self-conscious and historically allusive stance of modern music. In the broadest sense we can identify 'modernism' as being characterized by an oppositional manner of utterance, with a marked tendency towards complexity (of form and of gesture) and a self-conscious sense of belatedness; furthermore, in music this is most closely linked to serial procedures from which the conventions of tonality are largely absent. Not all modernist music uses serial procedures, of course, and not all reactions away from it are minimalist. Indeed, minimalism is more correctly viewed as part of a more general wave of reactions to the perceived complexities of modernism, in which the re-emergence of tonality (both functional and non-functional!) serves as the most salient common denominator.

Whether Pärt's music can usefully be described as minimalist is a moot question, to which the answer is irredeemably relative. It depends on what meanings are collected together under such a heading, and it depends, equally, on who is asking the question.

Minimalism has been one of the most powerful, yet still critically undernourished, movements in the arts of the past forty years or so.[25] Intensely derided by modernist theorists and traditional symphony audiences alike, minimal music has nevertheless managed to be uncommonly popular as well—which has not necessarily helped its case. The austerity of some of its core works[26] stands in stark contrast to the limp 'New Ageism' that is sometimes seen as an outgrowth of it. In many circles 'minimalism' is simply a label of convenience by which a composer can be dismissed as unworthy of serious attention; in this kind of context it functions as a reflex action telling us very little about the music, but indicating the presence of certain limitations in the mind that uses it.

In my understanding, the term 'minimalism' is not limited to one specific kind of musical technique or one particular time, but refers instead to an ancient attitude towards sound which has resurfaced in recent decades. Of course, locally, in terms of both historical and cultural perspectives, this attitude or quality is most readily identified with the American repetitive style, usually employing steady pulse and gradual changes, of Terry Riley, Steve Reich, and Philip Glass, with LaMonte Young's name usually added to the list as something of a founding father. The term has at least two points of origination, if not more, and this of course makes it more difficult to specify any single meaning.

But first, the *Oxford English Dictionary's* definition of 'minimal': 'Smallest, least. Extremely minute in size; of the nature of or constituting a minimum; of a minimum amount, quality, or degree; that is the least possible. . . . See also *minimum*: The smallest portion into which matter is divisible; an atom. Also, the hypothetical smallest possible portion of time or space.' And so we have a suggestion of economy—the least amount necessary (by implication) to perform the task at hand. We also encounter the concept of going to an extreme of time/duration or space/size. Extreme smallness is a relative term. A dot or a single thin line are ideas, concepts vivid to us because of their

---

[25] There was certainly an outpouring of documentation contemporary with early (visual arts) minimalism (see especially Battcock), but in music there has been little in the way of a balanced, sympathetic, yet non-partisan literature. There are signs, however, that this is beginning to change. The principal books so far are Mertens and Strickland.

[26] Steve Reich's *Drumming*, Louis Andriessen's *Hoketus*, and Philip Glass's *Einstein on the Beach*, for example.

formal purity; but who can determine the size of a dot or the width of a line? Utterly pure concepts such as these may be placed in size or duration anywhere on a scale from microscopically small to immensely large without losing their 'minimal' essence.

The term 'minimalism' was originally developed with reference to paintings and sculptures in the 1960s using very elemental, simple forms, often with repetitive geometric and symmetrical features. The apparent 'work content' was minimal—as the critic Richard Wollheim observed in a 1965 article that was probably the first use of the term in print. He cited Duchamp's 'ready-mades' (such as the urinal exhibited in 1917 as *Fountain*) as a precursor of this movement, whereby the artist's decision to choose a certain object or configuration of objects renders them works of art—despite the fact that, technically, anyone might have executed this action—or could indeed now do so.

Other important precursors of minimalism abound, and include the Russian suprematist Kasimir Malevich, the composer Erik Satie (both producing their most important work in the heady years prior to World War I), while Gertrude Stein's use of asymmetric repetition created a literary model which at times uncannily prefigures similar activity in the music of the American mimimalists.

Minimal art derives its significance from the confrontation, or meeting-point, between the artwork and the viewer, the viewer's experience thus completing the artistic act. And although this is true of all art, of course, in highly differentiated art (Rubens, Beethoven) the artwork is so specific in its expression that we reasonably assume each person's experience of that work to be broadly and even in detail similar to everyone else's. On the other hand, in minimal art the responses can be much more varied as so much is left open—to be completed by the viewer. If this is so, who can deny that minimalism is potentially rich in artistic experience?

Many minimalist artists were not concerned with this conceptual approach, however, and were more interested in the fact that by reducing the elements in their work to a bare minimum they could focus attention on the isolated object or on a process *per se*; this gave their approach a cool sense of discipline and purity, which for some was a much needed counterbalance to the preceding decades of intense expressionism that had characterized high modernism.

Minimalist music was developed in both San Francisco and New York in the early to mid-1960s. Nearly all of the early performances of many minimalist works were given in the art galleries and lofts of the New York art world, and only later moved into more conventional concert-halls. This meant that many different kinds of people heard the music, people who would not normally consider going to a symphony concert; and indeed, minimalism has had a strong influence on rock music as well.[27] Many composers both within the United States and in other countries have been influenced by the four principal American minimalists, and have themselves written music that can to varying degrees be called minimalist (though its stylistic diversity suggests both the richness of minimalism and at the same time its inadequacy as a term of reference).[28]

American minimal music was originally characterized by the repetition of sound modules within a constant environment of pulsed rhythms and unchanging tonality. Such a bald description holds true only for the earliest works, but it remains the ab-origin of the style. Musical material is thus reduced to its elemental essence, very often having a single tempo, a single timbre, a single dynamic, so that the ear focuses uniquely on the process of change, which becomes the only identity the music is left with.

Although extremely consonant, the sense of tonality is non-functional (there is no progressively structural use of modulation). The traditional narrative manner of common-practice tonality is thus absent; the dramatic tension, the sense of conflict and drama which motivate the structures of symphonic form, have little or no place in this music. Many pieces tend through length and repetition to establish a sense of timelessness or a continual present; the use of drones (which are in a sense a continuous repetition) reinforces this effect.

Above all, the music unfolds a single process which is both form and content, foreground and background, inside and outside, at the same time. The musical process is not only transparent, but is the music's object-subject in one.[29]

[27] Especially through the work of Brian Eno, as both a musician in his own right and a producer of other musicians. The music of Meredith Monk and, less directly, Laurie Anderson also suggests the influence of minimalism.

[28] These include Gavin Bryars and Michael Nyman in England and Louis Andriessen in Holland, while younger composers such as Kevin Volans and Michael Torke, and Lepo Sumera in Estonia, have also composed in the light of the minimalist example. John Adams has also become widely known as a 'minimalist', but apart from some early works this epithet is not accurate: he makes use of minimalist textures, certainly, but mostly his works eschew the focus on process and extended time which distinguish the minimalist essence, and he is more properly seen as a member of a tradition extending from Samuel Barber, Aaron Copeland, and David del Tredici to Adams himself. His latest works (such as the 1994 *Chamber Symphony*) confirm this observation even as they enrich the texture of his *œuvre*.

[29] See Reich, especially the essay 'Music as a Gradual Process'.

There is another aspect of new music which could also be considered 'minimalist'—though in practice it has not been, at least not in a direct manner. In addition to the emphasis on *process*, the 'linear' aspect of minimalism, there has been a focus on the internal qualities of sound such as may be found in the work of LaMonte Young[30] and (though differently) Morton Feldman, which we might call the 'point' aspect of minimalism. Ultimately these two aspects fuse together: an isolated musical event and a continuously repeated musical event both force our attention on to the inner details of the event itself, rather than its relationship to a distinctly other event.

This interest in the internal quality of sound is of course strongly manifest in Pärt's tintinnabuli music, in which the triad functions as a single entity (both symbolically and actually), permeating and containing a musical work in its entirety. It is a music in which the linear and point aspects are inseparably woven together.

Pärt's music generally avoids the fast, steady pulse of the American genre, and while it is in some respects repetitive, the repetition in and of itself is not the driving force of the music. It is, however, reductive; it is tonal; and the playing out of a clear process is very often the essence of a piece, especially the instrumental works. Finally, we have to conclude that while the *word* 'minimalist' is highly appropriate to describe some important aspects of Pärt's music, the *label* 'minimalist' is misleading, too culturally determined, to stand uncontested or at least unexplained.

Both the emphases just discussed—music as process, music as sound—are of course prefigured deep in the heart of modernist music. Where is the fusion of form and content more beautifully revealed than in the canons of Webern's Symphony? Where is the inner content of the harmonic series more extensively meditated upon than in Stockhausen's *Stimmung*? (And such examples can easily be multiplied.) No, as in all periods of change in music history, nothing is completely new, or completely different, or completely unprepared. And this holds true, too, within the scope of Pärt's own music. In the 1960s he composed music in which a fixed state obtains, music which unfolds gradual processes every bit

[30] Although recognized as the first minimalist, LaMonte Young's later music has moved away from almost every aspect of minimalism's aesthetic except the use of long time periods. Some of his early works, however, are reductive to an extreme degree. His *arabic number (any integer) to Henry Flynt*, dating from April 1960, calls for an unspecified sound to be repeated *x* number of times as regularly as possible. Another early work, *Composition 1960 #7*, consists of a single open fifth chord ($f_\sharp'$ above b) 'to be held for a long time', while other works are conceptually beautiful but verge on the inaudible, even mentally.

as logical and unswerving as those which underly the tintinnabuli later works (though admittedly bringing different processes into contentious opposition, and with very dramatic results). The sharpest change and the most obvious difference lies quite simply in the use of tonality.

In most minimalist music the use of tonality is endemic, though the familiar functionality which we so readily associate with the word is normally absent. Looked at broadly, we may draw a parallel between the development of perspective in European art and the slightly later development in music towards functional tonality. Both create the illusion of a depth of field which allows a powerfully directed sense of movement, whether visually or across time, to permeate the whole composition with subtle cross-references that give it a unified sense of drive and motivation. Within the compass of such a work, various contrasted elements can each have their appointed station, reconciled in the ultimate linear goal of getting somewhere. But in many other forms of art (especially, though not exclusively, medieval and non-Western) the sense of perspective is excluded—as is the case with icons. In its place we find idealized or geometric representations of the natural world in which shapes or sounds coexist in the same plane. The content of such art moves before us as in a procession, one thing after another; whatever particular detail may be foremost at any given moment, the procession is always simply there, and will continue until it is over: it does not have to get anywhere else—it has no appointments to keep.

It is possible that the fixed-state, non-narrative content of minimalist music serves the need for a sense of ritual. The use of repetitive patterns and harmonic stasis suggests an awareness of time quite different from the materiality of Western 'clock' time, though just as real to the person who experiences it. Even if we have the sense that newly invented rituals are spurious—the music may seem 'ritualistic', but culturally there is no pre-ordained pattern to which it conforms, no inherited iconography—even so, minimalist music does articulate the possibility at least of a bona fide existential ritual, if only, quite literally, for the time being.

With Pärt we are taken one step further, though we are obliged to accept, or at least take on trust, the framework of Christianity within which he works (this is easier with the instrumental works, for obvious reasons). The ritual aspect of his music derives both aesthetically and spiritually from its function as a sounding icon. The music ushers us into the presence of a recurring process: for ritual is not simply the

17

repetition or re-enactment of structured events, but rather a return to a perennial condition.

Bells

When someone comes to write the full history of minimalist music, they may have to recognize that the English were there first! I refer that future historian to the art of change ringing, which has been a familiar part of the soundscape of the English shires for several centuries.[31] There are more than five thousand churches in England that house five or more bells (normally tuned to the diatonic major scale), and it is here, over the centuries, that the curious yet fascinating art of change ringing has evolved—to serve no other apparent purpose than the satisfaction of sounding out the mathematical potentials that can be derived from a series of fixed diatonic pitches. The bells are rung to a steady rhythm in carefully ordered, changing sequences. The names given to these sequences are evocative: Cambridge Surprise Minor, Plain Bob Major, Stedman Caters, names entirely meaningful of course to ringers, as are the sequences they call forth, though they are as mystifying to the uninitiated as are the terms used in cricket. It is easy, however, to learn that the last word in each name indicates the number of bells involved; in the examples just given these are six, eight, and nine, respectively. One example must serve here to indicate the process that underlies change ringing: it is one of the simplest patterns, known as Plain Hunting, here shown with four bells; note the position of the treble bell (1) which 'leads' a path from the beginning smoothly across the sequence back to its original position. The other bells follow the same path, but necessarily beginning at four different points in the pattern.

1234
2143
2413
4231
4321
3412
3142
1324
1234

[31] For further information on bells see especially Price and Johnston.

Larger numbers of bells and more complex patterns of changes quickly create substantially longer 'compositions'. We refer casually enough to a 'peal of bells', unaware perhaps that a peal requires a minimum of 5,000 changes, which is about three hours' work. The earliest recorded peal took place in Norwich in 1715, though the bell-ringing movement can be dated to at least a century earlier than that, and received its first major impetus with the publication in 1668 of Fabian Stedman's *Tintinnalogia*.

Pärt has recently spent part of each year in England, so the sound of English change ringing will (I trust) become an actuality for him. But there is already a coincidence of interest which arises not only from the tintinnabulating bells themselves, but also from the steadiness of purpose with which the patterns of changes are unfolded. We can observe the evolution of comparable patterns (different in substance, but not so much in kind) in several of Pärt's works, and also in the earlier minimalist works of Steve Reich and Philip Glass. The length of some of their works, consisting of seemingly endless rapid, repetitive notes and slow patterns of change, seems small in scale when set beside the endurances to which bell-ringers customarily aspire.

The precise meaning of 'tintinnabulum' is given in the *Oxford Dictionary of English Etymology* as a 'small tinkling bell'. The word's onomatopoeic origin is attested to by St Isidore of Seville in his *Etymologiarum* (*c*.AD 630), while later (*c*.800) there is report of a tintinnabulum which 'gave a joyful sound as if struck by an angel' (Vita Primini prior).[32]

Bells are made to sound in one of two ways: either struck on the outside using a hammer, or 'chimed' on the inside usually with a clapper suspended from the apex of the bell. In church the main purpose of bells was (and still is) to act as a signal, the larger sounds calling the faithful to worship and announcing the monastic hours, the smaller bells being used within the services to mark the most sacred parts of the rite (the Sanctus bell, for example), to accompany the movements of the priest (by small bells actually attached to the priest's vestments), or to cue directions to the choir. In addition to the regular liturgical customs, there are many kinds of special occasion which call for bell-ringing, from the peal of celebration at a wedding,

---

[32] In general, 'tintinnabulum' is to be distinguished from 'campana', a term normally reserved for larger, deeper-sounding bells, and derived from the name Campania, which is the province around Naples famous since antiquity for its bronze casting.

to the 'passing bell', tolled while someone is dying, to ward off any evil spirits that might be waiting to seize the departing soul. In 1610 Pope Paul V established the custom of ringing the *De Profundis* bell on All Saints' Day to rouse the faithful (at 1 a.m.) to pray for the souls of the dead by reciting Psalm 130: 'Out of the depths have I cried unto Thee, O Lord'. We may perhaps listen to Pärt's *De Profundis* with this in mind, or to the bell in *Cantus—In Memoriam Benjamin Britten*.

If a single bell is struck, and we contemplate the nature of its sound—the *Klang* at impact, the spread of sound after this initial gesture, and then the lingering cloud of resonance—what we hear takes us to the heart of tintinnabuli. A finely wrought bell makes one of the most mysterious and creative sounds: a sound that certainly 'rings out' and reaches towards us, yet at the same time pulls us in towards it, so that soon we realize we are on the inside of it, that its inside and outside are in fact one and the same.

This quality of sound is carried over into Pärt's tintinnabuli music intact. We hear individual bells in some pieces, but we may also notice that the music as a whole is somehow similarly structured, that the form of some tintinnabuli compositions (or sometimes just a phrase or a chord) resembles the way (the shape) in which a bell sounds. But the connection also extends into the more complex manner in which sounds are combined and repeated to make a musical composition. The way in which Pärt uses a single triad to illuminate an entire work is also a response to the natural sonority of bells, a development of it by extension. Yet we have also to reckon with the simultaneous multiplicity of sound. A single sound is already quite a complex phenomenon, a web of overtones—in a sense, there is no such thing as two sounds, merely a rapidly proliferating, multiple sonic reaction. The ringing of bells together never loses its unanimity: two bells simply create a more complex version of the sound that one bell makes. As more bells are added, we may feel the sonority expanding and blossoming, certainly, so that there is a sense of growth, even climax; but the sound remains rooted in one place, and its identity singular, however complex the manifestation of it.

Many different kinds of bell music have been created throughout the world, ranging from concise melodic idioms, through simple repetitive tolling, to a clamorous sounding of bells together in no particular sequence.[33] A bell has many notes in it (partials) as it vibrates

---

[33] I must confess to finding the playing of conventional melodic and harmonic music on carillons sometimes charming, but less than inspiring, precisely because it seems to ignore the true sonic nature of bells altogether.

across its whole length, and while the constituency of the bell metal and the nature and action of the striking agent are obviously extremely important, the resulting sonority depends very much on the way in which the partials are tuned, and on the bell's shape, which will intensify certain partials over others. The partials along the full length of the bell set up a magnificent 'hum', and when several bells are rung together, the result is a powerful texture of shifting and changing tones, the lower pitches deep and liquid with a strong undertow, while the middle and upper registers create a lighter, kaleidoscopic mixture of sound. Such music corresponds strongly to the sonorities at play in a work like *Cantus*, not so much in terms of the actual notes played, as in the manner in which the total sound envelops the ear. This surely is more than a fortuitous connection, though the correspondences called forth by Pärt's adoption of the term 'tintinnabuli' do not end here. We can listen to the deep 'enchantment' of *Cantus* and ponder the mutual origin of these two words, which have to do with the spell that song weaves: words that have a ring of their own.

In one of his most minimalist works, *Sarah Was Ninety Years Old*, Pärt uses a very spare, rhythmic knocking, slowly articulating an additive-reductive pattern, to evoke the long years during which Sarah waited, barren, hoping to give birth. This bare percussion calls to mind the semantron, an instrument that came into use during the early centuries of Christianity before bells were introduced. The semantron is usually a long narrow wooden board struck by a wooden hammer, though semantra can vary quite considerably in size and sound, stones and, later on, metal also being used. The simplest of instruments, it none the less produces a strong resonance and a variety of different intonations, so that quite subtle results can be obtained.

When bells were introduced into the Russian Orthodox Church, the playing techniques and idiomatic system of signals developed for the semantra were retained. (The semantron is still in widespread use in southern Orthodox countries, Greece especially, and could still be heard in the more obscure, rural parts of Russia[34] at the time of the Revolution.) Russian bells, though at first struck like semantra, were later played by means of ropes fixed to the clappers, so that a skilful ringer could play several at once. The bells themselves, therefore, remain stationary (whereas in English change ringing, for example, they are fixed to a wheel and 'swung': rotated through 360 degrees in alternately clockwise and anticlockwise directions), and this makes for

[34] In Russia the wooden semantron is called *Bilo*, and its metal counterpart *Klepalo*.

a generally softer sound, while also permitting an astonishingly subtle touch. Indeed, listening to different types of Russian bell-ringing one may be reminded of many things, ranging from Cage's prepared pianos (!) to the extreme tenderness of some of Pärt's most introverted moments[35]—while in addition, of course, there are the more conventionally jubilant timbres and moods, though even here the particularity of each sonority is impressive and never overreaches itself to become brute strength. The summons of these bells is not insistent: come—if you wish. The onus is upon the listener to discover what lies behind the sound, just as the Orthodox Church is not noticeably evangelical in its approach: it remains open to those who seek it—nothing more. The same may of course be said of Pärt's music.

The collection of bells in a Russian Orthodox Church is called a 'zvon', and a unique style of music was developed for it during the seventeenth to nineteenth centuries, often involving a number of different rhythmic patterns simultaneously and at times, seemingly, arbitrarily. The bells are not tuned to a particular scale, but simply have higher and lower pitches and varied tone-colours (again reminiscent of the semantron). Because of its religious associations, zvon ringing was virtually banned by the Soviet regime, and many of the bells were destroyed, though something of a revival was later permitted when 'folksiness' became politically correct in the 1960s. Fortunately the religious context was sustained in other Orthodox countries, the largest zvon being located on Mount Athos and in Jerusalem. It is to be hoped that the events of 1989 will eventually lead to a full restoration of zvon ringing in its native country.

In an article of great interest to anyone exploring the topic of bells, 'Aural Icons of Orthodoxy',[36] Edward Williams refers to the sound of Russian bells being perceived by the Orthodox as 'aural icons of past and future trumpeting'. He traces the source of this characterization back to the Sinai peninsula in the middle of the thirteenth century BC. 'The continuous voice of a trumpet was among the aural and visual phenomena reported during the giving of the Law on Mount Sinai'

[35] I am aware, of course, of the highly subjective nature of these observations (though there is some basis in fact for them), and therefore warmly commend the recording of Russian bells detailed in the discography to the reader's attention so that he or she may form their own opinion. A recording of funeral bell-ringing at Pskovo-Pecora (track 2 on this CD) offers a seemingly random sequence of the most varied and often delicate timbres and evokes—for me—the kind of atmosphere in which I imagine Pärt drawing sustenance for his musical explorations in the early 1970s, during which time (according to friends) he made various visits to Orthodox monasteries and expressed considerable interest in bell-ringing.

[36] Brumfield and Velimirovic, pp. 3–13; see also Williams for a more general study of the whole topic of Russian bells.

(reported in Exod. 19 and 20); 'but by the beginning of the sixth century . . . the *semantron* had replaced the trumpet as the agent of convocation in the monasteries of Egypt, Palestine, and Sinai. The rhythms struck on wood were soon vested with the aural memory of rhythmic blasts from earlier trumpets.' Eventually, 'the semantron's iconography of trumpeting was transferred to the *zvon* of Russian bells.' And he quotes the mid-nineteenth-century Russian Archimandrite Leonid:

[I]n Russia our motherland . . . the variety of calls to church, at first with wooden, and then with cast iron, beams and finally with the ringing of bells, has its own significance and deep meaning, even an acoustical one between our time and that more distant—the past and future. . . . The weak sounds of the wood and iron remind us of the prophet's vague, cryptic language, but the clamor and harmonious ringing of the bells is a proclamation of the Gospel, its exultation to the ends of the universe, and reminds us of the angel's trumpet on the final day.[37]

Again I am reminded of a particular work by Pärt (*Fratres* in this case; *Sarah Was Ninety Years Old* has already been mentioned in connection with the semantron); but it would be wrong of me to suggest that Pärt intends us to hear such meaningfully specific echoes of bells in his tintinnabuli music.

Hesychasm, minimalism, rites, icons: these are the dominant motifs which have come to surround my response to Pärt's music, and I will leave the reader to accommodate them at will into the following account of the music itself. While I am aware that the music stands by itself (as it must), I have found these motifs inescapable, and to avoid them would be to accept the (to me) unacceptable premiss that Pärt's music is simply an accident of time and circumstance, a mere reaction to prevailing conditions. I have tried to show, below, first of all that his *œuvre* should be considered as a whole (and not merely to celebrate its core in the popular tintinnabuli works); and second, that the influence of early music is not a superficial imitation or borrowing, still less an escape from modernity, but represents a reconnection with our collective musical unconscious, and is thus as much a way forward as a way back.

[37] Ibid. pp. 3–5.

2

BIOGRAPHICAL NOTES

Estonia

ALTHOUGH Pärt was born and grew up in Estonia, any suggestion that his music could be characterized as 'Estonian' would be misleading: it makes no use of Estonian themes or motifs,[1] and offers no imaginative evocation of anything that might be interpreted as having a national identity; nor, apart from a couple of early cantatas, does the composer choose the Estonian language for his texts. Yet it is unlikely that the composer's unique musical and spiritual identity could have been created anywhere else. Pärt has avowed that his musical education is Western, while his spiritual education is Eastern. But the particular significance of these compass points only becomes meaningful if we know the central reference point from which they emanate. In Pärt's case, of course, that is Estonia, wedged between East (Russia and the Orthodox Church) and West (Germany and Scandinavia). His 'Western' musical training dwelt on the conventional canon of great composers, though it also owed a great deal at a local level to Russian models. However, despite its proximity to Russia, the Estonian capital, Tallinn, has the unmistakable air of being a European city, attached firmly to a cultural perspective that links cities along the Baltic coast and eventually winds round to places like Amsterdam and Copenhagen, and across land to Berlin and Prague; intellectually, this is primarily a Germanic heritage.

The history of Estonia, like that of most small nations, is one of dominance by one or other of its more powerful neighbours. These have included the Teutonic Knights,[2] Denmark (Tallinn means 'Danish fortress'), the combined force of Poland and Lithuania, Sweden, and, bringing us well into modern times, Tsarist Russia. Such a pattern of subjugation has not prevented the survival of a distinct Estonian identity, which has certainly been helped by the fact that the

---

[1] It is true that there are a few places where a (thin) case could be made for hearing a distant impression of the overlapping, repetitive patterns of traditional rune singing common to various Baltic peoples, but the connection is too remote to be of great significance.

[2] Tallinn (under the name of Reval) was part of the medieval Hanseatic League.

24

Estonian language, a member of the Finno-Ugrian family, bears no resemblance to the neighbouring Indo-European tongues (apart from a superficial residue of various loan-words).[3]

Even under the Russian Empire, the Baltic German land-owning classes retained their hold on local power, and this assured the continuing importance of German as the language of administration and as a cultural filter through which styles and ideas arrived from the West. It also meant that the Lutheran Church became the dominant religious force. Yet the proximity of Russia had inevitably encouraged the introduction of Russian Orthodoxy, and there were times when the peasantry were openly drawn to it as a counterbalance to the Lutheranism of establishment and privilege. It was during the early nineteenth century, at the hands of Baltic-German 'Estophiles', that Estonian language and culture assumed a more objective identity with their own national epic: the *Kalevipoeg*. This was a literary construction assembled from genuine folk sources (by Friedrich Robert Faehlmann and Friedrich Rheinhold Kreutzwald), and played a role similar to that of the Finnish *Kalevala*, with which it has many narrative themes in common. Another aspect of this growing nationalism was the establishment (in 1869) of the large-scale choral song festivals that have continued down to the present day.

The armistice that ended World War I in November 1918 was followed in Estonia (as in Finland) by a war of independence against the Bolsheviks, and in February 1920 an independent Republic of Estonia finally came into being. The ensuing decade was largely a prosperous one, both economically and culturally. However, the economic woes of the 1930s were felt in Estonia too, and a new, more authoritarian constitution was passed in 1934. Then in 1940 the Soviets returned, to be ousted temporarily by the Nazis. But in 1944 they returned yet again, as 'liberators', and this time stayed for 50 years.[4]

Pärt's youth was passed in the shadow first of war, then of lingering occupation. For the formative decades of his youth and early career, the artistic pulse of the country lay exposed to whatever mood prevailed in Moscow, its sense of cultural autonomy severely compromised, to say nothing of the material degradations wrought in the name of social progress. But to children of Pärt's generation this

---

[3] It is close to Finnish and a handful of other Baltic languages, most of which have a small and dwindling number of speakers. *Forgotten Peoples*, a set of choral song cycles by Veljo Tormis, explores this shared heritage.

[4] I write this sentence just a few weeks after the final withdrawal of Russian troops from Estonian soil in the summer of 1994!

history was woven into the fabric of their lives, so that it had the appearance of normality. 'We had what we had—my parents and professors told me that the time before the Soviets was quite different. We listened wide-eyed, open-eared, but for us it was nothing. Later, when I was older, in the Conservatory, then I began to appreciate what it was to live in the Soviet Union, everything enclosed or forbidden. But as a child I didn't know anything different.'

Early Life

Arvo Pärt was born on 11 September 1935, in Paide, a small town lying some 50 miles south and somewhat to the east of Tallinn. His parents separated when he was 3 years old, and he and his mother went to live in Rakvere (a smaller town, almost due east of Tallinn). There, from the age of 7 or 8, Pärt attended a children's music school (outside regular school hours), where he was given sound musical instruction in piano and music theory and literature. At home, the family had acquired a venerable Russian grand piano on which he could practice, though, as only the extreme registers functioned properly, he felt encouraged to spend much of the time experimenting and inventing compositions of his own.

As a teenager, Pärt developed a voracious appetite for listening to music on the radio—any kind of music whatsoever, though he was drawn above all to the sound of the symphony orchestra. The broadcasts included programmes from Finnish Radio, which could be received quite clearly in the northern part of Estonia; and the story has often been told of how he would circle the town square on his bicycle while symphony concerts were being relayed over the loudspeakers there.

At school the piano remained his principal instrument, and he often performed in concerts, particularly as an accompanist. He also played oboe in the school orchestra, percussion in a dance band, and sang in the school choir. He progressed gradually from creative improvisation at the keyboard to more formal compositions, which he began to write down at the age of 14 or 15. The first public performance of a composition by him came a little later when, aged about 17, he entered a young artists' competition, performing a piano piece he had written called *Meloodia*. He did not win: his composition was commended, but the lack of any overtly Estonian roots or influence was apparently a big disadvantage. Pärt remembers that it showed the influence of Rachmaninov—in any case, 'It was not personal music.'

The years following Stalin's death in 1953 are aptly termed a 'thaw'. The immediate sense of terror receded, and a degree of liberalization and radical enquiry crept into the arts. It soon became apparent, however, that the basic direction of Soviet policy was not going to change, nor the underlying adherence to 'Social Realism'. If there were any lingering doubts about this, events in Hungary in 1956 made everything much clearer.

In 1954 Pärt began a course of study at the Music Middle School[5] in Tallinn, where his teachers included the composer Harri Otsa (b.1926). The subjects included composition and theory, piano, music literature, analysis, and folk music. This was abruptly interrupted a few months later by two years' compulsory military service, during which he played oboe and drums in a military orchestra. Pärt has described this as a time of much suffering, though 'it perhaps helped me as a composer'; in fact, he contracted a serious kidney ailment, and his health remained severely impaired for more than a decade. Afterwards, he returned to the Music Middle School for the academic year 1956–7, where his theory and composition teacher was now Veljo Tormis (b.1930).

At the end of the year he was judged sufficiently advanced to move on directly to the Tallinn Conservatory, which he entered in the autumn of 1957. The Conservatory maintained the rigorous standards and comprehensive approach of the Middle School, but included some obligatory extra subjects as well: political economy, history of the Communist Party, and the 'science' of atheism.

To his contemporaries at the Tallinn Conservatory it was clear that Pärt was outstandingly talented. Already in Middle School he stood out as someone to whom the art of composition appeared to come easily. As one follow student[6] put it: 'He just seemed to shake his sleeve and the notes would fall out.' He was extremely fast to assimilate any new idea, whether it came from his teachers or elsewhere, and this facility would extend to his later adoption of various avant-garde techniques often gleaned from the merest hint of a new idea from the West. Assessments vary as to the nature and extent of what Pärt learned from his teachers: on the one hand, it has been said that his teachers did not need to teach him anything much, or so it appeared

---

[5] The equivalent of undergraduate study, whereas Music High School would be the equivalent of graduate or post-diploma study.

[6] Ave Hirvesoo.

to some of his contemporaries, and that he seemed to have an innate sense of timing and musical form (which the clear dramatic profile of many of his subsequent compositions certainly bears out); on the other hand, we have Pärt's own high estimation of his composition teacher, Eller (see below), and his general sense of indebtedness to the integrated instruction he had received, modelled largely on Russian principles. These are not contradictions, of course, but rather reflect the different perspectives involved.

Throughout his time at the Conservatory, Pärt studied composition with Heino Eller (1887–1970), at that time the leading musical figure in Estonia. Eller was a fine violinist and chamber musician, as well as a composer. He had studied at the Conservatoire in St Petersburg, where he attended the classes of the legendary violin teacher Leopold Auer and studied composition with Glazunov (whom Pärt in turn acknowledges as his 'musical grandfather').[7]

As a teacher, Eller was loved and respected by generations of student composers, who came to comprise an Eller 'school'; these included the symphonist Eduard Tubin, who later settled in Sweden, and many others, such as Jaan Rääts, Heimar Ilves, Jaan Koha, and Lepo Sumera, the last-mentioned born in 1950 and recently Minister of Culture in the new Estonian Republic. When Pärt came to study with him, Eller was already in his seventies, and Pärt speaks with great affection of this man, not only as a teacher, but as a father-figure as well. The lessons were held on a one-to-one basis, and normally took place in Eller's house. As with all of Eller's students, there was a tendency to concentrate on instrumental composition somewhat at the expense of vocal music.

The music history that was taught at the Conservatory covered the full range, from earliest times to a rather narrow version of the present, though at this juncture Pärt was not interested in early music or counterpoint, which he found irksome. Eller recognized this and gave him special instruction, so that in a short time he was able to pass the required examination in fugue. It was only later, after Eller's death, that Pärt found a need to focus anew on polyphony: 'I was then quite alone and had to teach myself everything; it was like a new beginning, a new contact with music.'

Although his own music was conservative in style, Eller did not discourage his students from exploring the new ideas that were beginning to filter through from the West. At the beginning of the 1960s

[7] Bradshaw, p. 25.

Pärt studied the few 12-tone scores he could find, and worked alone at two books of exercises by Eimert and Krenek.[8] At this time only a few contemporary Western works had ever been heard in Estonia—pieces by Webern, Boulez, Nono, but little else beyond a few scores and illegal tapes.

It was not only at the Conservatory that Pärt acquired his craft. Quite soon after he began studies with Eller, he also found work as a recording engineer with Estonian Radio. There was little preparatory training for this work; skills were acquired on the job as and when they were needed. During this period Pärt also composed music for the theatre (he was for a while Musical Director at the Pioneer Theatre in Tallinn), and received numerous commissions to write film scores, so that by the time he graduated from Eller's class in the spring of 1963 his career as a professional composer was well under way.

The film and theatre work continued over the years, and the total number of film scores to his credit is estimated at around 50. However, Pärt seems to have derived more fulfilment from the music he wrote for theatre productions, especially children's theatre and puppet productions.[9] In retrospect, Pärt is less than kind towards his film music, dismissing it quite categorically as having no importance whatsoever, although he does seem to have enjoyed the studio's workshop atmosphere.

Early Works

Pärt's earliest published works—two Sonatinas and a Partita—were written shortly after he began studies at the Conservatory, when he was approximately 22 years old. They were followed by a string quartet, two cantatas, and *Nekrolog* for orchestra. All these pieces, with the exception of *Nekrolog*, can be considered as student works or (in the case of the cantatas) as a form of *Gebrauchsmusik*. They reveal an impressive technical fluency and a consuming energy and sense of urgency, and while they do not say anything particularly new, their air of controlled assurance is immediately noticeable.

The piano works are strongly imbued with neoclassical mannerisms, though held under tight rein and permeated with a marked

---

[8] Herbert Eimert's *Lehrbuch der Zwölftontechnik* (Wiesbaden, 1953), and Ernst Krenek's *Studies in Counterpoint—Based on the Twelve-Tone Technique* (New York, 1940).

[9] A group of songs from this period were published *c*.1960 as *Five Children's Songs*. An earlier set of piano pieces, *Four Easy Dances for Piano*, has recently been reissued by Eres Edition, Bremen (1993). Written for a children's theatre in 1956–7, the titles are: 1. Puss in Boots. 2. Little Red Riding Hood and the Wolf. 3. Butterflies. 4. Dance of the Ducklings.

severity of mood. The Partita is the most individual of them, and is notable for its avoidance of any clear suggestion of tonality in the opening section. Whereas the shadows of Shostakovich and Prokofiev bestride the piano pieces, it is more the spirit of Bartók that animates the three-movement String Quartet, particularly from a rhythmic point of view. The two cantatas are another matter. *Meie Aed* ('Our Garden'), a cantata for children's choir and orchestra, must be viewed in the context of an extensive engagement with children's music. For his text Pärt drew on the work of Eno Raud (b.1928), a well-known children's author in Estonia who had also written scenarios for film and puppet theatre. The musical style is of course tonal and the mood spontaneous and cheerful, and while this may have been politically appropriate, one senses also the composer's direct involvement in the task of writing for children. The vocal lines and harmonies are simple enough, yet effective and expressive in an economical way, the impression of the whole being enhanced by colourful orchestration, punctuated here and there with deft touches of idiomatic vocal writing.

In the composition of *Nekrolog* (1960-1) Pärt began to employ serial technique. He was the first Estonian composer to do so, and came under strong criticism for this espousal of Western 'formalism' (the work will be discussed further in Chapter 3).

A year after *Nekrolog*, another cantata was written—*Maailma Samm*—presumably to mollify some official feathers that had been ruffled by the earlier work's decadent Western tendencies. Where *Meie Aed* breathes a certain fresh *naïveté*, the later cantata seems heavy with forced optimism and artificially inseminated international benevolence—though, as always, the musical ideas are boldly portrayed and skilfully articulated. The librettist for this work was Enn Vetemaa (b.1936), who would subsequently become well known as an author of short stories and plays, but whom Pärt probably met at the Conservatory, where Vetemaa was also a student of composition (graduating in 1965).

Merike Vaitmaa, an Estonian musicologist and author of several articles on Pärt, has commented on the origin and purpose of such works:

It is common knowledge that in those years here the composers, and young composers in particular, were being asked, ordered, sometimes employed privately by music officials to write cantatas and oratorios using the ideologically 'proper' texts; in the Estonian musicians' slang such works are called 'the emperor cantatas' (*die Kaiserkantaten*; *keisrikantaadid*). An emperor cantata was a kind of indulgence: having written it, a composer could write in peace what he wanted.[10]

In 1957 the Second All-Union Congress of Composers in Moscow had rejected the rigid conformism of the previous decade, and the following year saw the setting up of cultural exchange programmes with countries in the West, which opened the way for contact with fresh ideas. After 1958 the music of composers like Schoenberg and Webern was no longer banned. While this was undoubtedly an important concession, we should remember that Shostakovich and his generation were themselves opposed to modernist dodecaphony and the experimental avant-garde—opposed, that is to say, on musical grounds, not merely out of ideological convenience. In the autumn of 1959 Shostakovich even advised the younger Polish composers not to be seduced by experimental modernism.[11]

Shortly after the twenty-second Party Congress (October 1961) an article was issued attacking Andrei Volkonsky (b.1933) for his 'experiments' in dodecaphony.[12] In 1954 Volkonsky had been a staunch defender of Shostakovich's Tenth Symphony; but after 1956, when he produced the first serial work by a Soviet composer, *Musica Stricta*, he found the atmosphere around him becoming increasingly uncongenial. The same article also singles out works by slightly younger composers for special commendation, among them *Songs of War and Peace* by Alfred Schnittke (b.1934), *Ode to the First Cosmonaut* by Jaan Rääts (b.1932), and *Maailma Samm* by Pärt. The following year at the Third All-Union Congress of Composers (Moscow, March 1962) the attack on dodecaphony was further renewed, with contributions from older composers such as Khachaturyan and Kabalevsky. It was on this occasion, as we have seen, that Pärt came under sharp criticism for his orchestral work *Nekrolog*.

The autumn of this complex year also saw the Cuban missile crisis and Stravinsky's historic return visit to Russia for the first time in 50 years. In November a series of concerts called 'The All-Union Survey of the Creative Work of Young Composers' took place in Moscow. These formed the final round in a competition for young composers under the age of 35 from throughout the USSR. Over a thousand compositions had been considered, and amongst the six prize-winners were two Estonian composers, Pärt and Eino Tamberg (b.1930). This

[10] Vaitmaa 1990.
[11] Quoted in Schwarz, p. 323.
[12] By a minor official named Aksyuk; quoted in Schwarz, pp. 344-5.

was useful recognition of Pärt's talent, though the works in question (*Meie Aed* and *Maailma Samm*) lie outside his real path and were passing acknowledgements, as it were, of the tuneful optimism that earned Soviet prizes.

Middle Years

Throughout the 1960s Pärt continued to compose a rich series of works using serial and collage techniques which made no stylistic compromises whatsoever. His works were quite widely performed in the various Soviet republics and satellite states, and sometimes also in the West. But then in 1968 another scandal erupted, after the performance of *Credo* for piano, chorus, and orchestra. Quite apart from the official displeasure occasioned by the implications of the work's title, this marked a huge crisis in his creative development, and for a number of years Pärt, to all intents and purposes, fell silent.[13] The crisis was not only a musical one, but reached into all aspects of his life at once, affecting his spiritual well-being and his physical health. Later, during the early 1970s, Pärt married his second wife, Nora (in 1972); he joined the Russian Orthodox Church; his health was restored; and, guided by his researches into early music, he moved towards a new tonal style to which he gave the name 'tintinnabuli'.

During the 1970s an exodus of Soviet Jews took place, that grew from an initial trickle to a veritable flood by the end of the decade.[14] As Pärt's wife was Jewish, he was urged to take advantage of the opportunity this presented—and thus doubtless to spare the authorities the thorn of his presence. But the Pärts at first had no desire to leave Estonia. However, as the official attitude towards his new music hardened, he was prevented from travelling abroad to attend concerts of his music, and altogether his ability to function as a composer was severely compromised, both artistically and economically. Eventually, in 1979, the Pärts decided to apply for exit visas to leave the Soviet Union. These were duly granted. On 18 January 1980, Pärt, his wife, and their two sons, boarded the train in Tallinn that would transport them across Europe to Vienna. Theoretically they were bound for Israel, though when they left they had no specific final destination in

---

[13] This period will be examined in greater detail in Ch. 4.
[14] Brumfield and Velimirovic and Levin are interesting sources of information on this subject.

32

mind.[15] Two mornings later they arrived at Vienna Hauptbahnhof, where they were met unexpectedly by a representative of Universal Edition, who offered them assistance to stay in Vienna.[16] This they were glad to do, and, as they had been obliged as a condition of leaving the Soviet Union to give up their Soviet citizenship, they acquired Austrian citizenship. The following year, with the help of a scholarship from the German Academic Exchange Service, they moved to Berlin—which remains their principal home today.

[15] Technically, all émigrés were destined for Israel, whose authorities were obliged to issue official invitations, but a considerable majority 'dropped out' *en route* and headed for destinations in Western Europe and North America.

[16] It seems that the composer Alfred Schnittke was instrumental in this arrangement.

3
SERIALISM/COLLAGE

Introduction

THROUGHOUT the 1960s, from *Nekrolog* to *Credo*, Pärt followed a distinctly personal path through the twists and turns of what we have now learned to call 'modernism'. Inevitably this period in his life has been discounted as 'the other', as the obverse of what he has since become famous for. Our view of this music, which has been lumped together as that of his 'serial period', has been distorted by somewhat superficial observation by writers hastening on to the richer pastures of the tintinnabuli music itself. Perhaps they should not be blamed for doing this; to a certain degree they have been encouraged by Pärt's own disavowal of the earlier style (not, however, of the actual pieces), to which must be added the foreshortening perspective of hindsight, reinforced by the clearly demarcated zones of tonal and serial languages.

The purpose of this chapter will be to answer two broad questions: what is the nature of this music in itself, and how does it lead towards an understanding of the later works? I have preferred to set aside the occasionally nagging question of which composer this or that section reminds us of. Berg may come to mind, Bartók assuredly will, also Penderecki and perhaps Ligeti. But the lines of influence cannot be mapped with any confidence; not all new music was readily available to Pärt, and many of his works suggest a unique stylistic synthesis owing quite as much to the composer's own vision as to any outside model. The deeper influences are, initially, quite simply the great composers of the European tradition, with special emphasis perhaps on 'local' figures such as Tchaikovsky and Glazunov. Later, of course, and more specifically there is the acknowledged use of Bach, and later still the exploration of early music and plainchant. In between, the currents of twentieth-century modernism make themselves plainly felt and are obvious enough, but the main issue concerns Pärt's inward journey towards the stylistic block that followed *Credo*, and not the relatively familiar outward circumstances that washed against him.

What precisely was lacking for Pärt in modernism? The binding strength of tonality certainly, but, more than that surely, its focus on a still centre as a point of radiant permanence. The glimpses of tonality in these earlier works are like intimations of a paradisiacal garden from which exile is felt to be increasingly futile. The quest is a spiritual one enfolded within an aesthetic one, and the worldly renunciation that we witness in his music of the 1970s is the decisive act of someone for whom the two realms are no longer separate.

If we were asked to pin-point the principal works in this narrative, we should cite *Perpetuum Mobile*, Symphony No. 2, and *Credo*—three works which together tell the essence of the story, and are fundamental to an understanding of Pärt's work overall. It should perhaps also be pointed out that the serial/collage works were composed over a period of just eight to nine years, which bespeaks a time of fairly intense activity. I begin with the first work which Pärt accepts as moving beyond his student works, *Nekrolog*, composed when he was about 25 and already making two kinds of names for himself in the strange musical world of the Soviet Union: prize-winner and *enfant terrible*.

Nekrolog

In the course of my life there have been several upsets. It started as far back as 1960–61, when I composed *Nekrolog*, which was my first orchestral piece. I was a student at the conservatory of music in Tallinn, and I had written a piece in 12-tone technique which was at that time and place extraordinary. As a result there was strong criticism from the highest circles. Nothing was considered more hostile than so-called influences from the West, to which 12-tone music belonged.[1]

Indeed, this work stimulated open quarrelling amongst critics and academics. There were performances in Moscow, Leningrad, Zagreb, Geneva, and later in Tallinn, so it could hardly be ignored. It was the first dodecaphonic piece by any Estonian composer, and although Pärt's skill and imagination were not in doubt, its blatant 'formalism' certainly clouded the official response. At the 1962 All-Union Congress of Composers, the Union's First Secretary, Khrennikov, spoke out vehemently against those who would compose in dodecaphonic style:

[1] Elste, p. 338.

35

I must speak here of an exclusive small group existing in the backwater of the broad stream of musical life and engaged in formal searchings and fruitless experimentation. Their striving to deck themselves in other people's cast-off clothes is undoubtedly the sign of immaturity of some of our young composers. . . . Our young experimenters should realize that there is a difference between freedom of creative searchings and lack of principles.[2]

Turning to Pärt in particular, Khrennikov remarked:

A work like Pärt's [*Nekrolog*] makes it quite clear that the twelve-tone experiment is untenable. This composition is dedicated to the memory of the victims of Fascism,[3] but it bears the characteristics of the productions of foreign 'avant-gardists': ultra-expressionistic, purely naturalistic depiction of the state of fear, terror, despair and dejection . . . so we see that the attempts to employ the expressive techniques of the avant-garde bourgeois music for the realization of progressive ideas of our time are discredited by the results they produce.[4]

For Pärt, the work's title meant quite specifically an obituary—but one for the living, rather than the dead. The original dedication, referred to above, was not supplied by the composer. He did not object to it at the time, as it was to a certain extent appropriate. The theme was indeed fashionable—but if one were to mourn the victims of fascism, why not also the victims of communism? 'The theme is larger than something which can be wept over; a condition of mourning for the whole of mankind'—implying essentially our modern civilization and everything that is worldly in it. The music's character is blackly depressive, offering no hint of relief or escape, still less of resurrection. In later years, Pärt came to accept the necessity of suffering as a means towards catharsis. But at the time he could not detect that life-giving source which can exist in moments of grief; he felt, and could express, only a pervasive sense of evil and tragedy, which he wanted to refute. It would have been madness, of course, to express such sentiments openly, and so the true import of the work's title remained a secret. The first mature work of Pärt's *œuvre*, it may be said to point towards the tintinnabuli style, but it does so from a great distance, and represents starkly the negative polarity of the later music.

Nekrolog is cast in a single movement, and bears the imprint of sonata form in its use of two contrasted blocks of material and ele-

---

[2] Quoted in Schwarz, p. 345.

[3] The original dedication, 'to the victims of Fascism', has been omitted from the score recently published by M. P. Belaieff (Frankfurt, 1990).

[4] Quoted in Schwarz, p. 346.

ments of development and recapitulation. Although there are points where a 12-note row is articulated, the music is not entirely governed by strict serial procedures. Despite variations of tempo and texture, its mood is almost unremittingly bleak.

The introduction sets forth the work's basic material, in which a series of falling sixths leads to the insistent repetition of a single pitch, which in turn generates an even more rhetorical gesture. Exx. 1*a–d* show the main thread of this introduction. The opening (Ex. 1*a*) presents this material in its most compact form: a motif in the top voice (comprised of a rising perfect fourth, bisected by a tone and a third, followed by a falling sixth) and simultaneously a chord (two minor thirds a semitone apart separated by octave transposition); the first three chords in fact contain all 12 pitch classes. In Exx. 1*b* and 1*c* only the most prominent musical line is shown. In Ex. 1*b*, the opening

Ex. 1*a*

Ex. 1*b*

Ex. 1*c*

Ex. 1*d*

Ex. 1e

vn. 1 soli

Ex. 1f

ob. solo

motif is repeated in sequence, each entry a major third lower (the accompanying parts, not shown, also correspond in detail to the opening chords). The repeated Es in Ex. 1c provide a model for similar gestures later in the work, but for the moment lead directly to the first statement of a push–pull rhythmic motif (Ex. 1d) which is repeated with obsessive intensity at defining points throughout the work. (The pitch classes of this chord are those of the opening chord transposed down a fourth.)

After the introduction there are two contrasting longer sections, one a nervous and spiky scherzo with aggressive dance rhythms, the other slower, more contrapuntal, and even at times lyrical in character. (The beginnings of both are shown in Exx. 1e and 1f respectively.) These materials are then combined and developed, leading into a frenzied finale like a dance of the dead with prancing triple rhythms. Eventually, the rhythmic figure shown in Ex. 1d is reasserted in an ominous tutti, and the music's energy collapses into a reprise of slow dissonant counterpoint, before fading away in muffled timpani rolls to nothing.[5]

Perpetuum Mobile *and First Symphony*

These next two pieces properly form a pair; both are highly tense, relentless works built around clearly defined systematic processes.

[5] Of the various orchestral works I will be discussing, *Nekrolog* is the only one currently unavailable on a commercial recording. I was fortunate in obtaining an old radio tape from Estonian sources, which allowed me to clarify my impressions of the work. It is to be hoped that this gap in Pärt's discography will be filled before long.

They also share the same 12-note row, the initial form in one being an inversion of that in the other, transposed through a tritone (see below, Ex. 3*a*). The symphony was begun first, and so carries the earlier opus number, but Pärt interrupted work on it to compose *Perpetuum Mobile*, which he completed before returning to the symphony.

Perpetuum Mobile (Perpetual Motion), was premièred in Tallinn in 1963, and was subsequently performed at the Warsaw Autumn Festival of Contemporary Music in September 1964, where an immediate encore was demanded. The sensational success of this performance was repeated shortly afterwards in other Soviet bloc capitals.

Though only four minutes long, *Perpetuum Mobile* calls for full orchestra. It is a work in which the organization of a growing mass of sound is strictly controlled by serial processes to create a musical shape whose simplicity is apparent enough to the listener even as it threatens to overwhelm him. This shape is a gradual crescendo and decrescendo (in a series of waves each bigger than the last), rising from nothing, and eventually returning to nothing. The relentless intensification of dynamic, rhythm, register, and harmonic density builds a wall of sound that finally climaxes three-quarters of the way through, at which point the music subsides, rather like a nightmare being put back to sleep. It comes as no surprise to find that the underlying structure is carefully calculated to bring this effect about logically, step by step.

The work is in six sections, each containing one of the four basic untransposed versions of a 12-note row. In each bar (4/4 throughout) a new instrument or group of instruments enters, with a single pitch class and specific note-value, which is then repeated a set number of times. (The diagram, Ex. 2*a*, shows the systematic pattern in which the pitches and durations are deployed.) The bar-to-bar array of pitches gradually enunciates the 12-note row, while the note-values become progressively shorter. When the first version of the row has been sounded, the rhythmic and pitch process begins again, using a different version of the row. During the first four sections, the overall range of note-values gradually shortens, and the number of repeats (of each individual pitch) increases, so that a dense texture is built up of different pitches and durations sounding together and steadily accumulating force. Then the rhythmic pattern is reversed for the final two sections (and two more versions of the row).

The order in which the instruments enter and the use of octave transposition and doubling are freely varied, though naturally the greatest density and range are found in the fourth and fifth sections,

Ex. 2*a*

Standard no. of
bars for each
pitch

N.B. 3/2 = 3 of the given unit in the
same time as 2 of the *same* unit;

thus ♪ = 𝄽𝄽𝄽𝄽𝄽 = ♩
    5/4

leading towards the highest point of intensity. This is marked by a
cymbal crash at the beginning of the sixth section, where the violas
initiate the final pitch/rhythm sequence. This point in the score is
also reproduced here (Ex. 2*b*). Each new pitch is given only once, and
thereafter only the rhythm is shown. The score shows concert pitches;
gradual crescendos and decrescendos are indicated by the direction
of the arrows: the violas' downward arrow at fig. 6 indicates a steady
decrescendo.

The use of such a closely predetermined scheme prefigures much in
Pärt's later music, of course, and it also sets a pattern for his general
application of serial technique. He does, however, allow himself a
certain flexibility: there are a few bars (at the beginning and the end)
which fall outside the strict pattern; the number of bars is not always

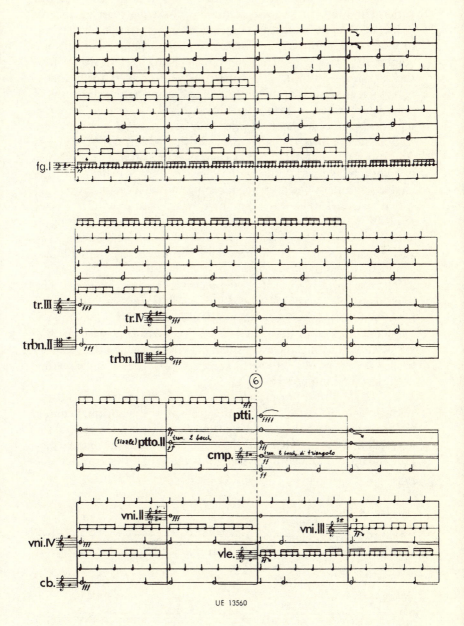

UE 13560

fully sustained by all instruments where two or more are doubling a pattern; and towards the end of the fourth section there is an early reduction from the 15 repeats of each pitch in preparation for the drop to nine in the fifth section. These essentially colouristic details are admittedly minor considerations, yet they show a close attention to the sounding result, at the expense, if necessary, of strict adherence to a preconceived system. Even so, an intriguing foretaste of minimalism emerges as one examines this work, especially if one ignores the precedence of 12 notes over 7. This arises not from any audible surface pattern (other than perhaps momentarily), still less from any dance pulse, but rather from the monolithic nature of what is going on. Notwithstanding the constant flux to which the title alludes, essentially one massive, uncompromising idea is taking shape, which accords well with the underlying nature of the earlier minimalist works (in art as well as music) that were beginning to appear in New York and San Francisco at this time, and in which the very apparent simplicity of form does not necessarily translate into simplicity of experience.

Pärt was unaware of such developments at the time, of course. The only likely influence for *Perpetuum Mobile*'s textural writing would have been the younger generation of Polish composers—though here we should notice that despite its expressive intensity, *Perpetuum Mobile* essentially avoids the expressionistic gestures which then characterized the music of Penderecki. *Perpetuum Mobile* is a single searing gesture several minutes in length.

Ex. 3*a* shows the basic tone-rows for *Perpetuum Mobile* and the First Symphony. An all-interval row (though the major third/minor sixth are obtained only by moving from the twelfth pitch back to the first again), it interpolates two chromatic hexachords in contrary motion: the upper hexachord (divided into groups of three, two, and one

Ex. 3*a*

Perpetuum Mobile

Symphony No. 1

pitches) is shown in the example by slurs, the lower hexachord by square brackets.

The First Symphony carries the subtitle 'Polyphonic', and is dedicated to Pärt's teacher Heino Eller. There are two movements: Canons, and Prelude and Fugue. 'Polyphonic' implies an imitative contrapuntal texture, which this work certainly has, though several of its many interesting features derive from interlocking rhythmic patterns, syncopation, and even ostinato, relying on a visceral sense of energy quite as much as polyphonic intricacy to propel the music forward.

The opening is an astringent fanfare, at once ominous and assertive, with more than a hint of melodrama. Ex. 3b shows the hemiola effect which obtains at the outset, and yields a brash melodic figure (bars 13–14), to which other instruments respond, building up the notes of the row as they do so. The opening chords are then repeated and

Ex. 3b

answered by dense string clusters which expand the rhythmic pattern, so that [♩ ♩ ♩ ♩] becomes [♩ ♩ ♩ ♩ ♩ ♩ ♩]. This leads directly to a change of metre (2/4) and a sprightly woodwind conversation based more clearly now on the row as a melodic entity. The row is heard in five forms simultaneously: four instruments play one version each, while between them certain tones are sustained so as to delineate a further version.

There follows a series of different canonic treatments of the row, each rising to a different degree of intensity. After the loudest of these has been dissipated by a solo hi-hat roll, dissolving in a ritardando and diminuendo, the final and most ingenious canon concludes the movement with a four-part texture worthy of the fifteenth-century Flemish school. Ex. 3c shows a passage from this section (rehearsal no. 29, 3rd bar), where the second and fourth voices are in canon (at the unison displaced by two octaves), as are, likewise, the third and first voices (the first pair playing the row P-11, the second pair playing the inversion of this transposition). There is also strict rhythmic imitation between the two slower-moving, outer voices (a bar apart), and more closely still between the two inner voices (just a single beat apart). The middle section of this canon then treats the row transposed to P-2 and its inversion with fuller scoring. At its loudest point, retrograde versions of the row are introduced, and it is with these forms and finally

Ex. 3c

str.
w.w.

* The published score has F natural
  which I take to be a misprint, given
  the strict canonic principles at work.

R-11 that the movement unwinds, with pizzicato cellos falling away to nothing.

The prelude which opens the second movement provides a brief lyrical core to the symphony, dominated by a solo violin. This is soon overwhelmed by a dense string texture of the sort which becomes a frequent characteristic of Pärt's string writing in the 1960s. Typically, the strings subdivide to play a melodic line in parallel or contrary motion, dispersed by semitones across an interval that may be as much as an octave. The result is very much like the piano clusters of Henry Cowell, though again, the Polish avant-garde may be the more immediate source. Surprisingly, this in turn gives way to a walking pizzicato bass and a fugato woodwind section which sounds positively light-hearted, for a while at least. This then yields to a rhythmic fugue, the most distinctively Pärtian passage in the whole piece. A rhythmic ostinato pattern is set up by the violas on their low C (beginning at rehearsal no. 43), while a bassoon sustains the same pitch. This is answered by the same figure displaced by half a beat and pitched a semitone higher, the bassoon also moving to the new pitch. This interlocking of the same rhythmic figure with itself is shown in Ex. 3d.

In this way the row is sounded out slowly by the woodwind, one note at a time; but in the process, each pitch in turn joins the gathering string cluster that grows ever larger and louder. After the row has been sounded once, the process continues, moving not only to a higher register, but with the row transposed up a semitone, so as to enrich the dissonance with a new array of the 12 tones. It is then the turn of the brass to sound forth across this pulsating texture with a steadier melodic line derived from the 'light-hearted' music heard earlier. Even the walking bass is alluded to by the woodwind, now almost running, in not quite parallel octaves.

The final and climactic section takes the prelude's violin solo and reworks it for subdivided strings playing the melody in twelve parallel seconds, so that each chord is a dense 12-note cluster. The percussion break into this strange rhapsody with a figure borrowed from the rhythmic fugue, which becomes increasingly aggressive, rising to a savage climax which leaves a high string cluster hanging, supine, in the air.

Ex. 3d

45

Although the contrapuntal and numerical ingenuities of serial composition clearly appealed to Pärt, he never seems to have settled happily into the idiom. This is an easy observation to make with hindsight, certainly, but it is very noticeable that the strongest features of these earlier works are those larger dramatic gestures in which musical time is frozen and a particular idea is allowed to attain its own organic shape, owing nothing particularly to the serial process itself. The corporeal substance of Pärt's musical ideas and his propensity for broad, clearly outlined dramatic reliefs have little to do with the fully integrated serialism advocated in the 1950s and 1960s at such centres as Paris, Darmstadt, and Princeton. For Pärt it seems that serialism was primarily a useful means of pouring pitch sequences into musical ideas that originated elsewhere. At first we harbour the suspicion that this is due to lingering shades of neoclassicism—which have, after all, haunted many of this century's composers, offering easy toccata and fugato formats wherever technique and will-power are all that is to hand. But Pärt has never lacked musical ideas or compositional motivation; we shall see that throughout the 1960s a growing struggle was taking place between textures that fill to screaming point and then empty to almost nothing and a steadier sense of being and contemplation which Pärt invokes, but then sets out with almost diabolical precision to destroy.

Whereas *Perpetuum Mobile* incarnates a compositional archetype with a rigour that is strongly suggestive of his later tintinnabuli structures, the First Symphony gives the lie to any suggestion that Pärt discovered imitative counterpoint and metrical canons during his period of early music study in the 1970s. It is clear that he already had a profound awareness of such devices and their architectonic potential: indeed, it is clear that they form the idiomatic essence of his musical thought. The later study of early music certainly involved technical issues, but was primarily an exploration of ways in which musical technique could serve spiritual ends, given his arrival at a point at which tonality was once again a necessity.

The 1964 Compositions: Diagrams, Musica Sillabica, Quintettino, Solfeggio, Collage sur B-A-C-H

With these compositions Pärt assumes a more rigorously abstract musical style, of which *Musica Sillabica* and *Diagrams* are the most extreme examples. The athematicism of *Perpetuum Mobile* may be said to have paved the way for these works, while they in turn—or rather, some of their technical procedures—are put to service in the Second Symphony and eventually also in *Credo*.

1964 also sees the first appearance of a reference to Bach, although this is only explicit in the work called *Collage*, which is both based on the B-A-C-H motif and also quotes actual music by Bach. But the B-A-C-H motif, variously transposed and inverted, can also be traced in several other works, suggesting a potential link between them. This reference and the link it proposes do not seem to have been always intentional, yet the motif's recurring presence is undeniable. The more conscious references to Bach continue after *Collage* with *Credo*, 1968, and on into 1976 with *Wenn Bach Bienen gezüchtet hätte*.

At first glance, the most surprising thing about the score of *Diagrams* (the only work for piano solo between Partita and *Für Alina*) is its colourful appearance. The cover of the original Estonian edition sports a bold design in red, black, and white, while coloured circles are used in the opening section of the music to connect groups of pitches into phrases (the colours being used in the order in which they appear in the colour spectrum).

The row again illustrates Pärt's taste for symmetry, with emphasis on the division of the octave into two halves (the second hexachord is a transposed inversion of the first), and a clear pattern created by the disposition of intervals (see Ex. 4). The first four pitches employ the intervals of the B-A-C-H motif transposed to begin on C. Altogether the work presents the row 48 times (though in only four different positions: P, I, R-2, and R-12, this last transposition and shape yielding the actual B-A-C-H pitches), which is a significant Bachian number indeed—notwithstanding a certain dodecadic inevitability where a 12-note row is in use.

There are two sections, markedly contrasted in character. The first is marked 'Rahutult' (agitatedly), and consists of a sequence of coloured circles containing first one, then two pitches, and so on up to 12. This process uses up 13 versions of the row, and leads directly to a series of 12-note clusters in each hand. The right hand remains in the top octave, while the left hand jumps in a systematic sequence down through the octaves to the piano's lowest register. This in effect

Ex. 4

no. of
semitones: 1   3   1   2   1   5   1   3   1   2   1   5

47

constitutes another 30 soundings of the row's chromatic content, although each one occurs all at once. The second section then follows, marked 'Aeglaselt' (slowly), and consists of isolated single pitches throughout, taking us through five more statements of the row. It is the central group of 30 (this could so easily have been another number) which reinforces the sense of an intentional allusion to Bach—although the composer does not remember this being the case!

Musica Sillabica is a chamber work for 12 instruments, although a conductor is required, who must play a thirteenth instrument at the very end (a timpani roll). Its overall texture is strongly coloured by the timbres of the piano, vibraphone, and electric guitar. Each bar is separated from the next by a short pause, and thus we seem to hear a succession of musical 'syllables' (of varying duration and complexity) rather than complete words or phrases. There is therefore an underlying sense of rhythmic pulse, defined by the regular alternation of sounds and silence—although the exact length of these is not specified. The pitches are notated as dots distributed equally in the space of a bar, no two players having the same number of pitches in the same bar.

The work is based on a 12-note row, the inversion of the one used in *Diagrams*. Two processes are at work, one ordering the number of notes in each bar, the other the distribution of pitches, and both processes unfold with strict precision. The row is always dispersed horizontally throughout the instruments, providing pitches as needed. First it is sounded in its four basic positions, in the order P, I, R, RI. This sequence is then repeated throughout, but with the row transposed to each of the row's pitches in turn, thus using up all 48 versions in strict sequence (this process is then repeated one and a half times).

The manner of construction of the work is altogether reminiscent of *Perpetuum Mobile* except that the pitches are isolated and without the duration being specified. As in the earlier work, a single, essentially cerebral process is given a starkly palpable shape by the clarity of the design and its execution: the alternation of sound and silence and the steady accumulation of detail to a maximum before a reduction of the texture back towards zero. The overall pointillistic articulation is not relinquished until the timpani roll at the very end and a concluding sweep of notes on the vibraphone. The composer described this work to me as an attempt to organize chaos, of penetrating to the heart of the atom.

The *Quintettino* is a lightweight wind quintet in three short movements, fast, slow, moderate, which again appears to employ the B-A-C-H motif, creating a 12-note set that divides the octave into three tetrachords. Although the first movement opens with a series of 12 staccato G major chords, it quickly veers off into faster, asymmetrical material, serially constructed. The second movement builds slow harmonic clusters out of each tetrachord, and in bar 3 the horn clearly announces the B-A-C-H motif, and further varies its shape every few bars. A slow flute cadenza leads *attacca* to the third movement, where the instruments enter separately, each with its own rhythmic ostinato patterns, before combining for a reprise of the first movement's chordal statements. The piece ends with a reassuringly whimsical gesture.

One of the most surprising works of this period is *Solfeggio*, a beautiful and delicate study in a cappella choral timbres, which uses the simplest material imaginable: a seven-note series—the C major scale—sung 10 times in succession, while the 'text' comprises the syllables of the tonic sol-fa. No strict system governs the distribution of the pitches among the four voices, but everything is most skilfully balanced to produce a constantly fluctuating texture of overlapping pitches. Subtle variations of dynamic, register, and duration enrich the meshing together of diatonic dissonances in a way that begins to resemble what will eventually emerge as an important aspect of the tintinnabuli style.

Whereas the degree of intention behind Pärt's use of the B-A-C-H motif in other 1964 works may be open to question, *Collage sur B-A-C-H* declares its allegiance openly. As the title implies, this work employs more than a simple allusion or quotation: in addition to the many contrapuntal and harmonic treatments of the titular motif, we witness for the first time the appearance of quasi-baroque textures and even quotations of actual music by Bach, both 'straight' and distorted. In addition, the titles of the three movements—Toccata, Sarabande, and Ricercar—openly proclaim the work's grounding in the heritage of the past. The work is scored for string orchestra with the addition of solo oboe, harpsichord, and piano in the middle movement. Considered in isolation, this work might appear to be just another neo-baroque effusion (of which there have been so many, particularly at this time from eastern Europe); but its place in Pärt's unfolding *œuvre* is more than happenstance, preparing the way for *Credo* and articulating the growing clash between irreconcilable elements which now emerges as Pärt's most immediate concern.

The Toccata consists of three sections, each framed by two of the B-A-C-H pitches, thus: BA AC CH. The first section begins with a pulsated B♭ major chord, contained in one octave, which quickly spreads outwards across the arpeggiated triad of B♭, moving in both directions at once, until it occupies a five-octave spread. This rapidly collapses down to a single unison B♭, which is gradually superseded by the following pitches: A-C-B(= H)-E♭-E-D-G-F-F♯; this sequence is then repeated, and in fact forms a 10-note row (see Ex. 5*a*). Against the prevailing pattern of steady quavers, one pitch is emphasized by being played louder and in semiquavers; as the row is repeated, more pitches are treated thus, until we reach a point at which all ten pitches have become semiquavers.

This in turn dissolves inwards, not to a unison, but to a chord of B♭, A, and C, which makes brief passing reference to A minor and establishes the movement's second section. A pulsating texture of considerable harmonic density is built up, with two sets of instruments, one playing on the beat, the other on the off-beat. There is another outward-spanning chord, as at the beginning (though now of course highly dissonant), and at the point of maximum expansion the double basses are added and tonality is restored with a resounding C minor.[6] The third section is thereby announced. This fuses into a total chromatic cluster, C♯ and A♭ having finally been admitted (though one's ear can hardly be expected to detect the fact), and there follows a protracted discourse echoing the quaver–semiquaver contrasts of the first section, but using the row now in each of its (untransposed) basic forms with emphasis on the retrograde and its inversion. The conclusion of this episode leaves a reiterated bass D treading not into silence, but on to a final chord of B minor.

The outcome of this movement is to confer a linear relationship between the opening tonality of B♭ major and the concluding B minor. Initially this is a consequence of the B-A-C-H motif heard as a macro-melody being slowly enunciated through the movement as a whole. But it is reinforced by the many repetitions of the foreshortened row which, never being transposed, allows the sum of its opening

[6] The E♭s in the published score are erroneous.

and closing pitches (in the row's four basic positions)—B♭ D F♯—to articulate a triadic ambiguity. This, with the helpful direction of the B-A-C-H motif, is ultimately resolved in favour of B minor.

The second movement is a rescoring of the D minor Sarabande from Bach's Sixth English Suite, chosen, we may guess, for the lyrical and somewhat disguised use it makes of the B-A-C-H motif (transposed to begin on F; see Ex. 5*b*). Its form follows that of the original—a binary structure of 8 and 16 bars, both repeated—except in one detail. For the first eight bars, oboe and harpsichord, doubled by strings, simply play Bach's music, cool and unmediated except for the particulars of the orchestration. The repeat is another matter, and it is here that the tonal/atonal conflict is most keenly felt: the strings absorb the melody by playing it in 12-part clusters of parallel semitones, doubled by the piano, over a low pedal D. The ear recognizes the melodic shape at first, but as the pedal drops away, the melody winds away from its model in an upward spiral. Tonality is restored, together with oboe and harpsichord, for the first eight bars of the Sarabande's second section. Again the repeat is distorted with string clusters, this time starting softly and high up over an A pedal (rather like someone gingerly treading barefoot through fragments of glass); a crescendo threatens, but then the safety of Bach's D minor is restored for the last eight bars.

The Ricercar, marked *deciso*, consists of strictly imitative counterpoint, in which relentless statements of the B-A-C-H motif (see Ex. 5*a* above) are variously inverted, transposed, and augmented, overlapping from the beginning in a continuous stretto texture. Just before the end, a rhythmic declamation of D major is announced, which contends with a dissonant chord—comprised of

Ex. 5*b* The beginning of Bach's Sarabande

The BACH motif is shown by the asterisks.

the B–A–C–H pitches!—and we are left with a D major glowing with promise.

1966: Second Symphony and Pro et Contra

The concerto for cello and orchestra *Pro et Contra* (For and Against) and the Symphony No. 2 were both written in 1966, and share many distinctive traits. They are in many ways the most confident and mature examples of Pärt's serial writing, even though they offer firm evidence of the mounting frustration which he seems to have felt with this particular dialect of modernism. The concept of collage still underwrites the music, even where no external references are being made. The music is mostly constructed by juxtaposing and alternating different motifs or textures, which typically expand or contract in a systematic way, either rising from the merest gestural scribble to a point of screaming, high density (whether in terms of volume, dissonance, or both), or being disassembled in a comparable manner. Very often one system is expanding at the direct expense of another which is in the process of shrinking. It seems that the music is unwilling or unable to stand still, to be at peace; that it can only exist by growing (and therefore, ultimately, by dying), and knows nothing of the subsistence economy which marks Pärt's later style.

In a compositional process that uses layers or blocks of contrasted sounds, a sudden assertion of tonality or even a direct quotation is easy to arrange. The fact that this can have an anachronistic effect is something deliberately cultivated by many composers, especially of this generation and stylistic orientation. Tonality is displayed as an alternative, sometimes to be quickly snatched away again, sometimes trifled with, and sometimes fingered longingly like a forgotten toy. Pärt is perfectly adept at handling such material, but there is something out of place: it is not the allusion itself or the stylistic contrasts which are troubling, but rather the need to make the allusion. It is the confession of a composer for whom a certain kind of expressiveness is unobtainable within the style that history has apparently ordained for him. The transcendent climax of this personal struggle is reached in *Credo*, where a more lasting solution is glimpsed. But with these 1966 works we are still in a world that chronicles despair, yet no longer feels that this is sufficient purpose. Here the desolation (musical at the very least, and pointing to some deeply personal crisis) reaches its apogee.

If the Symphony No. 2 is Pärt's most disturbing work, it is not the level of aggression that makes it so, for there is as much, if not more, in other works; nor is it simply the uneasy mixture of serialism and tonality, which also occurs elsewhere. Rather, it is the unique chemical reaction of the different elements, and the feeling of savage, bitter scorn unleashed, barely relieved even by the dulcet conclusion. At the outset we are knocked off balance by the unexpected sound of children's squeaky toys, the alienating effect of which lingers in the memory and permeates the whole piece; indeed, the beginning and end of this work may be said to inhabit childhood, the purity of which is invoked as something that might eventually overcome all the evil in the world.

The symphony has three movements, each of which variously juxtaposes and alternates versions of two very basic musical ideas: short notes and long notes, both of which 'thicken' and grow more alike as the piece develops. Even the final quotation from Tchaikovsky[7] sustains this pattern, consisting of a legato melody (and bass line) accompanied by detached, off-beat chords.

The row devised by Pärt for this work does not entirely abandon the world of B-A-C-H, for each tetrachord, a major third apart, features the same inversion of the B-A-C-H intervals; however, the sequence is so changed that we may claim simply a family resemblance to rows in the earlier works (see Ex. 6).

The first movement opens with a random pizzicato texture (*pp* after an initial *f*) and, as mentioned above, the curious sound of children's toys; this is followed by three sustained pitches on a French horn (the first three pitches of the row R-10); this in turn is followed by staccato flutes, asymmetric like the strings, but *f* and precisely notated. The pattern of these three alternating elements is repeated three more times, the second and third elements growing in complexity and length, until, once a complete 12-note row has been played (RI-0), a new section is begun. As in *Collage* Pärt now sets a full tonic triad on top of a pitch sequence: in this case pitches 1–7 of the row. We hear the major triads of B, D, C, D♭, and so on, with the fifths at the top of

Ex. 6

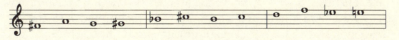

[7] See below, p. 54.

each chord playing out the pitches of P-o (while of course the roots of each triad produce P-5, and the thirds give P-8). These triads are each sustained for seven crochet beats, but each is punctuated by a 12-note cluster (the length of the clusters varies, and is itself subject to serial organization). At the eighth pitch this enunciation of the row reverts to single pitches, increasingly spread across the orchestra and, like the clusters, organized into varying lengths. Gradually, a string chord of D major with a dominant seventh is established and left suspended *fff*, to mark the movement's end.

A rapid patter of loud brass opens the second movement, answered *ppp* by six horns playing irregular groups of staccatos. As in the first movement, a third, quasi-melodic element is added (here superimposed on the other two). This consists of the row as a line of pitches (the sequence and direction of its intervals slightly reordered), but now each note is presented more in isolation, and highly differentiated in register, length, and dynamic shape, and dispersed across the whole timbral range of the orchestra. This leads into a second section of nervous, pointillistic writing, soon dominated by percussion and piano clusters. Again, this is counterpointed by a sustained line of pitches, beginning low on the trombones, but soon proliferating across the entire wind and brass into increasingly dense clusters. Eventually these also break up into short notes (of indeterminate pitch), leading *attacca* to the third movement.

A massive string chord, dense as concrete, introduces a typically Pärtian construction in which *ff* E♭s on the timpani, struck with relentless regularity, make a diminuendo as if towards silence, only to advance back again in a menacing crescendo. The opening of each of these rhythmic statements has 12 beats, which is reduced each time by one, followed by a crotchet rest. During each crotchet rest a fluttering string motif is heard, which also becomes louder and more complex until, after the last timpani strike has been answered anticlimactically by a staccato cymbal crash, the dynamic drops suddenly to *pp*. The work's final buildup now takes shape as different textural elements contend with one another, eventually overlapping in a carefully constructed 'chaos' of loud anguish. Uncertainly at first, there is a gleam of tonality, which, having cleared the stage of dissonance, now quietly takes charge: a passage from Tchaikovsky's 'Sweet Day-Dream' from his 1878 album of children's piano pieces, orchestrated with cooling delicacy. Dissonance threatens to intrude again, but is abruptly dismissed by open-string fifths, and the children's music continues, confirming that this brief vision of purity and simplicity will endure.

This ending can easily be distorted in performance by over-romanticized phrasing; it should be played without guile, so that its pristine nobility does not descend into kitsch.

There is an almost cinematic quality to Pärt's writing in this symphony—by which I mean decidedly *not* film music (in the accompanimental sense), but rather an equivalent approach to material and structure: the cut and dissolve technique, the sense of movement and shifting perspective sometimes at the viewer's expense, the juxtaposition of contrasting, seemingly unrelated images. In particular, the opening and closing moments can be thought of as image sequences which require no explanation, but are deeply imprinted on the rest of the work.

Pro et Contra was written at the invitation of Mstislav Rostropovich, and is loosely modelled on the baroque concerto grosso, with the performers in three groups: solo cello, a concertino grouping of various solo instruments, and the full orchestra. In fact, it is not so much a concerto as a histrionic representation of what a concerto might signify, highlighting elements of conflict and contrast not only between the three groups, but also between the 'ordered' world of tonality and the increasingly disturbed chaos in its absence. By setting these contentious opposites within a somewhat melodramatic framework, we are spared the extremity of feeling that marks the Second Symphony. *Pro et Contra* has its moments of outright aggression, certainly, but the issue seems less momentous, the outcome less bleak.

At the very beginning the significance of the title is made plain. The first movement is marked *maestoso*, but observes this mood only for the opening chord of D major: *Pro*. Then, after a brief pause, comes an aleatoric frenzy that sounds as if the orchestra is being broken into tiny pieces: *Contra*. The cello emerges from this still holding on to part of the D major triad (*f♯* and *a*), but, left alone, falls away in a wandering glissando rather like a dog with its tail between its legs.

The immediate function of these two opening gestures may be likened to that of a cadence in a conventional concerto which introduces a virtuoso cadenza, except that in this case the soloist responds with a parody of a cadenza, treating the cello's body as a percussion instrument to produce a tenuous series of random clicks and knockings. Eventually a pitch emerges, then another; a solo violin joins the cellist, followed by other concertino instruments in turn; and gradually a new, dodecaphonic order of sound is propounded. Soon this process inaugurates an orchestral tutti comprised of three elements which successively interrupt each other in a highly disputatious manner: (1) rapidly dispersed collections of wind, brass, and percussion pitches (the latter strongly coloured by marimba and piano) in which each instrument has a different number of pitches to play within a given bar, with no precise rhythm indicated (as in *Musica Sillabica*); (2) 12-note string clusters of superimposed minor thirds (the push–pull rhythmic gesture from *Nekrolog* can also be detected); (3) the solo cello playing rhythmically indeterminate groups of pitches as in (1). No sooner has this pattern been established than the texture of the first group begins to thin, and the string clusters grow progressively shorter. Eventually, the soloist is left alone, though hardly victorious, and in turn also disappears, note by note, with increasingly longer rests between each phrase.

The second movement, Largo, is in D minor, and consists simply of a short four-bar bridge passage (a cadential modulation, the bass descending by step, from D minor to A major) leading to the *allegro* third movement. The Allegro begins with the solo cello (*pp sul ponticello*) giving out short broken phrases at first (segments of the work's row), building these into a thematic shape which is gradually taken up by the whole orchestra save the strings, who maintain a motoric rhythm spreading from a single low D to cover all 12 pitches and eventually shifting to the higher octaves (see Ex. 7; the circled numbers, referring to numbered instructions in the score, tell the soloist which part of the instrument to tap or strike).

The soloist's thematic gestures are answered by the orchestra with increasing insistence over the *moto perpetuo* of the strings. During this fast and often exciting ride to nowhere in particular, there are many abrupt, dramatic gestures from the soloist and other instruments (most noticeably, the flourishes drawn across the strings inside the piano and a horn's whooping glissando). A trio of trombone, horn, and trumpet call out the series in canon at different speeds, which is later imitated by other instruments. Eventually the music can get no louder, and with a cymbal crash the orchestra cuts out, and the solo cello comes screeching to a halt on *g″*. (For the third time the poor soloist is 'discovered' at the end of a tutti and retires covered in embarrassment!) The opening *maestoso* then returns, in spoof baroque grandeur, to end the work in E♭ major.

There are only three brief moments of tonality in this work (which is itself quite short, lasting barely nine minutes), but they are sufficient to establish the baroque concerto grosso as a reference point,

which is totally at odds with the harmonic language otherwise used. Yet the spirit of manic play which suffuses the piece is almost sufficient to bring these opposing elements to a temporary reconciliation. If the work's title summarizes the conflict underlying Pärt's music at this time, it also alludes to the ambiguity inherent in the word 'concerto' (and related terms such as 'concerto grosso', 'concertante', and of course simply 'concert'), which is further reinforced by the word's etymology: the Latin *concertare* giving us 'to contend, dispute, debate', while the Italian meaning of the same word gives us 'to arrange, agree, get together'.

In *Pro et Contra* Pärt composes his own 'baroque' music; the idea of collage is still useful, affording him not only a readily recognizable stylistic reference (to play with and against), but coming more and more to stand for the elements at war within him. Soon, rather than quote a sense of affirmation and tranquillity, he would seek a compositional means of creating his own version of these qualities.

The pivotal work in Pärt's *œuvre* is *Credo* for piano solo, chorus, and orchestra. This is the last of the collage works in which tonal and atonal forces are set in confrontation; it is also, significantly, the first choral work (excepting the tiny, textless *Solfeggio*) since the early prize-winning cantatas, and initiates a substantial series of important choral works that continues to this day.

The work's première (conducted by Neeme Järvi) led to a scandal—though it was a great success with the public, and was immediately encored. In fact, even this first performance took place only due to an oversight on the part of local officials. One of the more vigilant bureaucrats was absent at the time, and his colleagues had somehow failed to take notice of the work, despite the strongly personalized religious declaration of the title. Soon, however, with Party authorities beginning to express concern, a scandal resulted that reached absurd proportions—all too typical of the system then in power. The work's title was interpreted as a gesture of defiance, and the authorities questioned Pärt as to his political aims—from Pärt's perspective there were none. By 1968 serial language no longer posed a problem, but the title and the personal nature of the declaration it enshrined did. At this first performance, the programme included Stravinsky's *Symphony of Psalms*, which also has a sacred Latin text; but Stravinsky was an outsider, Russian, yet not Soviet, and psalms could be regarded as 'mere' poetry. Pärt however was local; his choices were seen as having immediate consequences, and his choice of the title *Credo* was interpreted as a direct provocation. The work was subsequently banned in the Soviet Union for over a decade.

Unsurprisingly, it was assumed that the work was a setting of the liturgical Credo, which it is not. The opening words, bad enough from a Soviet point of view, are 'Credo in Jesum Christum' (whereas the liturgical Credo begins 'Credo in unum Deum' and mentions Christ only four phrases later). The remainder of the text is taken from the Gospel according to St Matthew (5: 38–9) and comprises two statements: 'Audivistis dictum: oculum pro oculo, dentem pro dente' ('You have heard it said: an eye for an eye and a tooth for a tooth'), and 'Autem ego vobis dico: non esse resistendum injuriae' ('But I say unto you: do not resist evil'). The word 'Credo' is then repeated in conclusion.

The work is based on Bach's Prelude in C major from Book 1 of the *Well-Tempered Clavier*. Pärt's use of Bach or a Bachian idiom in earlier works had already ushered tonality into his sound-world, as had other collage elements. But while those works propose somewhat intermittently the possibility of serenity and certainty, their glimpses of paradise remain tragic, for nothing is fulfilled, nothing forgiven. They are in this sense truly nostalgic. In *Credo* the elements of conflict are more violent than ever, but for the first time we encounter moments of tonality with an enduring quality; what had seemed catastrophe is now redeemed through catharsis in music of a newly calm intensity.

The text makes explicit the elements which are to form the work's basis: its proposition is that the pacifist response to violence is ultimately stronger than violence itself. The use of 12-note and eventually aleatoric textures symbolizes the gradual distortion of this teaching and its eventual restoration: thus we are shown how an idea can be slowly corrupted from within, until it turns into its opposite.

Superficially, the work presents a confrontation between the forces of good and evil, and their musical characterization will come as no surprise: a pristine C major for the former (the white piano keys), and aleatoric cacophony for the latter (notated at its most extreme by thick bands of black). This would be naïve if it merely juxtaposed tonality and some form or degree of atonality like characters in a melodrama; the strength of the work lies in the way tonality is negated, step by step, using its own most powerful element: the cycle of fifths. In this context serialism functions not, as might be anticipated, as a willing agent of evil(!), but as an almost unwitting step in the process that leads to chaos. Whereas in previous works Pärt had juxtaposed blocks of tonal harmony within a menacing atonal context, in *Credo* the two extremes of order and disorder, good and evil, are presented not as separate blocks of energy, but as linked forces, each containing the seeds of their opposite, with a continuum of gradual disintegration (and reconstitution) lying between them.

Musically this is achieved by building a 12-note series step by step out of the most solidly consonant of intervals, the perfect fifth. Beginning with the fifth from C to G, then dropping a perfect fourth for the next fifth (D to A), and so on, a chain of perfect fifths, each a whole tone higher, quickly completes the 12-note cycle in the most consonant of fashions (see Ex. 8*a*).

Ex. 8*a*

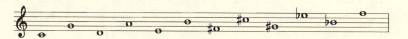

In outline the work falls into three main sections:

1. A tonal opening in C moving towards G: 'Credo in Jesum Christum'.
2. A long central section of dodecaphony (spanning outwards in fifths from the C–G core to a totally aleatoric representation of chaos): 'Audivistis dictum: oculum pro oculo, dente—pro dente.'
3. A tonal conclusion reasserting the C–G–C axis: 'Autem ego vobis dico: non esse resistendum injuriae. Credo.'

The Bach Prelude fills the first and third sections, while the central section consists of a series of expanding and contracting processes whereby the row is used to generate waves of chromatic intensity building up to a savage climax.

The work begins with the choir quietly repeating the word 'Credo' over a pedal C, their harmonies outlining a simple sequence: I II V I. A huge burst of sound follows for the third enunciation of 'Credo' and the words 'in Jesum Christum', by which time the harmonic sequence is beginning to sound very familiar. When the piano solo enters a few bars later, the reason for the familiarity becomes apparent, as most ears will now identify Bach's C major Prelude, which provides the exact harmonic model for the first 30 or so bars. Indeed, it becomes rapidly apparent that this is to be Pärt's supreme 'Bach' piece, with the C major Prelude at its core.

When the pianist reaches the Prelude's most dissonant point (a diminished-seventh chord—E♭ F♯ A C—over a pedal G) the pitch is lifted first an octave, then another octave, while a timpani crescendo projects us towards the next chord, the second inversion of the tonic, traditionally a preparation for a cadenza; but the piano stops abruptly at this point, and the male voices of the chorus declaim the 'Audivistis . . . pro dente' section of the text on a unison G. A perfect cadence is outlined (still following Bach), but cheated of its full force as the tonic C is played by a muted horn *frullando* without any additional harmony.

A transformation now takes place. Gradually, with increasing harmonic density, dynamic, and tempo, the orchestra introduces the row, building from a single note sounded once, to the sounding of all 12 notes together 12 times. When this process has been achieved, the piano re-enters, more or less at the point it had reached previously, only now at a faster tempo and playing a retrograde inversion of the Prelude (signifying the maximum distortion of Christ's teaching). The chorus declaims 'oculum pro oculo, dentem pro dente', a syllable at a time, and both piano and chorus are punctuated by the orchestra retreating back through its 12 times 12-note complexity towards a single 12-note chord. (Is it entirely fortuitous that the text 'oculum . . . dente' has 12 syllables?!)

Now it is the chorus that builds up from a single pitch to a 12-note cluster, at which point it declaims this portion of the text in full (rendering it 11 times in all), first in a loud whisper, then making a gradual transition to full voice and highest register. The orchestra meanwhile recommences another construction from one times one to 12 times 12 pitches, and when both chorus and orchestra have reached their fullest complexity, Pärt abandons conventional notation for an improvised section marked *Feroce* and *fff* throughout. Black bands indicate which instruments are playing when, while a set of three signs indicates whether to use a high, middle, or low register. The dramatic appearance of the score in this section, where the sense of chaos reaches an unbearable climax, is shown in Ex. 8*b*. At rehearsal no. 41 the beginning of a restoration of conventional notation can be seen (the wind and brass play 12 simultaneous transpositions of the row) and the first of a series of four low-octave Cs, which now gradually affirm the restoration of tonality. The fourth of these heralds the male voices of the chorus, who declaim on a unison middle C 'autem ego vobis dico'; and the whole choir sings in octaves 'non esse resistendum injuriae' to the pitches of the row in retrograde (see Ex. 8*c*). The 11 syllables of this statement leave the choir on unison Gs; the twelfth pitch, *c″*, is then sounded as the piano proceeds to play the entire Bach Prelude in a high register, this time without interruption. The orchestra is still unwinding the 12-note process begun at rehearsal no. 41, though the later stages of this are inevitably diatonic. The choir repeats the words 'non esse . . .', now joining in the Bachian harmonies from the bass up.

As the Prelude comes to a close, the orchestra supports and amplifies the piano soloist. There is a final resplendent outpouring of 'Credo, credo' from chorus and full orchestra (with C forming the seventh of a D major chord, an echo of the sixth bar of the Prelude); the work then comes to rest in a wide-spanning *pp* triad of C major, spread across seven octaves on strings and piano.

No verbal description can do justice to the powerful effect of this work, which is one of Pärt's finest. It is, furthermore, a compendium of techniques developed by the composer throughout the 1960s and, in its revelatory treatment of the C major triad, points unerringly forward to the music to come. That it quotes the music of Bach soon becomes so obvious as to be meaningless; in a sense *Credo* is composed

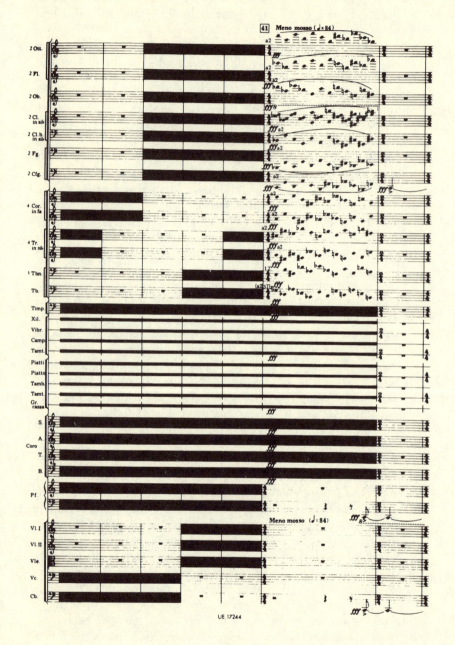

UE. 17244

choir (in octaves), str.

Non es - se re - sis - ten - dum in - ju - ri - ae

from *within* the Prelude, rather than from without, so complete is Pärt's identification with the earlier music. It is true that at first hearing the Bach may loom too large, too readily identifiable for the music to make its full effect; it is only on subsequent hearings, as the familiarity of the Prelude begins to evaporate and ceases to be 'Bach', that the full integration of the work's musical elements is able to achieve its effect.

One might propose the art-science of alchemy as a metaphor to describe this process; but alchemy involves the transformation of base metals into gold, and Bach's Prelude is hardly a base substance of any kind. This in turn highlights the nature of Pärt's achievement—and his remaining quandary. He had certainly penetrated in this work to the very heart of what tonality is and means; furthermore, he unfolds from tonality's most fundamental intervallic relationships (a perfect fifth and a perfect fourth) a statement that is openly 'contemporary', with its use of 12-note and even aleatoric techniques, but is still able to return to C major as the most natural thing in the world. But the quandary remains: how to move on from this point (of tonality regained) without continuing to refer back to pre-existing music. In this regard, alchemy is an appropriate symbol, for it is tonality itself that has been rendered base by exposure and sheer usage.

The elements that have gone into the making of this work are employed every bit as methodically as the processes of construction and deconstruction already noted in works such as *Perpetuum Mobile* and *Musica Sillabica*, and which will soon be brought to bear in the tintinnabuli works. Systematic processes govern details such as the length of rests and individual pitches or pitch clusters, even the disposition and timing of each percussion stroke; as one system is expanding, another is contracting, so that the entire score seems to breathe. It is a hymn not only to the splendour of Bach's music, but also to the splendour of tonality, and finally to the splendour of religious belief.

4

AFTER *CREDO*

After Credo

WITH *Credo*, Pärt had written himself into a cul-de-sac: he had reached a position of complete despair, in which the composition of music appeared to be the most futile of gestures, and he lacked the musical faith and will-power to write even a single note. It was from this creative death that there gradually arose in him a search for an entirely new way to proceed.

Pärt had disappeared, so to speak, into the nodal point, the central figure of Western music, J. S. Bach,[1] and seemed thereby to refute the notion of progress which had hitherto underwritten the course of modern music. He is not the only composer to have done so, of course, and in today's postmodern context numerous musical idioms are busy creating their own individual whirlpools. There are many who coolly profess to see this pluralistic situation as somehow, comfortingly, an expression of multiculturalism. There are others who view the loss of a central tradition as a bewildering tragedy. Others appear simply to dismiss those musics which do not conform to *their* central tradition, however they perceive it. This splintered, factional condition is certainly potent and excitingly fertile; but its restlessness cannot continue for ever. The biggest problem is the severing of 'serious' music from its vernacular roots. To the extent that composers such as Pärt and Steve Reich, among others, have restored a certain use of tonality (a non-functional, 'abstract' tonality, as I suggested in Chapter 1) and discernible rhythmic pattern, their music has found a wide, rapidly growing audience, internationally. Inevitably this process has sucked in fellow-travellers, allowing for a weakening of the image, justifying at times the accusations of New Ageism and faddishness; this only accentuates the need for a disciplined appraisal of the best of such music. But this cannot take place until the criteria by which it functions are more fully accepted.

In an interview on Estonian Radio in 1968, Pärt expressed himself in a way that shows he had strong intimations of the forces guiding

---

[1] 'Central' from a historical perspective that embraces medieval and Renaissance music.

him, and already at this stage there is a potent glimmer of the solution he would eventually find. The discussion seems to have centred on Pärt's use of Bach and what this implied about the notion of 'progress' and the future of music:

I am not sure there could be progress in art. Progress as such is present in science. Everyone understands what progress means in the technique of military warfare. Art presents a more complex situation . . . many art objects of the past appear to be more contemporary than our present art. How do we explain it? Not that genius was seeing two hundred years ahead. I think the modernity of Bach's music will not vanish in another two hundred years, and perhaps never will . . . the reason is not just that in absolute terms it could simply be better than contemporary music . . . the secret to its contemporaneity resides in the question: How thoroughly has the author-composer perceived, not his own present, but the totality of life, its joys, worries and mysteries? . . . It is as though we are given a problem to solve, a number (ONE, for example), terribly complex when broken up into fractions. Finding a solution is a long process and requires intense concentration; but wisdom resides in reduction. If it is now conceivable that different fractions (epochs, lives) are united by a single solution (ONE), then that ONE is something more than the solution to a single fraction. It is the correct solution to all problems, to all fractions (epochs, lives)—and always has been. So the boundaries of a single fraction are too confining for it and it goes through all time . . . always the most contemporary is that work in which there is a clearer, bigger correct solution (ONE). Art has to deal with eternal questions, not just sorting out the issues of today.
In any case, if we want to reach to the core of a musical work, no matter what kind, we cannot forgo the process of reduction. In other words we have to throw out our ballast—eras, styles, forms, orchestration, harmony, polyphony—and so to reach to one voice, to its 'intonations'. Only there are we eye to eye [with the question]: 'Is it truth or falsehood?'[2]

It has become almost a convention to describe the period of Pärt's career between *Credo* and the appearance of the first tintinnabuli works in 1976 as one of silence punctuated by only two works: the 'transitional' Third Symphony and the forgotten (and subsequently withdrawn) symphonic cantata *Laul Armastatule*. These two works are large enough to belie the appellation 'silence'; yet even if we allot a year to each of them, that still leaves a total of five years ungraced by any work completed and publicly performed. But to regard these years as a renunciation of all that pertains to the act of composing would be misleading indeed. At first Pärt's silence was real enough,

---

[2] Quoted in Vaitmaa 1970, part of which was also printed in the magazine *Sirp ja Vasar* ('Hammer and Sickle'), 22 Nov. 1968.

but it was hardly the meditational calm we might suppose—rather the frustrated immobility of an engine fully revved up, but unable to set off. Later still, after the composition of the Third Symphony, Pärt wrote reams of stylistic and technical studies resulting from his exploration of early music; he also continued to support himself and his family by writing film music, though only until 1974. But at the centre of this activity and searching there was indeed a silence—over which we can imaginatively supply both a fermata and a large crescendo sign.

After *Credo* Pärt instinctively knew that early music held important answers for him, though as no ready access to such music existed, studying it was no simple matter. The phenomenon of early music as an increasingly integral part of the twentieth-century musical world is well enough attested to. Early music compositional techniques have had a widespread influence on many composers, while the issues pertaining to performance practice have also had far-reaching consequences, even in the way we perform and listen to nineteenth-century music. More generally, we can cite the rise of a mode of performance, or performance ethic, which espouses 'objectivity': objective sound, objective manner or style of phrasing, as opposed to the subjective personae which are perceived to dominate the eighteenth- and nineteenth-century traditions. This aesthetic shift (to which not everyone subscribes) has permeated the work of many contemporary composers. Early music has influenced (flowed into) new music, surely enough, but one might also surmise that the cultural currents that have created our new music (or some corner of it) have also been directly responsible for the rediscovery[3] of early music—and to such an extent that it, too, has become part of the music of our time. Indeed, an ethnomusicologist's appraisal of the situation might well come to this very conclusion, relieved of any necessity to evaluate thereby the state of the culture's health.

In Eastern Europe, and in the former Soviet Union especially, the dogma of Social Realism served to perpetuate the hegemony of the symphony orchestra and its related performance traditions, so the impetus of (pre-Bachian) early music was much slower to acquire the cultural force it held in the West. An additional and significant factor in this state of affairs was the predominance of the sacred in most areas of extant early music repertoire, which could not have helped endear early music in general to the mentors of Communist taste.

[3] This 'rediscovery' is nothing new of course, and has been slowly gathering momentum since the 18th century.

As Western early music groups grew in number, invitations to tour in Eastern Europe grew apace. Those of us who undertook such visits will remember—perhaps with nostalgia—the intense thirst for early music that existed and gave a unique value to the experience of performing it in such situations, where one could almost hear the audience listening. It would be wrong, however, to suppose that there were no early music performers in the former Soviet bloc countries at all; but they were certainly few in number, and lacked the material resources (music scores or edited manuscripts) that could facilitate their work.

In Moscow itself, the music of Andre Volkonsky, the first Russian composer of serial music (pre-dating Pärt's *Nekrolog*), had encountered such sustained hostility that he virtually abandoned composition as his primary activity and turned instead to harpsichord performance. He also founded an early music group called 'Madrigal'. An Estonian early music group, 'Hortus Musicus', was founded in 1972 by Andres Mustonen, and it was this group that would shortly become the first to perform Pärt's early tintinnabuli compositions. Mustonen had come to know Volkonsky through their shared interest in new music, and probably found in Volkonsky's 'Madrigal' both encouragement and a model for Hortus Musicus—with the difference that Volkonsky's interests inclined towards Baroque music, while Mustonen was attracted to the earlier Renaissance and medieval periods. Volkonsky emigrated to the West in 1973, and part of his extensive collection of early music scores went to Mustonen.[4]

Pärt and the younger Mustonen had met around 1970 through a shared interest in the music of the fifteenth-century Netherlands school. Scores of this music were extremely scarce, as of course was information about its history and performance. Pärt was able to obtain some materials in Moscow libraries, but had also to copy a large number of works by hand (including *ars nova* ballades and Italian madrigals, as well as sacred works). This task was not mere drudgery: one of the most effective ways to understand a piece of music is to copy it, attentively, by hand.

In Tallinn at this time there was also a circle of musicians and intellectuals gathered around the central figure of Heimar Ilves, a composer and teacher of music history at the Tallinn Conservatory. Against a background of pervasive (and even institutionalized) atheism and a general lack of spiritual education and, indeed, experience,

---

[4] The connection is further cemented by the fact that Volkonsky's son became a member of Hortus Musicus.

Ilves stood out for his bold and original views on spiritual matters, which, moreover, he expounded at the Conservatory without any sense of fear—which was most unusual. He had a strong influence on the development of Pärt's personality during the years 1964–71, and may be considered as the teacher next in importance after Eller. He was broadly dismissive of all contemporary music, however, and one is naturally led to surmise that his views powerfully fuelled Pärt's own growing disenchantment with modernism.

Pärt himself is dispassionate about the effect of any external stimuli on his work at this period, beyond the essential quality of the music to which he was drawn and, inevitably, the spiritual support opening around him. It was around this time that Pärt met his second wife, Nora, and from 1968 on through the early 1970s it is clear that the whole structure and direction of his life found new meaning, encapsulated in his eventual turning to the Russian Orthodox Church and crystallized in the discovery of the tintinnabuli style, the two being inseparably intertwined.

Symphony No. 3

By 1971 Pärt had composed a third symphony very different in language and texture from anything he had written hitherto. Into this work Pärt seems to have poured the joy of his discovery of early music: there is not a dull page in the score, and after several years of collage, of 'For and Against', we now encounter a work that is richly sustained by one central thematic source, and a musical structure that avoids—and indeed does not require—being swollen to the limits of expression, but contains an understanding of those limits even at its quietest moments. This sense of a single element expanding and contracting, as opposed to the confrontation of two or more separate elements, marks the distinctive new path that his music would now follow.

Symphony No. 3 is in three movements, joined *attacca*, so that the whole work has the seamless flow and organic sense of development that we associate, for example, with the symphonies of Sibelius. The main thematic elements of the work are recognizably drawn from early music idioms: above all Gregorian chant and *ars nova* polyphony, with special emblematic use of the so-called Landini cadence. These elements can be reduced to three short motifs (for convenience these are shown in D minor in Ex. 9a); the first of these, X, is an 'opening' formula poised on the fifth of the scale, and is a simple turn, an embellishment of a single note; the second, Y, could equally be an opening phrase in a polyphonic work, though it carries its own sense of closure, and its shape could also be likened to a psalm tone, with its *intonatio* rising (in this case) to the third of the scale, which is the *tenor*, or recitation tone (the square note F in the example), and then the *terminatio* falling back to the tonic, or final; the third phrase, Z, is a 'closing' formula, and is familiar as such from many *ars nova* compositions (the Landini cadence).

The symphony begins in A minor with the opening motif, X, developed by oboe and clarinet in unison (Ex. 9*b*), briefly counterpointed by a solo trumpet, low in its range, and coming to rest on a unison E. This pitch is deftly transformed into the third of a C♯ minor triad cadencing in E major, a moment of gratuitous beauty (from strings and celeste)—still 'borrowed', however, from the motifs in Ex. 9*a* (see Ex. 9*c*). This is then answered in G♯ minor (bell, brass, and timpani) with a resolute gesture here labelled 'Q' (Ex. 9*c*, bars 4–6), that announces the Landini cadence, Z, but also incorporates the other two motifs from Ex. 9*a* in its three-part texture: X is on top, Z (Landini) in the middle, Y at the bottom.

As Ex. 9*c* shows, this immediately gives way to a sequence of flowing triplets based on Y (bars 8–9) and a settling of the symphony's tonality on G♯ minor (where, eventually, it will end). These triplets have a dance-like potential which for the moment is held back, but they soon begin to generate longer phrases and scales rising over an octave.

This first main section is brought to an arresting climax with a rhythmical variant of Q, followed by more legato contrapuntal treatment of Q's constituent phrases (X, Y, Z), and then their gradual fragmentation is phased into a new motion of semiquavers, both embellishing and counterpointed by different versions of X, Y, and Z. Two developments of this are worth highlighting: interpreting Y as a

Ex. 9*a*

Ex. 9*b*

Ex. 9c

Ex. 9d

Ex. 9e

psalm formula, its reciting tone (shown by the square note in Ex. 9a) is first reiterated and then accelerated (see Exx. 9d and 9e) in a foretaste of the work's final moments.

The ending of the first movement (after a resounding B♭ minor) retraces the pitches of the very opening, and eases us imperceptibly into the second movement (beginning at the double bar in Ex. 9f), in which slow legato phrases, based largely on X and Z, are counterpointed by Y as a cantus firmus (Ex. 9g). The triplets heard early in the first movement now return, but ff, and soon give way to a series of short, quiet statements based on the type of harmonic progression outlined in bars 1–2 of Ex. 9c. The first of these is answered by the tiny sounds of a solo celeste (playing a conflation of X and Y). The harmony darkens towards B♭ minor, through which we hear a solo timpanist playing steady sforzando strokes. Soon the timpanist is left alone, to build a crescendo accelerando of massive proportions until the sound collapses in a *fff* tremolo which quickly drops down to *p*. This solo, properly executed, can have a spellbinding effect.

The music picks up again, and continues quietly in D minor, but has now merged into the third movement, passages of slower string music alternating with a dance-like variant of the same material; Ex. 9*h* shows the beginning of this movement.

The extension and variation of these contrasting textures and moods provides music of unfailing variety. At one point the music shifts into 3/4 metre and a new thematic treatment of the material is heard, which is worth quoting here (Ex. 9*i*) for the resemblances it bears (especially if the accidentals are overlooked) to Pärt's tintinnabuli melodic style; a passage from *An den Wassern* (Ex. 9*j*) is given for comparison.

The *memory* of chant and early polyphony in a passage such as Ex. 9*j* is clear enough, but it is also clear that nothing is being quoted, whereas Symphony No. 3 is built on borrowed material, albeit transfused into a totally new and indeed living body. The derivation of Ex. 9*i* from similar origins is also clear enough, but it is certainly an evocative moment, especially as it is played alone by the double basses, echoing the different, but also single, melody of the celeste some moments earlier in the same work.

As mentioned earlier, the symphony concludes in G♯ minor, which is established in a recapitulation of the first movement's flowing triplets and motifs X, Y, and Z, heard now in slow and measured tones. Ex. 9*k* shows such a passage and the final incisive form assumed by the Q material. The ending itself rises from a low G♯ (held by the strings), to which upper octaves and fifths are added, as the whole orchestra joins in a massive crescendo. This open-fifth chord pulsates faster and faster in the strings, leading to a final assertion of Q in its ultimate form.

This is indeed a transitional work—but it is a splendid crossing with some glorious scenery, and sometimes we are looking in on an interior landscape that is taking shape in Pärt's imagination as early music and especially chant begin to formulate a world of new pos-

Ex. 9*i*

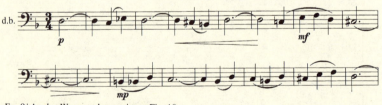

Ex. 9*j An den Wassern*, bass voice at Fig. 10

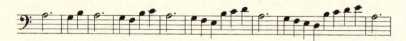

Ex. 9*k*

sibilities. Had Pärt been content to continue in the vein of the Third Symphony, there is little doubt that he could have contributed nobly to the history of that curious phenomenon, the late twentieth-century tonal symphony. His feeling for dramatic form and mastery of orchestration suggest that he would have been highly regarded in such a context, though sorely limited by its essentially reactionary vocabulary.

At this time Pärt was studying the work of Dante and the medieval Georgian poet Shota Rustaveli. His next composition, the symphonic cantata *Laul Armastatule*, completed in 1974, sets words from Rustaveli's masterpiece 'The Lord of the Panther-Skin'. The music sustains the general idiom of the Third Symphony (and even echoes one or two of its motifs), though perhaps less memorably and less compactly. There are seven movements, of which the last, the title movement, is the strongest; although a version of the work was performed, Pärt considers it unfinished (and unlikely to be), and has withdrawn it.

In the early 1970s Pärt continued to find free-lance work composing film scores. The music he assembled for this purpose has practically nothing to do with his real work as a composer, although occasionally a motif is used that recalls a moment in one of his published compositions. For example, a 1972 film about Estonian arts and crafts has a pizzicato figure reminiscent of the Third Symphony's motif Q as it appears in Ex. 9*k* above; but this is followed by pseudo-baroque jazz,

73

lyrical flute solos, experimental percussion writing, even some slight electronic 'bending' of sound. This wage music is imaginative in a fragmentary way, but inconsequential—as indeed the composer has often declared when questioned about it.

Intimations of Tintinnabuli

As we have seen, the quality of Pärt's compositional silence during the years 1968–76 fluctuated considerably. It is none the less characterized by an underlying searching out and stripping away of all that was alien. Already in the Third Symphony there are many passages of two-part counterpoint, and the concept of pairing things off, of fusing two into one, became an *idée fixe*. After Symphony No. 3 Pärt began his most radical attempt yet to 'learn how to walk again as a composer'. With Gregorian chant as his source, he studied how to write a single line of music. Writing semi-automatically, page after page, filling book after book, he sought to enter a different sense of time, to fully assimilate all that might be meant by the idea of 'monody'. Sometimes he would draw a shape, such as the outline of wings or a landscape, and then create a melodic line that would fill that shape. Or he would quickly read a text, set it aside, and then immediately write music to mirror what he had just read. In this way he sought to steep himself in a new tradition, not artificially, but assimilating it bit by bit, pulling it gradually to the surface in such a way that it might become second nature. During this process of what amounted to a purification of his musical roots, he became highly sensitized to all noise, and separated himself from all other musical life (even performances of his own works). An image haunted him of an impenetrable wall through which he must pass.

This rite of passage was necessary, he felt, not just for himself, but as part of the wider process of rejuvenation which Western culture must undergo. A culture that attempts to live without the sustaining power of myth is a culture that is not whole, that has no connection with the past. And it is in this manner that we may understand Pärt's sense of purpose: as an attempt to reconstitute art within a sense of past and future time, to fly in the face of the disconnectedness of postmodernism and seize a cultural meta-narrative from time so distant, yet so potently realized, that it has the force of new life.

Eventually in his exercises Pärt moved on from monody to explore ways of combining two tonal voices and constructing forms out of rhythmic patterns and related processes.[5] From time to time elements of the yet to be discovered tintinnabuli system would drop in, as if by chance, but his progress was essentially steady and intuitive, and revolved around the understanding that the two voices he was now working with were in fact one. Once this principle was established, the possibility existed of composing again, and things went quite quickly. The tension of this long period of preparation had built up a massive inner need to compose, and in 1976 this exploded into an outpouring of new works, which continued unabated for three years. During this initial period of tintinnabuli composition, many of the most important (and still most played) works were written: *Fratres*, *Summa*, *Cantus*, *Tabula Rasa*, and even an initial version of *Passio*.

The List of Works gives seven titles for 1976; these were subsequently performed as a group under the collective title 'tintinnabuli'. But in the first two of these, *Modus* and *Calix*, the tintinnabuli style was still not exactly formed. The two basic components were there—the triad and the diatonic scale—and the all-important idea of fusing the two together, two voices as one. But still missing was the principle that would bring them simultaneously into focus and bind them together.

Although many of these early tintinnabuli works had quite precise religious themes (whether a spiritual concept or an actual text), Pärt judged that these should not be made explicit, at least in the title, so that their performance would not be prevented; the earlier titles can be regarded as a form of camouflage, but subsequently all the original titles have been restored. *Modus* itself has subsequently been revised and given its proper, more explicit title of *Sarah Was Ninety Years Old*, referring to the biblical story in which Abraham's aged wife, Sarah, joyfully discovers that she is pregnant. The various sections of this work, Pärt's most minimalist, give us an idea of the kind of material we might have found in Pärt's sketch-books from the previous year or so: play with rhythmic and pitch symmetries and use of both monodic and two-voice textures and even sequences of purely rhythmic patterns. This work also suggests itself as an allegory of Pärt's own progress through the mute years of exploration towards the uncovering of a new musical language and his own personal sense of renewal.

[5] He continued to use the writing of such exercises as a replenishing discipline from time to time, and still does so today.

75

The Latin title may be translated as 'way, manner', but my Langenscheidt pocket dictionary gives a cluster of further meanings, each of which has relevance not only to this piece but to the process of stylistic discovery in which it marks the turning-point: (a) size, extent, quantity; (b) time, rhythm, metre, melody; (c) bound, limit; (d) moderation, due measure. The music is comprised of the sparsest of textures and most methodical of processes, and presents in alternation two distinct sequences: one of rhythmic, one of melodic patterns (the rhythms have no designated pitch, the pitches little or no rhythmic differentiation). These sequences gradually and relentlessly construct an atmosphere of aridity strangely filled with expectation, which is finally released in an upward surge of sound, leading to a benediction in the form of the soprano's concluding, wordless song.

It is especially interesting to see how closely the second section approaches tintinnabuli technique, yet neither voice is a 'tintinnabuli' voice (see the section below on tintinnabuli technique for comparison). In fact, both triadic and stepwise motion are integrated into a set of seven pitches which form a two-part texture articulated sequentially across a rhythmic pattern so that each phrase begins and ends at a different point in the sequence (see Ex. 10). This resembles

Ex. 10

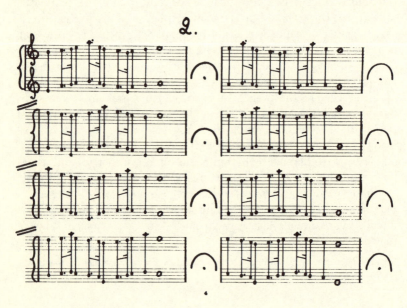

the interplay between *color* and *talea* in the *tenor* of a medieval isorhythmic motet.

The notation in this section also provides a visual pun (HI = hee) on the name given to Sarah's child: Isaac means 'he will laugh'. 'And Sarah said, God hath made me to laugh, so that all that hear will laugh with me' (Gen. 21: 6). Pärt had entertained the idea that the singer in this work should herself be pregnant: by chance, when the première took place in Riga, she was—visibly so!

Calix (chalice, cup) was the second work to use the nascent tintinnabuli style, and Pärt made several versions of it without quite achieving what he wanted. The 'camouflage' title symbolizes the Last Judgement. In essence, it is the original version of a setting of the *Dies Irae* (for mixed choir and instruments) which Pärt later modified for inclusion in the *Miserere* in 1989. In the earlier version the musical material is formed entirely of scales and triads: however, the relationship between them is not governed by tintinnabuli principles, but each element is part of a self-contained pattern, simultaneously given at different speeds in the form of a metric canon. At the word 'Rex' the music stops abruptly, and the stepwise patterns are inverted to rise slowly in a hushed conclusion. This general shape was folded directly into the *Miserere*, with the important difference that in the later work the major portion of the *Miserere* text is heard between the loud and soft sections of the *Dies Irae*.

While he was still composing *Calix*, Pärt one day produced a little piano piece in B minor (*Für Alina*) in which a triadic left hand and a melodic right hand were linked by a simple principle: the left hand always plays whichever pitch in the B minor triad is nearest to the pitch of the right hand, though remaining below it at all times. Thus the tintinnabuli style was born, though only in his next work *In Spe* (composed in a single day, 15 August 1976) was the tintinnabuli principle fused into a formal process generating both triadic and melodic parts and structural concepts as well.[6]

Early Music

Around 1976, at the moment my own tintinnabular style was about to be born, my life was tightly bound up with the Estonian Hortus Musicus and its leader Andres Mustonen. At that time the world of ancient music opened up before us and we were all full of enthusiasm. This atmosphere had the effect of a midwife for my new music.[7]

[6] *Für Alina* is discussed further in the next chapter, *In Spe* as *An den Wassern* in Ch. 6.
[7] Elste, p. 339.

As Mustonen's early music group took shape, Pärt frequently attended rehearsals and, when the time was ripe, had the opportunity to hear his new music played by the group. Pärt has always cherished close contact with performers of any new works, not only to guide their interpretation, but to adjust his own score if necessary, in order that the music might 'sound'.[8] Mustonen and Pärt met frequently to discuss how the new pieces should be performed, in what order, which instruments should be used, and so on. The first public performances took place in 1977. Eventually Hortus Musicus would perform them all over the Soviet Union, often in large venues. At their first Tallinn performances the reaction to the new style was mixed. According to Mustonen, other composers either disregarded the music or thought Pärt had gone mad; nobody seemed to think that much would come of it. Mustonen's support at this time was very important to the composer, sharing the element of risk which is always involved in bringing new music before the public, but in a context which provided added complications and frustrations.

The sources of tintinnabuli music can be loosely described as drawn from early music and Pärt's growing sense of the spiritual. More specifically, they lie both in the general nature of Pärt's compositional style (methodic construction and relatively clear dynamic relief) and in its historical context, where it forms part of a wide reaction to integral serialism that has yielded new approaches to tonality on several fronts—though Pärt was at the time unaware of similar developments elsewhere. It remains true, however, that in the eyes (or ears) of most people, it is the influence of early music that has had the most readily discernible impact on his style, and the rest of this chapter will be devoted to a consideration of the nature of this influence.

Pärt has said that it was primarily the spirit of early music that interested him, far more than the technical procedures by which it was put together.[9] What is this 'spirit'? And to what extent can it be separated from technique? As a student, Pärt's counterpoint lessons had included music of Palestrina, but this was a Palestrina reduced to textbook examples, dissociated from any live experience of the music or its spiritual background, and the whole thing meant little to him. Later he returned to this music, not by looking backwards through the eighteenth and nineteenth centuries, but by going much further back still, to its origins in plainsong. From there he moved forward to the earlier developments in polyphony, to the Notre Dame school,

[8] The German word *klingen* better conveys the ringing quality Pärt is looking for.
[9] See e.g. McCarthy.

Machaut, and the *ars nova*, and thence on into the Renaissance. Among the later composers he studied were those of the Netherlands school, such as Ockeghem, Obrecht, and Josquin; and this led in turn to the music of Palestrina and Victoria—an approach which gives a very different perspective indeed.

For centuries, plainsong lay at the core of Western art music. At the very least, it provided the daily musical fare of those great monastic and lay institutions which were the source and sustenance of the art of polyphony. But as that art developed, plainsong remained embedded in the musical experience; partly, of course, it was used as thematic source material; but, more important, it formed the very bones and marrow of a musician's training. Until the later sixteenth century, most composers received their initial training as singers, and many of them (Dufay, Ockeghem, Josquin, and Lassus are examples) either sang as boys or gained employment as singers before they were known as composers. Indeed, singing and composing once went together as naturally as keyboard playing and composing have done in more recent centuries.

This intimate acquaintance with plainsong reveals itself in the expressive linearity of polyphony. Almost any motet or mass by Dufay, Ockeghem, Josquin, or their contemporaries contains vocal lines whose contours and general poise are informed by those of plainsong. It is a question not of quotation, but of a certain melodic sensibility: an understanding of how to create a fluid melodic line, which effortlessly renews itself through constantly displaced stress-points and half-cadences, but which, viewed as a whole, is satisfyingly balanced and expressively refined. This will most likely be counterbalanced by other factors, such as sequences of motivic imitation and variation (e.g. Josquin) and by rhythmic stylization (e.g. Obrecht); but the root of the style is plainsong.

If polyphony grew up around plainsong, it did so not only stylistically, but to serve the same basic purpose: to be part of the daily worship of God in a complex liturgy whose central ingredients were prayer and sacrament. At the heart of these lies a mystery, which it is beyond the power of words to construe, though it is prepared for in the liturgy by the expression of words. And it is the words that provide the creative impetus for the music, just as God is the Logos, the procreative power bringing the cosmos incessantly into being. To the religious initiate, the words of a ritual are not symbols of a greater reality, but actually possess and are possessed by the thing they name.

It is no accident, then, that as Pärt turned to religion, he also turned, as we have seen, to words (e.g. *Credo*); and words have remained the source of almost all his most significant works since. Nevertheless, with very few exceptions, Pärt has not composed music for liturgical use. His music is sacred in subject-matter and tone, but remains concert music, albeit ideally for a very special kind of concert venue in which the focus is not on the faces and personal idiosyncrasies of the performers.

Compared with polyphonic music, the expressive range of monodic genres such as Gregorian chant might appear limited, its beauty as restrained as the asceticism we generally associate with it. But to anyone who spends any length of time with it, such music reveals subtle and profound beauties and, perhaps most surprisingly, an intense strength. This strength is shared by monodic music around the world, and resides in the purity and simplicity of its essence: one line outlining an area of sound built around either a single pitch centre or a collection of closely related pitches. Such music proceeds by some kind of mixture of recitation, repetition (of melodic formulae), extension (of already given patterns, by processes of addition and small variation), and invention (by the introduction of new but related material).

Plainchant may be divided into three broad styles, according to the number of notes sung per syllable. The simplest is of course 'syllabic', one note per syllable, and is found in prose settings such as of the Credo of the mass ordinary and in the intoning of psalms. The second may be described as 'neumatic', generally two to four notes per syllable; while the third, termed 'melismatic', has many notes to one syllable. The three styles are very often found together in one piece, and anyway they represent a gradual transition from straight textual declamation to a more ornamental idiom. It is the latter which affords the maximum opportunity for display and purely musical invention, but it is the syllabic and, to a lesser extent, neumatic styles that we find most directly in the tintinnabuli style. Ex. 11*a* shows the beginning of the Canticle *Benedictus* in which the bulk of the text is recited on a single pitch, with some slight variations at the beginning, at the caesura between the two halves of the verse, and at the final cadence. This same approach, albeit modified, underlies many of Pärt's tintinnabuli settings of texts, including some of those in the *Passio*. The chanting of psalms was normally done in a responsorial manner, alternating between soloist and choir (or simply 'others'), or antiphonally between two sides of a single choir. The idea of recitation and patterns

Be - ne —— dic —— tus Do - mi - nus —— De —— us Is —— ra - el,

qui - a vi - si - ta - vit et re - de - mit po - pu - lum su - um.

of alternation play a very important role in tintinnabuli music, and are
deeply embedded both in the construction of the works and in the
resulting sound.

In chapter 17 of the *Micrologus* by the eleventh-century theorist
Guido d'Arezzo is a passage entitled 'That anything that is spoken can
be made into music'.[10] Then follows an explanation of a method by
which the five vowels can be allotted to a series of pitches so that any
text may be used, syllable by syllable according to the vowel, to create
a simple melody. This method should be compared to Pärt's melodic
construction in the tintinnabuli technique outlined in the next chapter, which it resembles not in detail, but certainly in spirit.

Even earlier than this we find the following statement in the anonymous ninth-century *Musica Enchiriadis*: 'Just as the letters of the
alphabet are the basic and indivisible parts of the spoken word, from
which are composed syllables, which in turn make up the verbs and
nouns from which is formed the complete speech, so the notes are the
first elements of song; from the way in which they are combined arise
intervals, and from the combination of these, musical systems.'[11] This
process, seemingly simplistic, underwrites a whole approach to music
theory which enjoyed great currency in the medieval period, and can
be read without much effort into Pärt's whole approach to music. The
analogy between language and music is especially significant for us
here, and Pärt would probably have encountered in his studies of
chant those concepts of liturgical recitative which translate fairly directly into the melodic and rhythmic processes of tintinnabuli. The
Liber Usualis (a book of chant for general liturgical use in the Roman
Catholic Church) prescribes tones for recitation of prayers and biblical readings which are essentially monotonal recitations with downward inflections at various punctuation points marked in the text,

[10] *Hucbald, Guido, and John on Music—Three Medieval Treatises*, trans. Warren Babb, ed.
with an introduction by Claude Palisca (New Haven and London, 1978), p. 74.
[11] Quoted in F. A. Gallo, *Music in the Middle Ages* (Cambridge, 1985), ii. 1.

such as the comma, colon, semicolon, interrogation mark, and full stop.[12] If Pärt learned from this source or one very similar, he none the less followed the principles in spirit rather than to the letter.

The earliest developments of polyphony consisted of improvising a countermelody to a given plainchant, following certain systematic rules note by note. This technique also has similarities to Pärt's tintinnabuli procedures, and the resulting texture is similarly homophonic. Once a certain freedom had been obtained beyond the strictest parallel motion (at the octave, fourth, or fifth), we can glimpse a musical world in which the interplay of passing dissonances is further evocative of Pärt's music—but with the significant absence of the triad. Ex. 11*b* shows the opening of an early English (*c*.1100) two-part setting of the verse *Ut tuo propitiatus* in which the voice parts cross and create interesting dissonances. (Whether these were originally savoured in the same way as we might is a moot point; what concerns us here is not an authentic interpretation of the past, but an 'authentic' understanding of its effect on us today.)

The brilliant effusion of polyphony that we know as the Notre Dame school of twelfth-century Paris seems to have special significance for many of today's composers. Its greatest practitioner (about whom next to nothing is reliably known) was Perotin, who created the first known compositions for four voices; these are justifiably famous,

[12] This brief description is condensed from Willi Apel, *Gregorian Chant* (Bloomington, Ind., 1958), p. 204. This book can be consulted for a fuller understanding of the methodology underlying Pärt's aesthetic.

o = 2 × ●

though I find that his special genius is manifest in all the various works that can be attributed to him.[13] The opening of Perotin's four-voice organum setting of *Viderunt omnes* (Ex. 11c) shows the two elements of style which make the strongest appeal to our senses: the long sustained tones in the lowest voice (which functions as a drone, and consists of the original plainsong pitches vastly elongated), and above these the interwoven exchange of three voices in continually varying rhythmic patterns. This example is followed by a passage from Pärt's *An den Wassern*, in which the texture is remarkably similar (though the tempo would be much slower). I have 'edited' both examples into a style of notation used by Pärt in some of his earlier tintinnabuli scores.

---

[13] And in some that cannot, suggesting that we adopt from art history the term 'school of' to indicate a very likely situation in which a master craftsman did not work alone, but at the head of an atelier which quite properly bore his name—the atelier in this case consisting primarily of the gifted soloists at Notre Dame.

four voices (SATB, vocalizing on the vowel 'o') above an instrumental drone

$o = 3 \times \bullet$

Drones[14] play an important role in tintinnabuli music, and for the simple reason that the continuing reference to a fixed pitch centre and triad implies a continuous sound even where one may not altogether exist. Actual drones are used quite sparingly by Pärt, though they appear in *An den Wassern, Trivium,* and *Fratres,* for example, and in later works such as the *Te Deum* and the *Magnificat.* The place of drones in medieval music is a topic that has received virtually no discussion, but (in addition to the stationary pitches in organum) they are freely supplied by almost everyone who performs monodic repertoire, often to great effect. Their use is predicated partly on instrumental construction (vielle, hurdy-gurdy, and bagpipe) and partly on certain non-Western practices, but the precise manner in which they are used is largely a matter of taste.

An anonymous thirteenth-century manual for singers uses the term *basilica* (building, thus foundation) to describe a 'manner of singing in two ways so that one singer continuously holds one note which is like a foundation melody for the other singer'.[15] Examples of such procedures can be readily multiplied by looking at non-Western vocal practices. A similarity can also be suggested by the function of the tambura in Indian classical music, which is to provide a fixed back-

---

[14] 'Drone' is hardly a happy expression, but of the alternatives, 'bourdon' seems too tightly related to instrumental procedures, and 'pedal' indicates only the lower registers and is too suggestive of a tonal harmonic framework.

[15] *Summa Musice,* ed. and trans. Christopher Page (Cambridge, 1991), p. 124.

ground for both the chosen *rág* and the extensive microtonal embellishments of the soloist; this is an especially appropriate example, because the tambura's use of the open fifth and octave, coloured by strong overtones, and its constant yet non-functional harmonic presence bring it much closer to tintinnabuli triads than the single pitch drone.

We do not need to search for early music exemplars of all aspects of tintinnabuli—though they would not be hard to find. My purpose is not to suggest that Pärt copied any one aspect of early music—which would be a fruitless exercise—but rather to demonstrate how certain of his characteristic methods of combining sounds and words do have quite precise models. By observing the development of sacred polyphony from plainsong forwards, rather than projected back across the intervening styles (Baroque, Classical, Romantic), we see how these models interact and reinforce the same basic approach to sound, which is rooted in plainsong. Although the sound of plainsong is relatively familiar today, it is probably enjoyed more for its atmospheric beauty than for the meaning of the words or the cultural and liturgical significance of the combined word–music artefact. The relationship between words and music in plainsong and medieval monophonic music is an important one, but not always obvious to the casual observer. The fact that a given melody may exist with more than one set of words, sometimes very different in character, may suggest that no real connection exists beyond a convenience of structure. It is true that at this syntactical level, different sets of words and music are potentially interchangeable. This does not mean, however, that the music has not been considered for its expressive suitability by a poet-composer when creating a new song by fitting an existing melody to words newly written. The meanings that music contains are purely musical—until and unless some extra-musical significance can be attached to them. Words, of course, have a more specific set of meanings. But in a song, the words can cause the music to become the carrier of those meanings too. If the verbal meanings are changed, so is the musical effect, but only at the level of verbal meaning; the musical nature is perhaps translated or transposed, but its innate musical character is not compromised. We are left with a musical language in which originality and self-expression are not the point. Instead, we find a unique complex of melodic and verbal power, in which a self-contained musical identity reinforces the moods and images of the text, which in turn lend their identity to the music.

5

TINTINNABULI

Introduction

IN the previous chapter I elaborated how, after *Credo*, Pärt did not entirely stop composing, but that this was an activity that consisted primarily of a series of explorations: how to write a single line of melody or combine just a very few notes. At first he studied Gregorian chant and early polyphony—and the Third Symphony and *Laul Armastatule* reveal his preoccupation with these styles, though at this point the result is largely mimetic. In further immersing himself in such music, Pärt sought not to imitate the mechanical devices of its composition, but rather to understand how and in what way these devices served the expressive function of the text. He had already ascertained that the triad itself (rather than simply 'tonality') was central to his purpose. To sustain the sounding triad, but be able to move within its all-embracing presence, required not only invention, but some form of regulating discipline, otherwise the energy accumulated within such a powerful and traditional source of stability would quickly turn into rigidity. Pärt has always demonstrated a need for the constraints of structure, not through lack of invention but from the threat of an excess of it.

During this period Pärt came to appreciate the special resonance of bells, both in combination and singly, particularly the small tinkling bells of the tintinnabulum. The nature of the sound of bells suggests a direction quite removed from the premisses of Western music, and is akin to the *Klang* which results from heterophony (and which likewise is familiar to us, though essentially rooted in non-Western music); both of these entail a complex of sounds, changing yet always basically the same. When a bell is struck, it continues to sound indefinitely: the ear cannot detect the point at which it ceases to vibrate. This sound-image may be compared to Pärt's manner of articulating the triad from within a musical process, so that the sonority which accumulates is intrinsically clear yet contains overtones and undertones far more dense than the notes on paper would suggest. The combination of melodic lines and triadic notes provided two sorts of continuity: one which leads step by step from one thing to the next, and one which rotates like a single object being viewed from different perspectives. Once these principles had been fused into a unifying technique, the first tintinnabuli could be written.

Tintinnabulation is an area I sometimes wander into when I am searching for answers—in my life, my music, my work. In my dark hours, I have the certain feeling that everything outside this one thing has no meaning. The complex and many-faceted only confuses me, and I must search for unity. What is it, this one thing, and how do I find my way to it? Traces of this perfect thing appear in many guises—and everything that is unimportant falls away. Tintinnabulation is like this. Here I am alone with silence. I have discovered that it is enough when a single note is beautifully played. This one note, or a silent beat, or a moment of silence, comforts me. I work with very few elements—with one voice, with two voices. I build with the most primitive materials—with the triad, with one specific tonality. The three notes of the triad are like bells. And that is why I called it tintinnabulation.[1]

Tintinnabuli—Basic Principles

The tintinnabuli style was announced with characteristic tranquillity in a tender piano solo: *Für Alina* (For Alina). This short work is reproduced here in full (Ex. 12), not least because it is technically easy to play. It also exemplifies that quality, which distinguishes so many tintinnabuli pieces, of sounding both ancient and fresh at the same time.

Für Alina highlights the basic manner of tintinnabuli composition: there are two parts in a fixed relationship, one moving mostly by step, the other filling in notes from the tonic triad; it is homorhythmic; there is no chromaticism and no change of key or tempo. It is, however, somewhat atypical of Pärt's work in that the melodic voice (right hand) is freely composed rather than adhering to some regular pattern or procedural method. The low B octaves are sustained by the pedal, which also permits an accumulation of overtones from the upper voices, dominated by the left hand's triadic B minor. This efflorescence is lifted away at just one point, marked by a single flower drawn in the score, where the left hand ventures outside the triad to play a *c♯″*.

The next few years, immediately prior to Pärt's emigration, produced a sudden spate of works in the newly created tintinnabuli style. Many of these works now appear to be something in the nature of

[1] Arvo Pärt, quoted in the sleeve-note to the ECM disc *Tabula Rasa*.

Ex. 12

études, working through a series of ideas or, rather, the different ramifications of one central idea: the tintinnabuli process. This is not to suggest that there is anything tentative or experimental about them. While they sometimes seem like parts of a larger process, each work focuses on a self-contained musical concept and, with one exception, neither repeats nor depends upon any of the other works. The exception is the use of a mensuration canon to elaborate different statements of a melodic idea (very often a descending minor scale) and its attendant tintinnabuli pitches, a process which Pärt has used with eloquent effect in works such as *Arbos* and *Cantus*. But before proceeding to discuss any of these works in detail, it will be helpful to examine the precise workings of the tintinnabuli system itself.

The tintinnabuli style is based on a simple system for relating the horizontal and vertical manifestations of pitch—melody and harmony (scales and arpeggiated triads). In medieval and early Renaissance polyphony, the harmony is formed by the confluence of the constituent voices to such an extent that harmonic analysis becomes at best secondary. Similarly, in tintinnabuli music, where the harmony does not 'move', the harmonic framework has been tilted sideways to form a musical line, and the relationship between two different kinds of melodic movement creates a harmonic resonance which is essentially the triad and the fluctuating attendance of diatonic dissonances. What we hear might be described as a single moment spread out in time.

The characteristic sound of tintinnabuli music stems from a blend of diatonic scales and triadic arpeggios in which harmonic stasis is underpinned by the constant presence (actual or implied) of the tonic triad. This sound is not just a texture compounded of scales and triads, but the result of a very specific compositional technique evolved by Pärt in isolation, and deeply influenced by (though not based on) his studies of early music. As a technique, it has very lucid principles, which were not created arbitrarily, but arrived at intuitively through a process of observing and re-evaluating the meaning of tonality.

As we have seen, Pärt was irresistibly drawn towards tonality even while composing serial music; but at that point it seemed to offer him a symbol (of a truth that he sought), rather than a means of composing. Thus he felt free to use tonal elements within the context of a collage, and often began or ended a piece with a major triad; but this was tonality as an emotively charged musical allusion, a gesture among other gestures, powerful yet isolated. And in fact, not once from *Nekrolog* to *Credo* did he compose original tonal music, unless we except the prophetic *Solfeggio*, which uses the diatonic scale yet avoids any use of tonal harmony, and the brief baroque imitations in *Pro et Contra*.

Pärt was certainly not alone in mixing tonal and serial or other modernist elements, or in quoting from earlier musical styles. Indeed, collage or, more generally, different levels of influence and cross-reference, may be regarded as a quintessential twentieth-century style, and not only in music. But with Pärt, it became increasingly clear that a synthesis of these different styles was not acceptable—not possible even. He desired a fully integrated means of musical expression that would come from within him, rather than be claimed from external sources. So he turned aside from composing (in the sense of producing new, finished pieces), in order to penetrate more deeply into the very nature of music, which has primordially been rooted in some kind of tonal or modal pitch centre. He sought to re-establish tonality as the common basis for musical expression, but without the functional stereotypes of the Classical and Romantic eras. This radical renewal of musical language has often been dismissed as a retreat into the past or as yet another twentieth-century example of recycling an earlier musical idiom. It is the contention of this book that such is not the case. Many composers in recent decades have felt a similar need for a redefined sense of tonality, though few have articulated a response as uniquely expressive or as self-defining as Pärt's.

The elements of tonal music can be reduced to the triad and the diatonic scale, which may be seen as two sides of one coin—a tonality which can be expressed both horizontally and vertically. A scale defines a particular set of intervals, moving by step from a central note either up or down. In tonal music, only two basic kinds of scale are used, major and minor, though the effect of these can be greatly varied by chromatic alteration, thus affording a means of modulating to another tonal centre or key. In this way we talk about 'functional' tonality, meaning the way in which a piece of music can be given a contrasted and dynamic structure through the elements of tension and release involved in the process of modulation.

In pre-tonal music, more subtle variations of scale were available, the different permutations of tone and semitone producing the various modes (which can be readily identified by playing scales on the piano starting with different pitches and using only the white notes). The problem with playing modal music on the piano is that its tempered tuning system does not allow the small modifications of intonation that are necessary (and which traditional singers and some choirs achieve naturally) for the music to function properly. Furthermore, 'traditional' modal music emphasizes movement by step or by intervals that outline the fourth, fifth, and minor seventh (the lowest intervals in the harmonic series), and has little or no use for the triadic arpeggio. Where a triad occasionally occurs, it is usually by way of emphasizing the fifth, and only very rarely as a means of rising to the octave.

There are many aspects of tintinnabuli music which lead people to think of it as 'modal': it does not modulate, and there is virtually no chromaticism; the harmony[2] is not 'functional'—it does not provide a structural sense of tension and release; and the constant triadic presence is suggestive of the drone that is frequently a feature of modal music. In truth, questions of tonality and modality are problematized by the confusions of terminology which already exist in music history. Pärt's tintinnabuli music is a new blend of tonal and modal forces. Its use of tempered tuning and its triadic emphasis categorically refute the idea that this music is neo-medieval. Equally, its tonal stasis sets it apart from conventional tonality, for the constant presence of the same triad neutralizes any functional capabilities of pitches outside it.

Pärt seems to have felt that the powerful force exerted by tonality in its simplest triadic state (and not, that is to say, as a revival of eighteenth- and nineteenth-century functional tonality) was a musico-acoustic fact which he should no longer avoid, and that only by entering its world completely could he now create a music of essentials, a music of few notes, but great strength and purity. To proceed from a knowledge of Pärt's religious disposition (evinced by his choice of texts and his own comments on music) and to connect his perception of tonality to a perception of God is both to state the obvious and to risk too bald an interpretation. In this sense we may regard 'tonality', embodied in the constant presence of a major or minor triad, not as a symbol, but rather as a manifestation of God. Such a sacralizing view of music is neither unique nor eccentric; it has correspondences throughout music history, and is found in abundance in non-Western musics—moreover, without the self-consciousness forced upon it by a secular and materialistic society.

The basis of tintinnabuli style is a two-part texture (working always note against note), consisting of a 'melodic' voice[3] moving mostly by step from or towards a central pitch (often, but not always, the tonic) and a 'tintinnabuli' voice sounding the notes of the

---

[2] The word 'harmony' is to be understood here in its most basic sense as the vertical aggregate of pitches at any given moment.
[3] I use the word 'voice' here and elsewhere to denote a single musical line.

tonic[4] triad. For brevity these will be referred to henceforth as the 'M-voice' and the 'T-voice'.

The M-voice may be constructed in accordance with a textual pattern or a purely abstract musical procedure; very rarely is it composed freely. But however the M-voice is composed, the T-voice is fitted to it in a relationship that is never casual, but is ruled by a single principle which can function in various ways: the tin-tinnabuli note is always a note in the triad (other than a unison or octave) related in some specific and constant way to the melodic note. Once a particular relationship has been chosen, it is adhered to consistently.

Before embarking on an exposition of tintinnabuli practices, it is important to stress that these are best regarded not as rules, but as guiding principles from which 'rules' can be deduced from piece to piece. In other words, the 'rules' may change, or at least evolve, but they emanate from the central principle of vertical and horizontal combination which lies at the heart of tintinnabuli composition.

Constructing the T-voice

Ex. 13*a* shows a sample of very basic tintinnabuli technique in which the T-voice is alternately the next triadic pitch above and then the next below the M-voice. In fact, the T-voice may be in one of two 'positions' relative to the M-voice; and it may either remain fixed above or below the M-voice, or it may alternate above and below. Thus we arrive at the following list of positions:

1. The T-voice provides that pitch in the triad which is nearest to the M-voice: '1st position'.
2. The T-voice pitch is the next but one in the triad: '2nd position'.

There are then theoretically three possible manners in which these T-voice positions may be applied:

Ex. 13*a*

alternating

---

[4] It is important to state that words like 'tonic', 'dominant', and 'subdominant' are useful here as familiar pitch indicators, but do not carry the conventional meanings we associate with them when we talk about functional, or common-practice, tonality.

a. Alternating above and below the M-voice: 'alternating'.
b. Remaining above the M-voice: 'superior'.
c. Remaining below the M-voice: 'inferior'.

In practice, the 1st position is frequently used in the alternating manner, whereas the 2nd position is normally used remaining superior or inferior.

In addition to this is the option of beginning an alternating sequence from either above or below; as tintinnabuli music is built on principles of symmetry, this is a small yet significant detail. Ex. 13*b* shows the application of some of these basic positions to a simple scale of A minor. Any T-voice can be transposed to a different octave. One such transposition gives the illusion of a third T-position. In Ex. 13*c* the superior T-voice provides the most distant triadic pitch within the octave from the M-voice; but it is in essence an octave transposition of the inferior (1st position) T-voice. Which way the ear actually registers this is a moot point.

Ex. 13*b*

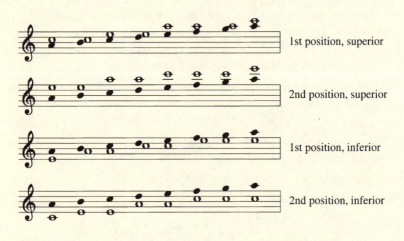

1st position, superior

2nd position, superior

1st position, inferior

2nd position, inferior

Ex. 13*c*

94

Constructing the M-voice

Although the composition of the M-voice always comes first, it is much more variable from work to work, and may range from the most basic pattern of scales moving strictly by step, to varieties of reiterated pitches or variations on the scale pattern with small interval leaps and melodic turns. None the less, the range of possibilities for M-voice construction can be condensed into four basic patterns, which are quite simply scales ascending or descending, to or from a central pitch; this central pitch is often the tonic (i.e. the tonic of the tintinnabuli triad), but it may also be another pitch (normally one of the other pitches in the tintinnabuli triad). In speaking of the M-voice I will refer to its 'pitch centre', to distinguish it from the triadic tonic of the T-voice (e.g. the T-voice may use the notes of the A minor triad, while the M-voice may use C as its pitch centre).

I have designated these M-voice types 'modes', because they are indeed scalar models; the word 'mode' has accumulated so many different meanings, rhythmic as well as melodic, that one more will surely do no harm! The fact that this is abbreviated to M, which can be conflated with 'melodic', only strengthens the meaning of 'mode' as used here (just as T can be seen to imply both tintinnabuli and triadic).

Ex. 13*d* shows the four modes, or ways of moving by step from or towards a central pitch—in this example, the tonic in A minor. In maintaining a systematic balance, the natural relationships between these four modes are clearly important: modes 1 and 2 are often combined in creating a melodic phrase, as are modes 1 and 3; we similarly find 3 and 4 as a pair, or 2 and 4. Less likely is a combination of 1 and 4, or 2 and 3.

When we add to these basic models the possibilities of different kinds of M-voice (the use of reiterated pitches or a melodic line that is not purely by step), the use of different pitch centres for the M-voice, octave transposition, and tacets for either of the two voices (these will be discussed later, especially in Chapter 7 on *Passio*), the manifold subtleties of this fundamentally simple concept will become quickly apparent.

Ex. 13*d*

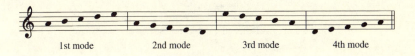

1st mode   2nd mode   3rd mode   4th mode

The need to create this small technical vocabulary arises not from any undue complexity in the subject at hand, but for the practical purpose of avoiding the repetition of cumbersome descriptions of musical procedures, simple enough in themselves, but for which we lack any distinct terminology. Equipped with this vocabulary, it will be easier to delineate clearly and succinctly the basic uses of tintinnabuli at any given point; it will also help to reveal the more subtle variations in technique from work to work and the precise scope of compositional choices with which Pärt has fashioned music out of a given text or musical idea.

As the reader examines the various examples of different tintinnabuli combinations, it should become apparent that, despite an overall similarity, subtle and even strong differences emerge, and some T-voices are clearly more effective in a particular context than others, or effective in different and significantly useful ways. The tintinnabuli system may be simplicity itself and appear easy to copy, but the burden of choice and invention is laid immediately upon the composer; as with all rules and systems of composition, the tintinnabuli style is only as good as the person using it! Further study of both the system and the music that Pärt has generated with it will only serve to strengthen our appreciation of the powerful and expressive *variety* of Pärt's achievements. Although Pärt discovered the tintinnabuli principle and codified it in his musical works, he regards it as something more than a subjective invention, something having indeed an objective reality of its own. Finally, I should point out that the terminology I have proposed is my own, and is offered simply as a vade-mecum within the confines of this book.

In one of our discussions about tintinnabuli, Pärt described to me his view that the M-voice always signifies the subjective world, the daily egoistic life of sin and suffering; the T-voice, meanwhile, is the objective realm of forgiveness. The M-voice may appear to wander, but is always held firmly by the T-voice. This can be likened to the eternal dualism of body and spirit, earth and heaven; but the two voices are in reality one voice, a twofold single entity. This can be neatly though enigmatically represented by the following equation:[5]

$$1 + 1 = 1.$$

[5] Proposed by Mrs Pärt, and warmly endorsed by the composer.

The intensity with which Pärt represented these ideas to me should be allowed to colour the entire preceding discussion of tintinnabuli 'technique'. In particular, he felt strongly that this equation expresses the kernel of the style, and is fundamental to the music's operation, and that it both precedes and dominates the actual process that underwrites each individual tintinnabuli composition.

Finally, it should be emphasized that Pärt's tintinnabuli style was developed intuitively. The association between the triad and the lingering manner in which bells resonate was initially made by Nora Pärt (and discussed in a 1977 concert programme note), so that the name tintinnabuli was adopted only after the technique itself had already been formulated.

THE EARLY TINTINNABULI WORKS

1976

THE name 'tintinnabuli' was eventually adopted as the collective title for all seven of the 1976 works. A 1978 programme lists their concert order as:

1. *Calix*
2. *Modus*
3. *Trivium*
4. *Für Alina*
5. *Kui Bach oleks mesilasi pidanud . . .*[1]
6. *Pari Intervallo*
7. *In Spe*

In the 1978 Tallinn Festival of Old and New Music they formed the first half of a concert the second half of which was a performance (using voices and instruments) of Dufay's *Missa L'Homme Armé* by Hortus Musicus. Although some of these pieces have subsequently been modified in various ways, they have all survived the composer's later scrutiny and been recorded in one context or another.

Modus, *Calix*, and *Für Alina* have been briefly discussed above, where it was noted that the first two works closely approach but do not yet, strictly speaking, employ the tintinnabuli technique, while *Für Alina* does have a 'regular' tintinnabuli part, though its melodic line is freely invented. *In Spe* was the first work to unite tintinnabuli principles with a systematic melodic process. Just as its title conceals the religious connotation that was confirmed when the work was reissued in 1984 as *An den Wassern zu Babel sassen wir und weinten* (Psalm 137: By the waters of Babylon we sat down and wept), so the singers' melismas conceal the actual text on which Pärt modelled the work: the Kyrie of the Mass. The work thus has a tripartite structure (Kyrie–Christe–Kyrie), using only the vowels of the text, and concluding

---

[1] The Estonian title of *If Bach had been a Bee-keeper*.

Ex. 14*a*

Ex. 14*b*

with an additional *i* and *e*, which reflects the title (perhaps coinciden-
tally) at the work's climax.

The music begins with a single melodic line (sung in turn by tenor,
soprano, and bass in three different octaves) which gently unfolds the
descending fifth from E to A by adding an extra pitch after each longer
note (see Ex. 14*a*). The three vowels sung (*i-i-e*) represent the word
'Kyrie'; the *i-e* of 'Christe' are sung to a different pattern, using E,
then B as pitch centres, accompanied by an E drone; the last 'Kyrie',
unaccompanied again, starts from a low A, and reverses the shape of
the opening phrases. Thus the vowels representing and thereby allud-
ing to Kyrie and Christe are sung by a single voice without the
'comfort' of tintinnabuli pitches.

A tintinnabuli voice is added only for the 'eleison' phrases, the first
of which is shown in Ex. 14*b*, where the M-voice alternates modes 3
and 4, and is accompanied by an alternating T-voice and an A drone;
the second vowel (*ei* is treated as a single syllable) is sung to an
inversion of the previous vowel's M-voice (with appropriate T-
pitches), while the two pairs of M- and T-voices are combined in a
tutti for the concluding vowel. The final *i(n)-(sp)e* are sung to variants
of the Kyrie–Christe models, providing a fervent climax which ends
with surprising abruptness.[2]

An den Wassern has become most familiar in the version for voices
and organ, though its original scoring calls for a wind quintet and a
quartet of strings (with double bass but no second violin) in addition

---

[2] The bass voice in Ex. 9*j* (see p. 72 above) is singing the equivalent of the second syllable of
the second 'eleison'; two T-voices and a B drone are not shown.

to the four singers. Similarly, *Pari Intervallo* was originally composed for four (unspecified) instruments, but later recast for organ;[3] it will be discussed in Chapter 9 together with *Trivium* and Pärt's two later organ works.

The remaining work of this first tintinnabuli year is the curiously titled *If Bach had been a Bee-keeper*. Originally described as a 'concertino' for wind instruments, harpsichord, and tape, it was rescored in 1984 for wind instruments, piano, and string orchestra. It is a strangely whimsical work; nothing in Pärt's new idiom prepares us for its chromaticisms, which seem to lie at an uncomfortably oblique angle to the tintinnabuli scales and triads. On the other hand, it can be read as underscoring the development of Pärt's language (if we compare it with *Collage*, the earlier work which it most resembles), and indeed as repaying a debt to the co-opted Bach of yore. At the very least, it introduces several arpeggiated motifs which have become hallmarks of the tintinnabuli instrumental style.

The B-A-C-H motif is brought into service once again, superimposed upon itself in various metrical formations to create a sonic impression of bees swarming. (If Bach *had* been a bee-keeper, he might indeed have heard the swarming of bees as variations on the motif formed by his name.) The motif is not only varied metrically, but transposed to begin on each of its constituent pitches in turn, and as this process is also superimposed upon itself, the bee swarm thickens considerably. Through this stalks the presence of tintinnabuli (the cosmic Bee-keeper himself?!), with reiterated chords and boldly fragmented rising scales, and an assertive triadic motif that foretells the kind of idiomatic string figuration that achieves such eloquent form in *Tabula Rasa*. As the harmonic density becomes saturated, Pärt introduces diminished seventh chords on F♯ and E♭, leading to a slower final section in B minor which now reveals that the work is closely modelled on Bach's B minor Prelude from Book 1 of the *Well-Tempered Clavier*. The scales of the first section now assume the character of a walking bass, and indeed, these, together with the earlier arpeggiated motifs, are now revealed in their original Bachian state.

1977

The flow of new works which started in 1976 was not only sustained during the following year, but actually increased. At least three of these 1977 works (*Fratres*, *Cantus*, and *Tabula Rasa*) have remained

[3] More recently a version for four recorders has been published.

pre-eminent examples of Pärt's new music, and are among his most frequently performed compositions.

The title of *Arbos* signifies the shape of a tree and the different tempos of life cycle it contains (branches, trunk, roots). A glance at the score of *Arbos* reveals how Pärt has encapsulated this image musically. The notes flow across the page at three distinctly different speeds, presenting three layers which form a mensuration canon in the proportion 4:2:1. In all three layers the same M-voice is constructed note by note, one extra pitch being added at the end of each phrase. The rhythm (an alternation of long and short) is the same throughout, but every second phrase reverses the pattern (from trochaic [♩ ♪] to iambic [♪ ♩]), so that the effect is of an alternating rhythmic current passing through the same ever-lengthening melodic contours. Ex. 15*a* shows the M-pitches (note the emphasis on certain foundation pitches—A, D, G, D—picked out thus: [o]); Ex. 15*b* gives the three opening versions (bars 1–5) of M in close score. (The T-voices are not shown.) The highest and quickest M-voice has a single T-voice below it (inferior); the middle M-voice is surrounded by two T-voices, one superior and one inferior; while the lowest and slowest M-voice again has a single T-voice, this time above it (superior). All T-voices are in 2nd position. Various versions of this work have been made (ranging from brass to recorders), but all incorporate some kind of percussion to articulate the phrases.

Ex. 15*a*

Ex. 15*b*

Compared to the stark reverberations of *Arbos*, *Cantus* offers a sense of peace and ineffable sadness. After an initial bell stroke has sounded three times, the violins enter with exquisite grace in their highest register, dancing slowly downwards; an octave beneath them the same pattern is unfolded in a slower tempo, while beneath that moves the same pattern, at ever slower speeds and lower octaves. In its underlying processes *Cantus* bears a striking resemblance to *Arbos* (and to the slightly earlier *Calix*): a compound triple metre, the note-by-note construction of a descending phrase, an alternating rhythmic current, the sounding together of the same material at proportionally slower tempos, and the overall descent from a high beginning to a low conclusion. Even so, the differences, and not only those of texture and tempo, are significant.

Cantus has five layers of tempo, which enter in turn, each one an octave lower and twice as slow as the one before, so that what began in the violins has slowed to a sixteenth of the tempo by the time it gets to the double basses. The top two layers (violins 1 and 2) and the bottom two layers (cellos and double basses) each consist of an M-voice and a T-voice in 1st position below it; the middle layer, however, consists of a single M-voice played by violas (and should sound slightly forward in the overall balance). The 'melody' is quite simply a descending A minor scale (Aeolian rather than melodic or harmonic minor). As the music unfolds, the faster-moving layers naturally cover a greater range than their slower counterparts, each layer coming eventually to rest on a different pitch within a low chord of A minor. These pitches are arrived at one by one, so that the first violins reach their low c' six full systems before the double basses finally come to rest on a low A_i.

Ex. 16 shows the beginning of the string entries (M-voices only) as far as the cello entry (the double basses enter four bars later). The bell sounds regularly throughout, in groups of three strokes followed by a

Ex. 16

$(\mathbf{J} = 112–120)$

vn. 1, vn. 2, va.

vc., d.b.

rest. Having begun *ppp*, the work reaches its loudest point, *fff*, just before the first violins reach their final long *c′*. There is no indication in the score that the strings should diminish this dynamic level, though the low tessitura acts as a natural constraint, and the bell is marked progressively softer.

Having no T-voice, it is the violas who play the most subjective role in this work, though their differentiation within the surrounding texture is a most subtle matter. Once they have completed their cycle and been enfolded, so to speak, in the work's final triadic entity, the bell falls silent. At this point also the T-voices in both the cello and double bass layers drop away; the double basses do not quite complete a regular octave cycle of the melodic pattern; having reached C, they continue directly on down to B,, and then the final A,. At the end of the long culminating string chord, the bell sounds softly one last time, and is left to merge into the awaiting silence.

The full title of this work is: *Cantus in memoriam Benjamin Britten*.

In the past years we have had many losses in the world of music to mourn. Why did the date of Benjamin Britten's death—December 4, 1976—touch such a chord in me? During this time I was obviously at the point where I could recognise the magnitude of such a loss. Inexplicable feelings of guilt, more than that even, arose in me. I had just discovered Britten for myself. Just before his death I began to appreciate the unusual purity of his music— I had had the impression of the same kind of purity in the ballads of Guillaume de Machaut. And besides, for a long time I had wanted to meet Britten personally—and now it would not come to that.[4]

Another work built on the diatonic scale is the set of six short *Variations* for piano 'on the recovery to health of Arinushka'. This added another piano piece to the previous year's *Für Alina*, though as yet these two delightful miniatures are the only works for solo piano in tintinnabuli style. The theme of these variations is quite simply a rising and falling octave scale; the scale is not constructed note by note, however, but is simply stated directly and subjected to various tintinnabuli and canonic treatments; the first three variations are in A minor, the last three in A major.

Nearly all the tintinnabuli works of Pärt's 'Estonian' period use the most consonant combinations of pitches, taking a 'white' scale (normally the white notes on the piano forming the Aeolian A minor), and using only the tonic and dominant as M-voice pitch centres. Treating

---

[4] Arvo Pärt quoted in the sleeve-note to the ECM recording of this work.

the bee-keeping Bach as something of a special case, *Fratres* distinguishes itself as the earliest example of a relatively dissonant tintinnabuli formation; though, having said this, it should be observed that the underlying triad—A minor—is serenely and perpetually present throughout. What dissonance there is arises from the use of a scale which incorporates an augmented second; on paper, this scale can be seen as the harmonic version of D minor. The harmonic texture is further enriched by having two parallel M-voices repeating the same six-bar pattern, but moving gradually down through a chain of thirds, so that, eventually, every pitch in this slightly irregular scale functions as a pitch centre. The melodic pattern itself (a three-bar phrase and its inversion) does not change, except insofar as it passes through varying combinations of tone and semitone.

In Ex. 17*a* the opening eight bars are shown (condensed to two staffs, with the right-hand music transposed down an octave). The M-voices construct an octave scale in two halves, using modes 2 and 3. The last three bars simply repeat the previous material with the melodic modes reversed. The A–E drone is sustained throughout the work.

Ex. 17*a*

The dry knocking of the opening rhythmic pattern is heard between each of these six-bar sections, and its effect is easily overlooked in any brief analytical description: but the repetition of this motif and the continuation of the drone together play a crucial role in delimiting the harmonic-melodic activity, and it is the contrast between these two separate elements (both of which suggest 'permanence' in their different ways) that gives the work its remarkable eloquence. This framing of melodic material within a repeated rhythmic motif occurs in many of the tintinnabuli works, especially the instrumental ones, and is a very satisfying musical device to offset the expansion and contraction of melodic material which give the works their particular dynamic shape; it also emphasizes the surrounding silence or stillness. But in addition to serving these purposes, the rhythmic puntuation is also, initially at least, a call to attention (rather like the wooden semantra which prefigured the use of bells in the Eastern Church); thereafter its unvarying repetition suggests the unchanging response in a litaneutical prayer.

Altogether, there are nine statements of the six-bar melodic subject, each one containing the same material: namely, two parallel M-voices a tenth apart and a single T-voice moving between them. Each statement is a third lower than its predecessor, and as the M-voices descend, they at first move further away from the A minor triad and then back towards it. Ex. 17*b* shows the initial pitches of each statement in turn, and it will be observed that the central three statements offer the most dissonant textures against the prevailing A minor. The term 'dissonance' is of course a relative one; we can speak of a tension between the triad and some of the pitches more distant from it, which is indeed used to determine the overall structure of the work; but this is not a functional dissonance in the note-to-note, chord-to-chord sense. The melodic C♯ is frequently countered by the triadic C♮, of course, but this dissonance has an effect similar to the 'false relation' in sixteenth-century music; it is chromatic in the purely colouristic sense of the word.

Ex. 17*b*

The title, *Fratres*, may be translated as 'brethren', the archaic plural of 'brother'. The word aptly describes the relationship between the two M-voices mediated throughout by a single T-voice. It is the operation of the T-voice in this work that is of particular subtlety, and that reinforces the growth of activity towards and then away from the middle of the work. The T-voice is frequently in 2nd position relative to both M-voices at the same time (i.e. triadically, the three voices are equidistant); there are, however, numerous instances where the composer must choose 1st position relative to one of the M-voices, keeping the T-voice in 2nd position relative to the other (see bar 3 in Ex. 17*a*, second and third chords). Pärt makes these choices so as to maintain a symmetry within each statement. In the first statement, for example, there are seven instances of (transposed) 1st position relative to each M-voice. The disposition of 2nd and 1st positions creates a symmetrical pattern from bar to bar, from phrase to phrase, and overall. The frequency of 1st position, taking each statement in turn, also creates a pattern: 7-7-6-9-10-9-6-7-7; again we notice an increase towards the centre.

In the original version, the question of scoring was left open. There are now numerous versions of *Fratres* (more of this work than of any other), but the underlying musical substance remains the same. The most marked difference occurs in the version for solo violin and piano. The harmonic material of the original is retained (mostly in the piano part), while the violin plays a series of variations above. These are often quite virtuosic, and range from rapidly arpeggiated figuration to harmonics and double- and triple-stopping, always, however, paralleling the piano part. The result provides an interesting gloss on the original—inevitably more varied and 'exciting', though it takes a gifted performer to meet the challenge of playing the notes in a way that does not do violence to the music's essential serenity.

Most of the tintinnabuli works discussed so far have been instrumental, and what vocal writing we have seen has employed procedures that are essentially 'instrumental' in conception. But the year 1977 also saw the composition of three vocal works—*Missa Sillabica*, *Cantate Domino*, and *Summa*—each of which depended on its text in a new way, and helped Pärt towards a melodic style similar to the one we have already witnessed—diatonic, moving mostly by step—but no longer wedded to abstract musical processes for the logic of its construction.

As its name suggests, *Missa Sillabica* is an entirely syllabic setting of the ordinary of the mass; but the connection between text and music is even closer. Setting aside the subjective interpretation of the text and even its manner of declamation, it is the structure of the text which Pärt uses to determine the structure of the music. It is not unusual, of course, for the shape of a text (such as, for example, the threefold Kyrie) to be reflected closely in the shape of its musical setting and for its division into smaller units to follow the natural pauses and breaks in the text suggested by both declamation and breathing. But in his search for an objective compositional style Pärt goes further, and uses the number of syllables in each word to determine its melodic shape. The division of the text into smaller grammatical units (by carefully graded punctuation) further assists him in determining not only the lengths of phrases, but also the rests between them; it also helps establish a pattern of initial and cadential note lengthenings, and changes of M-voice mode and T-voice direction.

Such undemonstrative music may seem to require touches of colour to 'enliven' it, yet its reductive purity permits only a minimum of variation by the composer. The composer's task is to uncover what 'musical' laws may inhere in the text itself and bring them to light as objectively as possible. Such an approach does not deny musical creativity, of course; indeed, as with plainchant and early polyphony, the process relies on a profound degree of musical craft and an equally profound affinity for a sense of tradition, of actively drawing upon a source—and where a disconnection with that source seems to have occurred, a reconnection must be made.

Exx. 18a and 18b show the initial Kyrie and Christe settings. The T-voice triad is D minor, and the M-voice pitch centre is D. Using first of all the third M-mode, the three-syllable word 'Kyrie' begins on F, the third note of the scale, while the four-syllable word 'eleison' begins on G, the fourth note of the scale. For the next phrase, the mode is reversed (to mode 4) and so 'Christe' (two syllables) begins on C, 'eleison' on A, the fourth below D. The opening Kyrie is then

Ex. 18a

Ex. 18*b*

repeated exactly (though only because the alternation of M- and T-patterns allows for this).

All composers setting the mass are confronted with two very different types of texts: the short prayers (the Kyrie, Sanctus and Benedictus, and Agnus, each having a threefold element) and the longer prose texts of the Gloria and Credo. Already in the fifteenth century it was customary to divide the longer texts into smaller sections for greater musical contrast. Pärt's syllabic approach side-steps the issue of musical form, and certainly does not give rise to problems of undue length, while any risk of *monotony* in the longer movements is nicely offset by a responsorial approach.

The Gloria has a three-part texture throughout, alternating two pairs of M-voices (A/T, S/B, both pairs in disjunct motion) and an instrumental T-voice. The pitch centre of the male voices is D, while the alto and soprano have respectively F and A as pitch centres. The T-voice (in 1st position, alternating) follows the upper voices, and its range is thus varied slightly.

For the Credo Pärt adopts a four-part texture, alternating tenor/bass and soprano/alto (each voice having its corresponding instrumental T-voice), and the contrast in their ranges creates a markedly antiphonal effect. This together with the text's length and an emphasis on the perfect fifth (the voices' pitch centres are A and D, using modes 1 and 3 respectively) combine to give the music a strongly hieratic cast. Even so, there is no absence of expression, though it emanates from the text's 'interior', duly strengthened by the compactness of the musical style. Ex. 18*c* reproduces sections 7–9 of the Credo, where the words exhibit a remarkable ability to inhabit and nuance such music with quite specific effect. Sections 7 and 8 are to be sung relatively softly; one may then enjoy in a perfectly conventional manner the musical repetition at 'et *homo factus* est', the dissonant cluster at the beginning of '*Cru*cifixus', the indefinite semi-cadence of

'Pi*lato*', the implied second inversion of the triad on 'sepultus *est*', and a renewed sense of energy in section 9.

All voices combine at the end of these two movements for an 'Amen'; again the prevailing processes determine the musical content of these, and a comparison of the two illuminates the different character Pärt has found in the two texts (Ex. 18*d*).

For the Sanctus Pärt moves to the relative (F) major for both T-triad and M-pitch centres, and presents a four-part tutti with each line doubled at the octave, resulting in a rich, jubilant declamation of the text. The D minor triad is restored for the Agnus and a quieter three-part texture, focusing on a narrow vocal range just above middle C; a second T-voice is added for the concluding phrase. The 'dismissal', 'Ite, missa est', and its response, 'Deo gratias', have not normally been part of polyphonic settings since the fourteenth century; Pärt sets these words in a reverberant tutti, which provides a fitting conclusion to this brief setting of the mass.

Cantate Domino is a short, lightly dancing setting of Psalm 95 cast technically very much in the same mould as the mass, though the key is B♭, with two pairs of voices (S/A, T/B) doubling each other at the octave and four instrumental lines, two of them T-voices, the other two doubling the voices at a higher and lower octave still. Again, in practice, various distributions of voices and instruments can be made.[5]

The third of these early texted pieces, *Summa*, already presents

Ex. 18*d*

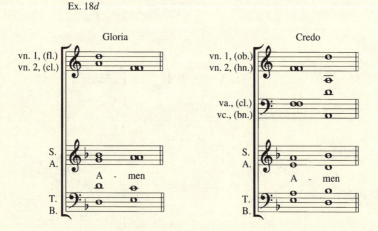

[5] One that was particularly effective, under the composer's direction, employed organ and glockenspiel.

some new departures. Originally composed for two solo voices (tenor and bass) and six instruments, *Summa* became better known first as an a cappella vocal work (both solo and choral) and more recently in various instrumental combinations, ranging from string quartet to string orchestra. Its quiet beauty seems straightforward enough, even if, while it is clear to the listener that the same basic musical material is being revolved through the text, the ear cannot readily detect any precise pattern either in the purely musical process or in the way the text is divided up among the two pairs of voices. But on closer inspection, *Summa* reveals itself to be one of the most intricately satisfying of the shorter tintinnabuli works. Beneath its undemonstrative exterior lie several interwoven layers of skilfully proportioned activity determining every note, but with such graceful subtlety that the impression is quite free.

The long text (364 syllables) is divided up into a fixed syllabic pattern: 7/9/14/9/14/9/14, and so on, ending with a final group of 7. (A five-note 'Amen' is used to close the pattern.) The nine-syllable groups are set *à* 4, the 14-syllable groups alternately for the lower and upper pair of voices, in strict rotation. This disposition of the text by syllable count takes no notice of its phrase structure, and results in a seemingly fortuitous setting, in which phrases stop or begin in the middle of words in one pair of voices, whilst continuing in the other (an approach which also occurs in some medieval pieces). In the exact centre of the work, however, this results in a significant and expressive break after a unison cadence at the words 'sepultus est'.

The M-voices form a pair of rising and falling scales, with one syllable allotted to each note of the scale; these scales move between a fourth and a sixth apart, though their parallel motion is somewhat disguised by the addition of passing tones, so that their motion might more aptly be described as 'curling' in either direction, rather than moving precisely by step. Both voices encompass ranges of a minor tenth, that of the bass being a fourth lower than that of the 'tenor'.[6] The upper voice begins with a descending phrase for the opening: 'Credo in unum Deum' (seven syllables). This phrase is normally sung as a solo intonation, and its length will have helped determine the particular syllabic divisions used by Pärt. In the next bar (nine syllables) the upper voice turns round and begins to ascend, joined now by the lower voice moving at first in parallel sixths; they turn around at different points to make their descent. The intervallic relationship

---

[6] i.e. the second part down, which is a tenor solo in the original version.

between the two M-voices gradually shifts from an emphasis upon sixths at the beginning, to predominantly fourths in the middle of the work, and then back to the more euphonious sixths again by the end. These opening phrases are shown in Ex. 19*a*.

If the T-voices are examined closely, it will be apparent that their connection to the M-voice does not strictly fit the 'rules' outlined in Chapter 4. Not only do they move around apparently freely between 1st, 2nd, and 3rd (transposed 1st) positions; there are even instances of octaves, which would normally be avoided. Instead, Pärt appears to have designed the two T-voices from a longer perspective so that they create their own pattern, both separately and together. The overall contours of the two patterns (M and T) do correspond, but the note-to-note logic of the T-voice is, exceptionally, self-contained.

To see this more clearly, we must strip away the passing notes and rhythmic values, leaving just the bare bones of M- and T-voices. In Ex. 19*b* I have superimposed the T-voices on one stave, and likewise the M-voices (and in order to do so, the lower pair has been transposed up an octave). This reveals both the separate patterns and the way they interlock, M with M and T with T.

Ex. 19*a*

● = sounding an octave lower

The M-voice scales are varied in a sequential fashion: every two bars a new beginning is made with the scale, always starting with E, then jumping to progressively one pitch later in the scale and continuing from that point. The pitch or pitches omitted in this process are then added at the end of the phrase. In Ex. 19*b* these two points are marked by an 'x'.

However, it is not quite so straightforward as that! Each M-voice pitch is sounded twice, once on the way up, once on the way down. Or we could say that the same sequence of notes (an octave scale) is repeated forwards and then backwards. Looking again at Ex. 19*b* we can observe that the opening scale from E down to F# is in effect repeated, starting on the sixth pitch of the second bar and working backwards to the same F#; but if we check the corresponding T-pitches, we will find a different part of the pattern. In other words, one part of the larger pattern is slowly emerging at a different point in the same pattern; the music begins to suggest the familiar unfamiliarity of a short story by Borges about a mirror which appears to dissolve, but is in fact slowly reconstituting itself elsewhere. And the process is circular: only at the very end of the work do the final pieces of the mirror slip back into place as the pitches (and rhythms) of the opening line are repeated exactly. Were it not for the 'Amen', bringing both sets of voices to rest on an open fifth, E–B, the piece could go on sounding to eternity.

This survey of Pärt's earlier tintinnabuli works may fittingly conclude with *Tabula Rasa* ('clean slate'), a double concerto for two violins and string orchestra with obbligato prepared piano. No new processes are introduced in this work, and in some respects it may be regarded as a summing up of the instrumental tintinnabuli works composed thus far, being both a more expansive piece of music (lasting over twenty-five minutes) and having two separate (yet complementary) movements, contrasted in mood and tempo. The underlying unity of these two movements is perhaps the most significant feature of the work as a whole, and serves to substantiate the tintinnabuli principle as something pervading all aspects of a composition, the larger structural elements as well as phrase-to-phrase construction, and not merely a means of moving from note to note.

The two movements are called *Ludus* (in A minor, marked 'Con moto', crotchet = *c*.120) and *Silentium* (in D minor, marked 'Senza moto', crotchet = *c*.60). The A–D cadential pattern outlines the natural polarity of these tonal centres; it also briefly affords a sense of resolution at the beginning of the second movement, but the ear is not given any expectation of a resolution, and this relationship cannot be regarded as functional except in the broadest sense. The work has two 'themes', bearing out the implications of the titles: *ludus* = game, to play (music); *silentium* = silence—or action and contemplation.

With a searing fortissimo A on both solo violins, four octaves apart, the 'slate' is wiped clean. This is the work's first 'theme'—a single note, from which is elaborated a process of melodic construction that is the same in both movements, though the first movement is founded on duple rhythms, the second on triple. After the initial sounding of the single note, there follows a bar of silence—the work's second 'theme'. The first movement is a 'game' full of silences that grow progressively shorter until they are overwhelmed by a loud cadenza. The second movement is slow and quiet, but has no actual silences until the very end; instead, it is a gradual preparation for silence, and a slow unwinding into it.

The beginning of *Ludus* is shown in Ex. *20a*. The first two bars announce the single A and the answering silence. At fig. 1 the first of eight variations begins: working in pairs (each pair comprising an M- and a T-voice) and starting with the first violins divisi, the orchestral strings sound the note A four times with T-pitches (1st position, alternating) C and E, all in equal crotchets. This pattern descends through the orchestra down to the low A, of the double basses. The soloists exchange more animated figuration based on the A minor triad, and the piano plays a single low chord of A minor; underneath, the orchestral strings reverse their pattern of entrances, ascending back to their initial octave. The second soloist plays a high a''' four times, accompanied by T-pitches from the piano. This is followed by a bar of silence (seven minims, one less than in bar 2), marking the end of the first variation. The second begins at fig. 2 and follows exactly the same sequence of events, except that the pitches B and G are added to the M-voice and, accordingly, to the patterns played by the soloists, and each event is longer by an extra bar.

This process of elongation continues steadily throughout eight variations, the stock of melodic pitches increasing by one in both directions in each variation; the concluding silences correspondingly diminish by a minim each time. By the eighth variation the M-voice has incorporated all seven diatonic pitches, and there are no more silences. In place of silence, there is a large crescendo that launches a cadenza. The prepared piano takes a major role here, leading the way in a three octave descending scale, with rapid tremolandos from all three soloists while individual pitches are sustained in the orchestra. This progression is arrested on the penultimate note, B, leading to a ninth variation in which two pitches are added, F♯ and E♭, to form a diminished seventh chord. The soloists articulate rapid arpeggios, while the orchestra pulsates loudly with a steady crotchet beat. At first the diminished triad is unchallenged, except by the piano's resounding chords of A minor, to which it responds by moving outwards in both directions, spreading its hold. The chord of A minor then contends more directly with these foreign pitches, gradually overcoming them. Finally, the soloists reach their respective high and low A's (as in bar 1), and a long single chord of A minor, low in the strings, brings

Ex. 20*a*

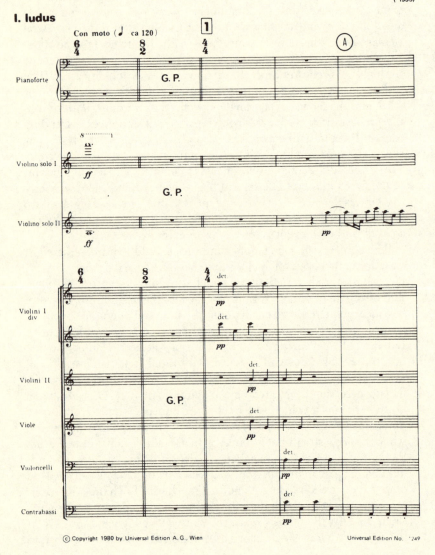

für tatjana grindenko, gidon kremer und eri klas

tabula rasa (1977)
doppelkonzert für zwei violinen, streichorcher
und präpariertes klavier

arvo pärt
(·1935)

I. ludus

Universal Edition No. '249

116

UE 17 249

the movement to an end. This latter struggle is remarkably reminiscent of passages in works written in Pärt's earlier style, particularly the Second Symphony and *Credo*, though here, of course, the activity is entirely generated from within the music's substance and makes no cross-references or stylistic allusions.

A D minor arpeggio from the prepared piano immediately establishes the tonal centre of the second movement. Ex. 20*b* shows the beginning of the same melodic pattern as was heard in the first movement, now centred on D and moving in triple rhythms and in a threefold metric canon, which begins simultaneously in the solo first violin and the tutti first violin and cello. Gradually they create a web of ever-widening melodic arcs, attended by tintinnabuli pitches. These T-voices are now distributed in three ways (as opposed to the single alternating 1st position in the first movement): the second soloist continues in alternating 1st position to the first soloist, while the second violins are in 2nd position inferior to the first violins, and the violas are in 2nd position superior to the cellos. The prepared piano rearticulates the opening arpeggio each time the M-voice soloist passes through its D pitch centre; naturally, this event occurs at increasingly longer intervals as the melodic arcs widen.

Eventually the cello arc grows to four octaves, and has to be assisted by the double basses; but their final descent towards the lowest D merges into inaudibility before it gets there. The last pitch actually sounded is E,, the penultimate in the scale, just as happened at the end of the first movement's cadenza. This time, however, it leads into silence.

The Late 1970s (Further Biographical Notes)

The first performance of *Credo* was neither the first nor the last incident in Pärt's Estonian period to provoke official displeasure. In 1972 it was suggested[7] that he could anonymously enter a composition which carried a substantial cash prize. Pärt seemed reluctant, but eventually delivered a score that opened up like a star and consisted of various contrapuntal variations of the Communist 'International'. The orchestral parts were not written out, and the work was never performed, but a copy of the score made its way to Moscow; in due course there came the inevitable visit by officials from Ideological Control. Pärt's friends defended him, saying that he was as precious to

---

[7] By Avo Hirvesoo.

Ex. 20*b*

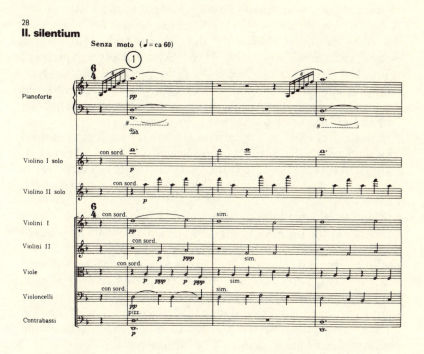

the Estonians as was Shostakovich to the Russians. 'Shostakovich is not so precious to us', came the reply. Pärt, they felt, had mocked one of their holiest symbols. The ramifications of this scandal did not disappear overnight, and of course Pärt's position as a professional composer was made less viable than ever. It was forbidden to buy or sell his music (though not to play it). A few years later, in 1978, with the tintinnabuli style already formed and as he was beginning to be sought after abroad, Pärt was prevented from travelling to attend some of these performances. Other Soviet musicians encountered similar problems, of course, and the period was one of sudden set-backs and petty frustrations.

In 1978 Andres Mustonen was the main instigator of the Tallinn Festival of Old and New Music, which he characterizes with some justification as a 'dissident' festival of great significance. Pärt's *Tabula Rasa* was performed, as were the seven early tintinnabuli pieces (mentioned at the beginning of this chapter). In addition, the music of Cage, Stockhausen, Xenakis, Webern, and Henze was heard alongside works by non-conformist Soviet composers including Edison Denisov, Vladimir Martinov, Valentin Silvestrov, and Viktor Suslin. Among the performers were the Lithuanian Chamber Orchestra, conducted by Saulus Sondeckis, and the violinists Gidon Kremer and Natalia Grindenko, who, with Alfred Schnittke playing prepared piano, had already taped *Tabula Rasa* the previous year for West German Radio, live at a concert in Cologne. This performance was destined to be included seven years later on the first recording to bring Pärt's name to prominence in the West.

Cologne was also the setting for a festival in March 1979 entitled 'Encounter with the Soviet Union', which infuriated Khrennikov, who was not exactly in agreement about the choice of composers to represent his country.[8] Several works by Pärt were performed: *Arbos*, *Cantate Domino*, *Fratres*, and *Missa Sillabica*.

Many people recall the day in 1979 when Pärt took the podium at a meeting of the Estonian Composers' Union, donned a long-haired wig, and proceeded to harangue those present about the restrictions placed on him and his music. Although he had been allowed to make a trip to Italy the previous year, he had been prevented from going to England, and more recently he had not been permitted to make the short ferry crossing to Finland, to attend a chamber music festival in Kuhmo. Grudgingly he was allowed to attend the London Prom performance of *Cantus* conducted by Rozhdestvensky.

The 'wig incident' highlights the increasingly uncongenial atmosphere that surrounded Pärt at the time. It was not entirely out of character for him to provoke criticism, even scandal, though the means of doing so had normally been a musical composition. Such public effusions were hardly typical of the composer, although the decisive emotion which gave rise to it certainly was; that circumstances led him to act so 'out of character' underscores the sense of frustration that motivated his decision to emigrate.

To us in the West his emigration might appear entirely natural on purely economic grounds, and certainly many families and individuals relocated themselves for such perfectly good reasons. Indeed, it was a truism of the cold war decades that life was better in the West. Materially, of course, it generally was, and during the 1970s the stifling bureaucracy of Soviet institutions seemed set to endure for another half-century at least. But it seems unlikely that Pärt would have made such a move if his musical life had been free of restrictions.

[8] See Schwartz, pp. 623–6.

He sought the wider audience for his music, as any composer would; but he came to the West with no guarantee of support, no promise of success, and, to judge by his comments in numerous published interviews, there are many aspects of its culture which he has found inimical.

7

PASSIO

Introduction: The Passion Genre

THE *Passio*[1] will probably stand as the quintessential example of Pärt's tintinnabuli music, in which the tintinnabuli principles function on a large scale to convey a long prose text of very special spiritual significance, and in such a manner that the two cannot be viewed separately. My main purpose here will be to examine the means by which Pärt has transformed the text—eight columns of closely printed prose in my copy of the Vulgate—into a unified musical utterance, whose power and beauty have been widely attested to by audiences throughout the world. But first I propose to trace the early history of the Passion genre, which forms an important background to Pärt's particular approach.

Of all sacred texts with a history of musical settings, of which we may therefore speak as a 'genre', the Passion stands apart from the rest, being pure narrative from beginning to end. The 'Christmas story' would be its immediate counterpart, though there exists no specific text which is automatically called forth by such a term, still less a specific musical tradition associated with it. Various text segments come quickly to mind, but they are not all narrative in content, and do not form a recognizable genre. That there are four distinct accounts of the Passion of Christ has not hindered the understanding of a special genre, which has indeed existed since earliest times. Whichever Gospel is chosen, the sheer length of the story already claims special attention, and its narrative content (including dialogue) has inevitably encouraged quasi-dramatic forms of representation. In the most famous examples, the Passions of Bach, the Evangelist's account is cast in a vivid recitative style that always reinforces the inherent drama of the situation, while various soloists comment on the events and make their personalized appeals to the suffering Christ. But these interpolations do not disturb the ritualized sense of process that underlies the retelling of any familiar story. The narrative sets up

[1] The full title is *Passio Domini Nostri Jesu Christi Secundum Johannem.*

its own sense of time and place, quite removed from the everyday world, and thereby invites meditation on the events even as the listener is being pulled along by them. The element of involvement in Christ's suffering—our *com-passio* for the protagonist—is always subsumed in the greater process of participation in a mystery that we cannot fully understand. However vivid the re-enactment, the outcome is known and foretold; the retelling of the story is a ritualistic act, whether it derives its function from an all-encompassing liturgy, or is sustained more broadly by a tradition of annual concert performances.

Notwithstanding its instrumental component and its status as a concert work (albeit, of a very special kind), Pärt's *Passio* shows the influence of sixteenth-century models, and in some respects takes its initial impetus from practices that date back to the ninth century and even earlier.

First we may make some basic observations concerning the origin of the Passion as a distinct genre.[2] From the earliest times a special reading of the story of Christ's Passion developed strictly within a liturgical framework; this rendition was distinguished by making plain the text's division into narrative and direct speech by the use of a special manner of utterance. The earliest evidence we have of liturgical readings of the Passion comes from the fourth century. From expressively heightened reading it is a short step to a manner of declamation or intonation that we can regard as singing; although the Latin verb *dicere* (to say) is used, it may be interpreted as implying 'recitation' on a single tone, rather than ordinary speech.[3] These readings sometimes presented a composite account drawn from all four Gospels, but already in the fifth century the St John Passion was selected for reading on Good Friday (since he alone of the disciples was thought to have been present at the crucifixion and to have stood at the foot of the cross).

By the middle of the eighth century the rendition of the Passion was given an introduction, or exordium: 'Passio Domini nostri Jesu Christi . . .', and from the ninth century onwards Passion texts exist with the addition of *litterae significativae* (letters of signification) indicating a varied manner of delivery, such as *c* for *celeriter* (quickly), *s* for *suaviter* (softly). These performance indications, concerning

---

[2] For this account of the early Passion I have drawn liberally on Kurt von Fischer's excellent essay *The Passion from its Beginnings until the 16th Century*, in Fischer, which is also the basis for his article on this topic in the New Grove.

[3] Ibid. pp. 12–13.

speed, dynamic, and relative pitch, further served to distinguish the Passion as a special genre.

By the twelfth century, Passion texts occur with specific pitches (indicated by letters rather than staff notation) ranging just over an octave from c to d', and therefore still suitable for one singer; the words of Christ are set at the lowest end (reciting on d and f), the Evangelist narrative is set in the middle (on a), while the Turba[4] is pitched at the upper octave d'.

It is in the thirteenth century that we first encounter evidence for performances of the Passion involving more than one singer. This move towards greater expressivity is explained by Fischer[5] as being rooted in the theological developments of that time: specifically, the influence of St Bernard of Clairvaux, whose followers sought to depict the agony of Christ with increasing realism. It was at this time also that paintings depicting the Crucifixion began to introduce greater numbers of figures, and generally to project a heightened sense of drama.

The earliest extant polyphonic setting of the Passion is found in the English manuscript known as Egerton 3307, dating from the early fifteenth century and probably compiled for use at St George's Chapel, Windsor. The exordium, the Turba (the crowd), and the solo characters—with the notable exception of Christus—are set in three-part English discant style. Thereafter the history of the Passion continues mostly in continental sources and in two distinct manners: one responsorial, generally reserved for accounts drawn from a single, specific Gospel and mixing polyphonic responses and solo recitation; the other through-composed, more often using a composite text drawn from all four Gospels. An important example of the latter type is the *Summa Passionis* of Antoine de Longueval (fl. 1507–22), probably the oldest extant four-part setting in this manner, which divides its abridged text into three sections (like a motet), and provides us with the first known example of the special closing prayer, or conclusio: 'Qui passus es pro nobis miserere nobis'—the same words used by Pärt, with the addition of a final 'Amen'.

A work such as the St Matthew Passion of Lassus retains some motet-style features in what is otherwise a responsorial setting: the individual roles are set in two- and three-part imitative polyphony,

---

[4] I use this Latin word for *crowd* to refer loosely to all the music sung by the singer or singers as 'chorus', who represent at different times an angry mob, the High Priest, or the various minor characters in the story.

[5] Ibid. pp. 18–20.

whereas the Turba settings are more homophonic in style, and chant is used for the Evangelist and Christ. In other settings we find precedents for Pärt's setting of the Evangelist part for four voices: a St John Passion (1587) by Jakobus Gallus is set for two four-voice choirs, one high, one low; the words of Christ are sung by the low voices and the Turba by both choirs, while the Evangelist text is set for a wide variety of combinations from four to eight voices. With the Reformation and use of the vernacular, it is not surprising to discern a tendency to more individual characterization of the various parts, though Schütz, in a related work, the *Auferstehungs-Historia* (Resurrection History), assigns the words of Christ to two voices.

Passio: *The Basic Structure*

Pärt's setting of the Passion according to St John reflects these early models in numerous ways, but it remains unmistakably a tintinnabuli work, not just in its sound, but in its manner of construction. While we may infer that Pärt has taken ideas from early music, ultimately we should say that he has found a means of working with a traditional fabric not by imitation, but by picking up the thread of that earlier tradition and continuing it. Each compositional idea, however readily we may assign to it an earlier model, emerges quite naturally from the manner in which *Passio* has been constructed; it is as if the same musico-poetic prototypes that enlivened the chant and early music models which I have described briefly above are once again active within Pärt's music.

To say that *Passio* consists of a beginning, a middle, and an end, is perhaps to court the reader's impatience; yet those are precisely the work's only clearly defined formal units, although within the main central unit there are certainly a number of discrete musical layers which together make up the narrative core. The beginning and end, the exordium and the conclusio, are brief but forcefully expressive moments, set apart by the long central structure which they abut. Without the centre, however, they would be virtually meaningless.

The words of the Evangelist, forming by far the greater bulk of the text, are delivered by a double quartet of four singers (SATB) and four instruments (violin, oboe, cello, bassoon), heard in every possible combination during the course of the work. The words of Peter, the High Priest, all the minor characters such as the servants and maid-servants, and of course the mob (Turba), are sung by the choir, sometimes doubled by organ, though Pärt does not make any specific colouristic distinctions to depict the various 'roles' represented by the chorus. The two truly solo voices are those of Christ and Pilate, the former a bass singing in a distinctly lower register than anyone else, the latter a tenor whose music is the most differentiated in the whole work. Both of these are accompanied throughout by organ.

Using a sequence of interconnected triads and pitch centres, the whole work draws upon three sets of overlapping fifths: D–A–E–B. This provides a residue of ninths, specifically D–E and A–B, which also emphasize the supertonic in the scales of D and A respectively, and these prove to have an important function throughout the work.

Ex. 21a shows the general scheme of *Passio* and the relative ranges of the different groups. 'Turba' is here used for the choir's collective role. The tintinnabuli chord for each group is always fixed and is shown thus: [o] ; a square [▫] note denotes a pedal or drone pitch; the puncta [•] show the melodic scales employed. The basic note-length is shown in brackets.

Ex. 21a

Before discussing these groups in more detail, a general account will be given of the rhythmic system used by Pärt in this work; the exordium and conclusio will then be discussed as a pair, followed by the work's main section, treating each of the four roles in turn in the order of their first appearance the Evangelist, Christ, Turba, and Pilate.

Rhythm

Looking always at the text, Pärt established a table of rhythmic values whereby to assign a specific length of note to each syllable, depending on its position in a phrase and that phrase's relationship to the other phrases around it. The same process is brought to bear on the complete text, but with certain variations. In effect, it is the punctuation (as it appears in the score) which determines these rhythmic values, though the punctuation is itself, of course, a realization of the meanings, emphases, and general pacing implicit in the text. The pauses at the end of a phrase may be marked by a comma, a question mark, a colon, or a full stop; each of these implies a different quantity and even quality in the following pause, and also determines the significance of the first word in the next phrase. Actual speech, of course, allows an infinite variety of nuance, to which different composers respond in different degrees. Pärt is less concerned with the intimate inflections of speech and more with the hierarchy of phrasing which underlies it; this is easier, certainly, to abstract from a written text, which can be rendered unambiguous at the level of punctuation. The subtle, manifold meanings that lurk within and behind all language are not smothered or weakened in this process: indeed, they are strengthened, for the music does not interpret the language (other than syntactically), but allows the text to speak for itself, unimpeded at the more intimate level, while its structural patterns are reinforced and enhanced through the the sustaining power of music. The 'meanings' are meanwhile allowed to reverberate fully, without the hindrance of rhetorical gesture so alien to the tintinnabuli style.

Accordingly, Pärt established a scheme entailing a scale of three relative note-values—short, medium, and long—and determined the following:

1. In the last word of a phrase ending with a comma, the stressed syllable would be medium.
2. In the last word of a phrase ending with a colon or full stop, each syllable would be long.

3. In the first word of a new sentence (or phrase beginning after a colon), the stressed syllable would be medium.
4. In the last word in a phrase ending with a question mark, each syllable would be medium.
5. Otherwise all syllables are short.

He then determined that this scale should operate at three different speeds, thus:

Evangelist   [♩ ♩ ♩.]

Turba and Pilate [♩ ♩. o.]

Christ   [♩. o ▯]

Ex. 21*b* shows a fragment from each of these three. The music is notated so that each word equals a bar. At the end of every phrase there is a bar's rest exactly half the length of the last word. But at the end of a sentence, where the same voice or group is going to continue, this space is occupied by a brief instrumental refrain, in which the final word just sung is echoed by the appropriate instruments, but with M-voice modes reversed and note-values diminished by half.

Exordium and Conclusio

The exordium and conclusio form a pair, whose function outside the main body of the work is reinforced by several details in their musical

Ex. 21*b*

128

setting. The title is announced in a descending chain of chords over a sustained pedal E (see Ex. 21*c*). There is a change of chord for each new word, separated by a comma. The alto voice has a descending A minor scale, and the bass moves in parallel a sixth below; these M-voices are both accompanied by two T-voices, in 1st and 2nd position superior. The syllabic structure of the text does not at this point determine the music, although the *number* of words in the phrase (seven) is put to remarkable effect: the alto's descending scale ends quite logically where the seventh word has left it, a step above the tonic. Its resolution is in effect the ensuing *a* sung by the bass Evangelist, and thence through the entire Passion narrative. The incomplete descending scale was used in earlier works such as *Tabula Rasa*, but here it neatly emerges from the text itself, and this process will be echoed in the conclusio with one significant difference.

About an hour into the work, the Evangelist vocal quartet comes to rest on two unison As an octave apart. As Ex. 21*a* showed, there have been other harmonies in the course of the work, but the overall impression is of a long sounding out of the A minor triad. As this tonality lingers in the memory, it becomes transformed into the dominant of the D major, which now rises quietly in the concluding prayer. It will be noticed also that the chorus and Pilate share the same M-voice pitch centre, B, as that played by the organ when accompanying Christ. This pitch forms the supertonic in A minor. The actual pitch centre for the voice of Christ is E, the supertonic in the key of D, the key in which the *Passio* finds its eventual conclusion.

The conclusio (see Ex. 21*d*) reverses the movement of the exordium, providing a rising scale of D major (choir and organ manual), while the exordium's E drone is now turned into a descending D major scale (organ pedal). The choir is divided into eight parts, consisting of soprano and alto M-voices (beginning the scale on F♯ and A)

Ex. 21*c*

choir

Pas - si - o Do - mi - ni nos - tri Je - su Chris - ti se - cun - dum Jo - an - nem

org.
pedal
(manuals double the choir, but sustain through each bar)

with attendant 1st position superior T-voices, this being doubled an octave lower by the male voices. The organ doubles the choral M-voices, but fills out the harmonic texture by providing different T-voices.

There is a gradual crescendo from *pp* to *fff*, and the words, divided into three phrases, are sung without commas. Here again it is the text which illuminates the musical structure, for there are now *eight* words, and the scales very naturally complete the octave in both directions, leaving the sopranos on a high *a″* and, indeed, the whole choir on a second inversion of a D major triad that aspires upwards, but is firmly grounded in the solid octaves of the organ's pedal register.

Apart from a general indication of *mp* at the beginning of the Evangelist part, the only dynamic marks in the entire piece are those found in the exordium and conclusio. The remainder of the work does not lack dynamic variations, though these arise spontaneously, both from the fluctuations in scoring and from the general musical motion and meaning of the words at any given moment. From time to time in this work (as elsewhere, but always very sparingly) the composer intervenes in the process he has set up to reinforce some expressive detail or to alter the course of a process with deliberate effect. Such a moment occurs in the conclusio when, at the end of the first phrase, the organ's pedal G is held across the following bar. Ideally this note should continue to crescendo, if the instrument can manage it technically; in any case, it serves to emphasize the harmonic resolution taking place.

The ability of tintinnabuli music to render a text expressively yet free of wilful interpretation is here beautifully encapsulated. Just to compare the passing dissonances of the first three bars (especially evocative at 'passus') to the more closed tension of 'nobis', which opens both times on to a pure D major, demonstrates the way in which Pärt can reflect the underlying rhetoric of a text, balancing its levels of emphasis perfectly and allowing its meanings to glow forth, even while following his rules here as elsewhere.

The Evangelist

Two main differences in tintinnabuli technique distinguish the central core of the work from the exordium/conclusio pair: all T-voices are here alternating 1st position, and the M-voices are all derived from the text's syllabic structure (as in the *Missa Sillabica*).

The exordium's pedal E (echoed by the part of Christ) is ultimately resolved by moving down a step to the conclusio's D major. The general ascent of the conclusio is a balanced response to the opening descent of the exordium, which gives the listener the impression of being lowered into the world of narrative, which is then left to run its inevitable course. Thereafter, until the concluding D major, the work is sustained by the Evangelist group, centred on A minor.

Although interspersed with the various words of Christ, Pilate, and the Turba, it is the text sung by the Evangelist or, more precisely, the structural methods with which Pärt articulates it, that determine the principal elements of form underlying this main section of the work, and it will therefore be examined first.

Pärt divides up the text of the Evangelist into its constituent phrases, which number 210, and groups them into four sections of 50 phrases each, with a final concluding set of 10. Each of these sections begins with a different solo voice, which sings two phrases. There is then a change of texture every two phrases (25 pairs, there-

131

fore, in each section), so that after the solo voice has begun, the other voices and instruments are added one by one until all eight are heard together; this pattern is then reversed back down to a single voice, and the process begins again. The final set of 10 phrases is sung by all four Evangelist voices, without the instrumental quartet; they converge on to a single pitch class, A, for their last utterance: 'Et inclinato capite tradidit spiritum' ('And he bowed his head and gave up the spirit').

This fourfold division is only a musical one, and does not reflect any pertinent change of pace or focus in the text; indeed, the music is woven seamlessly through the text, so that a break at any point, according to the text's demands, always appears perfectly logical. It is only at the end of this musical process (which coincides with the beginning of the final 10 phrases) that a break in music and text occurs simultaneously, and to beautiful effect: the last section begins 'After this, Jesus knowing that all things were now accomplished' (John 19: 28).

Each of the four main sections is constructed in the same way, and is part of a recurring pattern that begins from a point which is in effect the same yet different each time. Ex. 21*e* shows the pattern of entrances for the first section (v for voice, i for instrument). It is impossible to account in prose for the numerous subtleties within this pattern which consists in several layers of interconnecting, perfectly balanced details, operating both within each section and from one section to another, so that at comparable phrases in each section a variation of the same idea is taking place. The four lines fill in from the bottom upwards, starting with solo bass and adding instruments one by one to the upper lines; then two voices alone, tenor and bass, adding instruments again to complete the four parts; then three voices joined by just one instrument, and finally all four voices alone. From this point the four voices continue singing, and are joined first by one instrument, then two, and so on, until all eight are sounding. The instruments are then subtracted one by one (from the bottom up), as are then the voices, leaving the soprano alone. The pattern repeats, but now filling in from the top downwards, leaving the bass alone once more. The tenor takes over and initiates the third section, the other lines filling in first downwards, then from above. When this process is in due course reversed, it is the alto voice that is eventually left alone to begin the fourth section, the music filling in first with the line above, then from the bottom upwards.

vn., S.		i		i		i	v	v	v	v	vi	vi	vi	vi	v	v	v	v	v
ob., A.	i	i		i	i	v	v	v	v	v	vi	vi	vi	vi	v	v	v	v	i
vc., T.	i	i	i	v	v	v	v	v	v	v	vi	vi	vi	vi	v	v	v	v	i
bn., B.	v	v	v	v	v	v	v	v	v	v	vi	vi	vi	vi	v	v	v	v	i

The alto and bass are M-voices throughout the work, changing at each new phrase from an alternation of modes 1 and 2 to an alternation of modes 3 and 4. The soprano and tenor provide a 1st position alternating T-voice to each of these. The only variation occurs when, twice in each section, one of the M-voice singers sustains an A drone (the M-voice being played two octaves away). The soprano and tenor always have T-voice patterns: sometimes this means that an instrument is playing the text-derived M-voice, while the text itself is heard only in the arpeggiating vocal line. When one of these voices sings entirely alone (i.e., without any M-voice), the T-voice follows the M-voice that the text *would* have produced, but is present for the time being only by implication.

The instruments function in a wider variety of ways. Although each is basically paired with a specific voice (soprano with violin, etc.) which it sometimes doubles or replaces, at various times the instruments also double or replace other voices or provide a T-voice mirror, sometimes operating an octave or two away from the vocal pitch. With two M-voices and two possible alternating T-voices for each of them, a texture of six different lines is possible, though by different permutations of octave transposition the intensity of the Evangelist group can be further varied quite considerably.

Christ

As observed above, the part of Christ moves at the slowest tempo, and is set in the lowest range of all the voices, giving it a solemnity and distinction that are wholly traditional in concept. Together with the organ accompaniment, the harmonic framework of the music for

Christ encompasses the two overlapping triads of A minor and E minor, in which the pitch E functions as a linchpin, and it is this pitch which the voice takes as its pitch centre. The organ part meanwhile is made up of three musical elements: a mirror image of the vocal line (but with B as its pitch centre), a tintinnabulating A minor triad, and the interval of a fifth (E–B) as a drone.

The A minor T-voice follows the organ M-voice, and thus is not based directly on the vocal line, though there is of course a connection via the mirror imaging. It is the E–B drone (heard in various registers) that constitutes an unchanging support for the vocal part, providing it with a triadic essence, but emptied of the potential ambiguities of the third, and motionless. The net result is to ensure a fairly constant sounding of all seven diatonic pitches, but in a most consonant environment, provided by the continuous presence of the E–B drone and the A minor triad.

The voice never changes its range, but the other three elements are disposed around it in four specific ways which are heard in strict rotation throughout the work, providing the part of Christ with a sense of variety (which will be further developed by a sensitive organist's choice of stops) yet remaining quintessentially the same music. These four combinations are shown in Ex. 21*f* together with an indication of the vocal part; the M-voice pairs 1–2 and 3–4 are alternated, so that the same pair always appears with the same combination of organ ranges. [ₒ] = T-voice; [.] = M-voice; [≡] = 'drone'; rhythms not shown.) After each vocal phrase, the organ either presents an answering refrain (at the end of a sentence, though not of questions) or sustains the drone; again, as with the Evangelist part, this is determined by the punctuation. Given the slow tempo of the part, some of

Ex. 21*f*

the drones appear very long, and emphasize the timeless quality of the Christ's utterances.

As the end of the work approaches, these utterances become distinctly shorter, the last two consisting simply of 'Sitio' ('I thirst') and 'Consummatum est' ('It is finished'). Pärt sets the first syllable of 'Sitio' as a double breve—an exception to the rules for expressive purposes? As this is the only single-word phrase in the whole text, it can in fact be seen as a conflation of Pärt's rules governing first and last words in a phrase; it is, none the less, a very telling rendition of this word. For the last phrase however (see Ex. 21g), Pärt again 'intervenes' to place the last word on a low A (where normally it would be an E), thereby producing a descending scale of the fifth down from *e*, the significance of which derives not only from the chain of fifths governing the work, but also from the use of scales in the exordium and, to be heard shortly after this point, the conclusio. At this point he also inserts an additional T-voice sounding the triad of D minor, which not only prepares the ear for the D major conclusio, but lets us hear all three of the work's governing fifths simultaneously. The descending bass voice is mirrored by an ascending line in the organ, and the contrast in their registers and directions seems to empty the sound before our ears, beautifully confirming the meaning of the words at this crucial point. In the last chord the D minor T-voice pushes down against the E drone; the Evangelist quartet then sings its final unison A, and the chain of fifths can now be completed, moving down to rest on a fundamental D.

Ex. 21*g*

Apart from the special circumstances of the exordium and conclusio, the choir's music is derived from the text in one single manner throughout. The altos and basses are mirrored M-voices (alternating modes 1–2 and 3–4 from phrase to phrase), using the Phrygian scale starting on E with its characteristic flattened second degree. Meanwhile, the sopranos and tenors are the corresponding T-voices, always alternating 1st position, but with the resounding difference that they use the triad of E major. These two harmonic entities mesh together with surprisingly rich and varied results, fuelled partly by the sometimes abrupt lurching from G# to G♮ and the frequent tensions of F against E, G# against A, B against C, but more generally by the fact that the ear simply cannot anticipate the contrasting flow of consonant and dissonant chords.

Ex. 21*h* shows four chorus phrases, each representing a different

Ex. 21*h*

character or group, and displaying the highly effective text setting of which Pärt is readily capable, even within a controlled 'closed' system. In no. 52[6] the words are those of an officer who slaps Jesus and pompously enquires: 'Answerest thou the High Priest so?' In no. 62 a servant of the High Priest asks Peter: 'Did I not see thee in the garden with him?', and the short words produce a series of similar chords allowing a quiet, insinuating delivery. In no. 95 the whole mob responds to Pilate's question as to whether to free Barabbas or Jesus with the cry: 'Not this one, but Barabbas!', and the chordal progression at 'Barabbam' ends in a G major chord in first inversion that is quite ugly in its exultant perfection. Finally, in no. 111 the same mob, in even filthier mood, yells: 'Crucify, crucify him!', and the four syllables of 'crucifige' give the sopranos a dramatic leap up to their first *g♯"*, duly reinforced by the major third it forms with the alto *e"*, while the basses and tenors converge on a blunt dissonance

---

[6] Cue numbers are as in the score.

moving in the opposite direction. This last phrase is also one of only a handful that are doubled by the organ (where some of the soprano pitches are transposed, and the bass line is lowered to the pedal register).

Pilate

Like Christ, Pilate is accompanied throughout by organ, but sings at a generally faster, more fluid tempo, using the same set of rhythmic values as the Turba. Pilate stands before posterity as one of history's true politicians, sacrificing principles for expedience, striving to be all things to all men, and washing his hands of the consequences. The moral ambiguity of this character is delivered to us in musical terms with simple brilliancy. The music for Pilate uses an M-voice centred on B (as does the chorus), but the attendant T-voice uses the triad of F major, thereby highlighting that most ambiguous of intervals, the diminished fifth—medieval music's *diabolus in musica*. In fact, except for this B–F conflict, almost nothing in Pilate's music is stable. The tenor mostly has M-voice patterns, but on some occasions switches to the F major T-voice, while the organ provides the M-voice (directly based, of course, on the sung text). The organ part ranges widely from the highest to lowest registers, sometimes playing an M-voice in octaves, sometimes providing both of the possible alternating T-voices to the vocal line, at other times playing just a single line of music. Occasional use is also made of not one, but three different drone pitches: B, F, and E, emphasizing again the tritone and flattened second degree of the Phrygian mode on E. However, none of these musical elements is deployed according to any demonstrable plan unless it be the avoidance of consistency. There is, none the less, a consistency of mood in the part of Pilate engendered by its harmonic environment, and words and music are matched in some very apt and imaginative ways. Ex. 21*i* gives two short examples, including Pärt's perfectly appointed setting of the famous rhetorical question 'Quid est veritas?' ('What is truth?'), in which Pilate has the M-voice over a B drone in the organ, which also plays both alternating T-voices; and the later exclamation to the mob, 'Ecce homo' ('Behold the man'), Pilate now singing the T-voice while the organ plays the M-voice in octaves.

Finally, having examined separately the contributions of soloists, Evangelist quartet, and chorus, it is important to recognize how

Ex. 21*i*

seamlessly the work is woven together. As in his earlier collage works, albeit in a very different musical language, the various, apparently self-contained processes in *Passio* interlock with powerful and fertile results, though this is something which only the experience of hearing the whole work can suitably demonstrate.

8

TE DEUM, STABAT MATER, MISERERE

Te Deum

THE words of this hymn, thought to have originated early in the fifth century, are among the most venerable of non-biblical texts still in use in the Christian tradition. Pärt describes them as consisting of 'immutable truths', which reminded him of the 'immeasurable serenity imparted by a mountain panorama'. In his setting of the *Te Deum* he sought to convey a mood 'that could be infinite in time, by delicately removing one piece—one particle of time—out of the flow of infinity. I had to draw this music gently out of silence and emptiness.'[1]

Although Pärt does not employ the Gregorian melody (also of considerable age), he creates a series of chant-like melodies using the tintinnabuli technique, and it is interesting to see how readily the chant *melos* floats to the surface (see Ex. 22*b*). These chanted sections alternate with choral statements and string responses, beneath which for most of the opening and closing sections is heard a wind harp drone, duly reinforcing the sense of endless time and space.

It is the sounding of this drone which helps to articulate the larger structure of the work, though the relationship between its principal pitches, D and A, is decidedly not that of a conventional tonic–dominant; the sense of D major/minor is present throughout. It is perhaps more appropriate to see the work as based on the lower overtones of the harmonic series, taking its own sense of 'mountain panorama' from the fundamental strength of the octave Ds and their fifth, moving on to the major and minor thirds above them. Thus, when the low D is removed, the A moves more clearly into focus; when it too is removed, then the upper pitches receive more individual attention (specifically E, F, and F♯), but even then the memory of the drone is still present. The whole of this work gives the sense of being raised and lowered through these triadic entities (D major/minor), rather like shifting one's view through a prism of light.

The work is scored for three choirs, a string orchestra, prepared piano (which resonates rather like a cross between a harpsichord

---

[1] Quoted in an ECM Records leaflet of 1993.

and an amplified clavichord), and the wind harp. The total number of singers need not be large. Choir 1 (female voices) and choir 2 (male voices) sing the more overtly chant-like material, which is rhythmically free and melismatic; while choir 3 (mixed voices) sings a more syllabic, rhythmically defined setting of the text in four-part harmony.

The work falls into three main sections, each separated by a short pause. These are further subdivided into six, six, and five sections respectively; thus there are 17 subsections in all, of irregular length, across which are spread the text's 29 verses plus a concluding Amen and Sanctus. Within the three main sections, although each subsection is treated in varying degrees as a self-contained entity, the music itself is continuous, either marked *attacca* or with part of a drone actually carrying the sound across from one part to the next.

Broadly speaking, each verse is treated in a similar fashion. Each is sung first in chant style (by part or all of choirs 1 and 2) and then answered in rhythmicized patterns, either by choir 3 (which repeats the same text) or by the strings (whose music is based directly on the text just sung). A detailed examination of Pärt's treatment of the words of the first verse will give a sense of how he has proceeded throughout (see Ex. 22*a*, *b*, *c*). Using the standard four melodic modes in turn, we can construct a phrase in which 'Te' produces a single pitch, D, and the two syllables of 'Deum' yield two pitches, D and E (mode 1); the three syllables of 'laudamus' call for three pitches (now in mode 3), giving F, E, and D. The phrase is then balanced by using modes 2 and 4 for 'Te Dominum' and 'confitemur' respectively. In addition, throughout this work, Pärt observes the stressed syllables by giving them two pitches, the second one anticipating the next syllable's pitch. This gives us a provisional working model, shown as Ex. 22*a*, which is close to what Pärt writes, but he in fact elaborates the more important syllables by embellishing them with triadic notes as shown in Ex. 22*b*.

We can identify the basic pattern of Ex. 22*a* more closely in the music with which choir 3 answers this opening statement (see Ex. 22*c*); however, the two M-voices (alto and bass moving in contrary motion) are based on A and alternate modes 2 and 4, while their tintinnabuli voices (soprano and tenor) are superior, but slightly varied for both harmonic and melodic effect. The note durations are more precisely notated, and use specific metres (though these vary according to the interaction of text and tintinnabuli procedures).

Ex. 22*a*

Te De - um lau - da - mus, te Do - mi - num con - fi - te - mur.

Ex. 22*b*

choir 2

Te De _____ um lau - da _____ mus, te Do _ mi-num con-fi-te _____ mur

Ex. 22*c*

choir 3

Te De _____ um lau _ da _____ mus,

te Do _____ mi _ num con - fi _ te _____ mur

Verse 2 works in a similar way; where as verse 1 began with mode 1, verse 2 begins with mode 3; choir 3's answer comes in D major, however. Verse 3 reveals a freer melodic formulation, built on each of the triadic notes in turn and carrying the male voices from low F to top *d'*. The answering string ritornello starts with the double basses, who elaborate the chanted melody (again using additional pitches from the D minor triad); they are joined by tintinnabuli fragments in the cellos. When the given chant melody has been completed, the violas join in, moving in contrary motion to the basses, and thus the music is passed up through the violins to the higher octaves; in all, we hear the embellished chant melody three times. (Exx. 22*d* and *e* show verse 3 and the beginning of the string response.)

As suggested earlier, the story of this work is outlined for us by what happens to the drone. All we hear at the beginning of the work is the wind harp, as a low D emerges imperceptibly from silence over a period of about 20 seconds. This is not presented as a musical 'idea'; the sound is merely revealed, uncovered, as something already there. And yet, paradoxically perhaps, the real musical content of the *Te Deum* resides precisely in the fundamental presence of this drone throughout the work, even while it is not actually being sounded in its deepest and physically strongest form. 'The [drone sometimes] ceases as an auditive factor, but not as a spiritual force. . . . We are witnessing here a process of sublimation where the audible fundamental drone turns into a "mental" center of tonality.'[2]

In the first section the low D is present throughout the first three verses, and then falls silent as the strings play their first music (where the tintinnabuli fragments dance in triplets). At 'Sanctus, Sanctus' a

Ex. 22*d*

Ex. 22*e*

² 'Drone and "Dyaphonia Basilica"', in Gerson-Kiwi, p. 23.

low A is introduced, which makes a gradual crescendo towards the words 'Pleni sunt coeli', first chanted making a large crescendo and rising through two octaves, to be answered by the work's first *fff* tutti. Beneath the final chords of this climax, the low D is restored, though it soon fades completely, leaving several verses during which no low drone is heard. Eventually, at the end of the first main section, the violas extend a middle *a* which in turn leaves the female choir holding a *d'–a'* drone (an echo of the lower octaves) through which choir 3 threads its text.

The middle section begins with an abrupt transition to the more declamatory 'Tu Rex gloriae'. At first no drone is present at all, but a few verses later (at 'Tu devicto mortis') an *a'–e″* fifth is introduced by the violins (always against a triadic D background in the choir); this is sustained as the low A drone is reintroduced, which now supports a massive crescendo towards the work's loudest point, at 'Judex crederis'. The combined choirs here retain the D tonality (but mixing major and minor together), the strings multiplying the vocal pitches with triplet and sextuplet figuration over a low pedal A, while the prepared piano pounds out three octaves of triplet As. At the end of this outburst a *subito pp* restores the D, in both high and low octaves, but the A emphasis continues to be felt until the end of the section.

The last section is introduced by three descending chords from the prepared piano (punctuating the chanted words 'Per singulos dies'), at the root of which in turn are *a'*, *F,*, and *D,*, the D minor triad thus reaffirming the centrality of D, which duly remains audibly in place for the remainder of the work. In the second verse of this section (where the words 'Dignare Domine' are repeated) the contention between D major and minor, hinted at earlier by the tutti at 'Judex crederis', is resolved when the D minor harmony with which the verse opens gives way to D major at the end. From this point on there is a final buildup towards the last tutti, at the words 'Et misericordia tua', and here the prepared piano (playing tintinnabuli pitches in different octaves) is at its most forceful, as the chanting male voices rise to a high *f'*, leading into the choral response, with D major and minor alternating. While less dramatically assertive than the middle section's climax, this is the work's point of catharsis, requiring a maximum sense of exhaustion and spiritual abasement, allowing the last words 'In te Domine speravi' to be sung quietly and thankfully. Again, the D minor triad is sounded, this time in a series of single violin pitches, leading us back down, after a brief hiatus, to the final low D.

After the 'Amen', there is a musical coda in which the words

'Sanctus, Sanctus, Sanctus' are heard receding from our presence back towards the silence of the opening. Where earlier these words had signalled the first A drone, they are now suspended over the final D; and while the earlier statement was in D minor, they are now heard in a dancing echo in D major.

Stabat Mater

Whereas many of Pärt's settings of sacred texts call for a choir with or without soloists, his scoring of *Stabat Mater*, for three solo voices (soprano, alto, and tenor) and string trio, suggests something more akin to chamber music. Even so, the text places the work firmly in a long line of musical compositions, ranging from the polyphonic settings by Josquin, Palestrina, and Lassus to the very different idioms of Rossini, Verdi, and twentieth-century composers such as Poulenc and Penderecki (whose St Luke Passion incorporates a setting of the first six stanzas only).

The poem, with its opening verses based on St John's description of the Crucifixion (John 19: 25), is considered to be of thirteenth-century Franciscan origin, though its earlier attribution to Jacopone da Todi is now generally discounted. It has the characteristic structure of the (late medieval) sequence, consisting of a series of paired three-line verses with the rhyme scheme *aab, ccb/dde, ffe/etc.*, and an underlying trochaic rhythm, relieved only by the proparoxytonic ending of each third line (two unstressed syllables). This unchanging pattern might seem to pose quite a challenge to a composer who uses the text to generate the music as rigorously as does Pärt. As might be expected, Pärt does not try to 'overcome' the text, but turns its unvarying pattern into the underlying theme of the work itself. Remembering that it is the number of syllables in each word with which Pärt builds his melodic lines, the irregular rhythms of prose would appear better suited than verse to the creation of varied melodic patterns. In the *Stabat Mater* poem not only is the rhythm uniform throughout, but the number of syllables in each verse is also regular: 8, 8, 7. Fortunately, there is variation both in the number of words in each line and the different combinations of syllables; the most common are lines of three or four words, though very occasionally there are lines with just two, such as 'Moriendo desolatum' and one with as many as six: 'Quis est homo qui non fleret'. As in *Passio*, the punctuation of the text is reflected in the music, though only to the extent of a break (of one main beat) after a comma.

Such material may appear uncompromising, but its schematic nature and measured response to the theme of suffering are, like the stanzaic patterns and formal repeats of ancient ballad poetry, well suited to the expression of passionate and tragic subject-matter, where the weight of feeling engendered might overwhelm a more immediate, expressionistic response.

Notwithstanding its theological significance, the subject of the *Stabat Mater* poem is a human one, the suffering of a parent watching the death of her child. Pärt's setting of the text is enclosed between two passages of instrumental music and almost wordless singing (the voices sing 'Amen' mostly as a melisma on the first syllable), which dispense an atmosphere of tragic serenity and compassion. These passages function, like the *Passio*'s exordium and conclusio, to mark out a ritual space for the setting of the text itself, and are built on a descending scale without reference to words. The scale in this case is not a straightforward descent, but carefully articulates the A minor triad and intermediate pitches, thus encompassing both T- and M-voice elements in one line, and building up a symmetric pattern in the process (Ex. 23a). This is first played by the strings entering on A, C, and E in turn, and their combined rhythms ensure that we hear the work's rhythmic theme [♩ ♩] in each bar. The voices then reiterate this passage (shown in Ex. 23b in the vocal range), doubled by the instruments who now also sustain the descending triadic pitches. This leads straight into the first verse, the voices prolonging the first syllable for two bars before launching into the shorter triple rhythm that prevails in the texted music.

The poem has 10 pairs of verses, which Pärt divides into four sections of 2, 3, 3, and 2 pairs respectively, with an instrumental ritornello between each section. This, together with the prelude and postlude, creates an arching pattern which strongly echoes that shown in Ex. 23a: [1]-2-i-3-i-3-i-2-[1].

Ex. 23a

no. of
pitches: 1   2   3   3   2   1   1   2   3   3   2   1

1   2   3   3   2   1

M-voice pitch centres

section: 1   2   3   4

The organization of the larger sections of the work is coherently balanced, though less rigorously symmetric than in some earlier works. Certain elements are constant (or constant in their variation) throughout: all T-voices are alternating 1st position; the M-voices always alternate either modes 1 and 2 or 3 and 4. The use of these paired M-modes also reflects the poem's rhyme scheme, in which the first two lines of each verse rhyme, but not the third; thus the M-mode always changes at the third line from modes 1 and 2 to modes 3 and 4, or vice versa.

Some criteria change in accordance with the fourfold division of the text. In the shorter sections, (1 and 4), modes 1 and 2 are used to begin each verse; in section 2, modes 3 and 4 are used, while in section 3, each verse begins alternately with modes 1 and 2 and 3 and 4. In every case but one, however, the same pair of modes is used for the first two phrases, switching to the other pair for the third phrase. (Verse 18 is an exception, for while the soprano sings the 'expected' M-voice modes 1 and 2, the cello plays modes 3 and 4.)

Although the T-triad is A minor throughout, the M-voice pitch centres create an overall movement through the triad, emphasizing each of its pitches in turn (see Ex. 23*c*).

The particular disposition of voices and instruments follows a general plan, so that in section 1, after the opening verse with all three voices and instruments, the texture is paired down immediately to one or two voices and an occasional instrument. In section 2, the voices singly and in various combinations are only ever accompanied by one instrument. In section 3 this is raised generally to two instruments, and in section 4 to all three. Within this framework Pärt appears to have exercised considerable compositional freedom in choosing a constantly varied combination of voices and instruments. Each verse (except the first in each section) is followed by a short instrumental refrain echoing the final phrase with inverted M-voice. (On three occasions, verses 7, 13, and 16, the three voices repeat the last phrase of text unaccompanied.)

Some verses are sung by a single voice, accompanied only in the middle phrase by one instrument. Sometimes a single voice has a T-voice based on the text's M-voice potential (as happens in *Passio*), even though no M-voice is actually sung. The tenor sings verse 4 in this way, joined by the alto singing the M-voice for the middle phrase only. Similarly, in verse 14 the soprano starts alone with a T-voice, but switches to the M-voice for the second phrase, joined on a T-voice by the alto (and viola); for the third phrase, the soprano is alone again, and reverts to a T-voice.

Apart from these variations in scoring, T–M function, and octave disposition, the strongest elements of potential contrast are rhythmic; though Pärt confines himself to just three patterns (outside the instrumental interludes, for which see below, though these are themselves variations of the basic trochaic rhythm). The first is the standard alternation of [○ ♩] , and the second simply its reversal, [♩ ○] . The second of these is confined to the instruments, and offsets them very effectively against the voices, especially in fuller passages such as verse 1 and throughout section 4 (but instruments *tacent* in the final verse). But the effect is also very eloquent with just a single instrument, as in the first phrase of verse 6, shown in Ex. 23*d*. (Note that here, as is often the case in Pärt's vocal music, the music is barred according to the words, 1 word = 1 bar, and not the musical metre; Exx. 23*d* and *e* are both effectively in 3/2, though the notation does not indicate this.)

The third rhythmic variation consists in shortening the pattern to two minims, with a silent first beat. This feature is employed quite frequently in the two middle sections, but not at all in sections 1 or 4. Its syncopated nature adds a sense of rhetorical gesture, as in verse 9 (Ex. 23*e*), here amplified by the unexpected entrance of the cello at the end of the second phrase, just before a longer pause (required by the comma). In the short ritornello the cello switches to M-voice, while

Ex. 23*d*

Verse 6

Quis non pos - set con - tri - sta - ri

Ex. 23*e*

E - ja ma - ter, fons a - mo - ris me

E - ja ma - ter, fons a - mo - ris me

sen - ti - re vim do - lo - ris fac, ut te - cum

sen - ti - re vim do - lo - ris fac, ut te - cum

lu - ge - am.

lu - ge - am.

the viola takes up the syncopated T-voice pattern; their music is an untexted repeat of the last phrase with the M-voice inverted (ignoring the comma, but not the final full stop).

The three interludes provide progressive diminutions of the basic rhythmic pattern, using an altogether faster tempo. Ex. 23*f* shows how the short–long elements are combined: the unchanging [♩ ♪ ♪ ♩] passed through each instrument in turn is itself a diminution of the combined [♩ ♩ ♩ ♩], in which the crotchet is then successively reduced by half and then a quarter. Like the shorter ritornellos, these interludes use the previous line of text for the derivation of pitches. A detailed examination of the opening of the third interlude will serve as an example of how Pärt has constructed these sections. The whole of the previous verse (16) is used, though the example (Ex. 23*g*) shows only the portion which covers the first four syllables, preceded by the corresponding phrase just sung by the tenor. The tenor's *text* provides an M-voice model which is picked out in minims by the violin [o] and viola [x]. Both take C as their pitch centre (whereas the tenor used E), and use the contrary motion of modes 3 and 4. The viola plays the original rhythmic shape (long–short), while the violin plays its reversal (short–long). The initial pitch of each group of four semiquavers creates an alternating 1st position T-voice. (The passing notes following these T-pitches alternate direction, always in contrary motion to the other part.) The cello combines all four M- and T-elements from the other two instruments into its single part; as the enumeration in Ex. 23*g* demonstrates.

Ex. 23*f*

Ex. 23g

Fac,   ut   por - tem Chris - ti   mor - tem

(Fac)   (ut)

(por-)   (-tem)

(The figures 1, 2, 3, refer to the pitches A, C, E,
by their position in the triad; [o] and [x] relate
to the corresponding M-voices.)

Miserere

Introduction

Against the background of tintinnabuli works examined hitherto,
Pärt's setting of the *Miserere* (Psalm 50 in the Vulgate) stands out as a
dramatic conception from beginning to end. This is not to say that
there are no small, quiet moments; there are many, but even these are
deliberately poised to create tension and expectation. We are aware as
we hear them that this is not the norm, that we are listening to a
reduced fragment of something large and powerful. This was not the
case in the other major tintinnabuli works. Notwithstanding their
moments of power and energy, the whole image or emotional frame-

work of each of those works could be gleaned from a few moments' listening at any point. A single Evangelist phrase in *Passio* contains the whole work in its scope. This is not so with *Miserere*. In this respect it marks a *rapprochement* with the more conventional world of concert music, and adds a new dimension to the tintinnabuli style itself. The presence of overtly expressive melodic lines, particularly those of the bass soloist and in some of the instrumental interludes, should not, however, blind us to the fact that the tintinnabuli principles hold sway here as strongly as ever, though they have been invested with a degree of harmonic intensity and a relentless sense of direction which have not typified tintinnabuli music up to this point.

The opening of the work might suggest the opposite to be the case. A lone tenor begins to intone the first verse, a word at a time, each word cloaked in silence; a clarinet delicately picks out a few triadic pitches, another silence, the next word, and so on. The second half of the first verse is coloured briefly by the presence of a low bass clarinet drone. Eventually a second voice enters, and the triadic echoes are parcelled out among new instruments. Over a ghostly quiet timpani roll, the bass soloist begins the third verse on a low E, and is joined by the other four soloists as he rises up over two octaves to f'. The timpani roll, left alone, moves from background to foreground in a massive crescendo, opening like a gaping pit right in front of us, and the *Dies irae* erupts in a wall of sound. This is the music of *Calix* (1976) reworked, and will be discussed in a moment. Suffice it to say that this interruption is itself interrupted, and the *Miserere* psalm is restored with the voice of the solo bass, quite alone, without even the comfort of tintinnabuli pitches at first. We are now in for the long haul. A new voice is added at the beginning of each verse, and there is a slow gathering of sound and texture, with instrumental ritornellos—some very brief, some more extended—after each verse, which eventually reaches its apotheosis on the word 'holocaustis', and from thence gradually retreats back to the sound of the solo bass. The music is then transformed by the return of the *Dies irae* poem, the stanza beginning 'Rex tremendae'; the music no longer anguished, however, but hushed in awe, a musical vision that entirely expresses the words:

> Rex tremendae majestatis,
> Qui salvandos salvas gratis,
> Salva me fons pietatis.

In outline the form of the work is simple enough:

1. *Miserere*, first 3 verses, soloists.
2. *Dies irae*, first 7 verses, choir.
3. *Miserere*, remaining 16 verses, soloists.
4. *Dies irae*, verse 8, choir (plus SA soli).

There are five soloists (SATTB) and a mixed chorus; the instrumental ensemble consists of oboe, clarinet, bass clarinet, bassoon, trumpet, trombone, treble and bass guitars, timpani, other percussion, and organ. The instrumentation varies considerably throughout sections 1, 3, and 4, but is tutti in section 2.

In the Vulgate, the text of the psalm itself begins at what is called verse 3, the first two verses being taken up by the title: 'A psalm of David, when Nathan the Prophet came unto him, after he had gone in to Bathsheba'. The score observes this numbering, beginning at 'III'; however, I have chosen here to designate the first verse of the psalm itself as 1, and so on. Readers consulting a score should therefore add two to the verse numbers quoted.

Like the *Stabat Mater*, the *Dies irae* is a sequence, and is attributed to Thomas de Celano, a thirteenth-century Franciscan (also a friend and biographer of St Francis). The poem is modelled on a trope of the *Libera me* responsory, which uses the same words, thus leading to its eventual inclusion in the Requiem mass, although before the Council of Trent the *Dies irae* was not normally set polyphonically. The structure of the stanza is even tighter and more regular than that of the *Stabat Mater*: three lines, eight syllables each, rhyming *aaa*, *bbb*, *ccc*, etc.

My discussion of this work will lay less emphasis on mapping the progress of its various processes, though it will indicate their presence, and will focus instead on specific compositional details, especially where these indicate a new direction or emphasis within the tintinnabuli style. These considerations began in bar 1.

Section 1

The first word, 'Miserere', is recited on a monotone; the second word, 'mei', followed by a comma, is set a tone lower. This opening section, with clarinet tintinnabuli pitches, is shown in Ex. 24*a*. (The tenor sounds an octave lower.) As the text continues, small pitch changes, always on a stressed syllable, occur towards the end of phrases, first in one direction, then the other. (As in *Passio*, the punctuation of the text, including commas, is reflected by longer pauses in the music.) Thus the principle of tintinnabuli melodic construction is retained,

153

but for the moment reflecting the balance of words within phrases (rather than syllable count), and, most significantly of all, the pitch changes follow the position of the main stressed syllable.

This specifically marks a turning away from the text purely as a written source, in favour of its spoken quantity, albeit within a stylized framework. Both the use of syllabic recitation and the manner in which pitch changes are determined by syllable stress are reminiscent of psalmody. Although this is the first large-scale tintinnabuli work to demonstrate these values (and certainly the first using a Latin text), Pärt had already used monotonal recitation in *Ein Wallfahrtslied* (1984), and had further developed this in *Seven Magnificat Antiphons*[3] (written just one year earlier), in which the pitch changes clearly respond to the stress patterns in the text. Both these works are in German, but in the same year as the *Miserere*, Pärt also composed a Latin Magnificat which marks the stressed syllables even more strongly.

The underlying rhythm in the *Miserere* is an alternation of [♩ ♩]; in section 1 this is used to produce a sequence of triple rhythms (see Ex. 24*a*), which is continued even more rigorously in section 2, the *Dies irae*. Thereafter, only one stress per word is observed, producing a much more varied sequence of verbal rhythms.

Another innovation in tintinnabuli practice concerns the placing of the T-voice, which in various passages in the first two verses is heard as a separate reponse to the M-voice, with an intervening silence. It then arpeggiates outwards in both directions (see Ex. 24*a*) except at the end of the half-verse, where it moves inwards first and then out.

In verse 2, a second voice joins the tenor, and they exchange M- and T-roles as they proceed, using G as pitch centre. In the third verse, the bass ascends through a two-octave range, using each E and B in turn as pitch centres. The tenor imitates this, entering, however, only on (higher) triadic notes, and so the interval of imitation varies varies between a fifth and a sixth. Soon all five voices have joined in, with soprano and first tenor singing conventional T-patterns.

Ex. 24*a*

Mi-se-re-re   me-i

3 Discussed in Ch. 9.

154

The setting of the *Dies irae* is another example of Pärt's use of mensuration canon. In this case a series of descending A minor scales (with attendant T-voices) is heard simultaneously in five tempi, each one progressively doubling the length of the notes so that the slowest is 16 times longer than the fastest. The patterns are most clearly audible in the choral parts (doubled by woodwind), with male voices paired against female voices. They exchange roles every other verse (the opening verse is repeated at the end, bringing the faster declamation of the words 'Dies irae' climactically to the female voices). Within each pair, the T- and M-functions are exchanged every four notes, the T-voice switching from superior to inferior, though always in 1st position.

The underlying rhythm throughout is an alternation of triple metre long–short for one octave scale, reversing to short–long for the next octave, and so on; this pattern operates at each of the work's metrical levels. As with *Stabat Mater*, it is the text's trochaic rhythm which has determined the musical one, and which has been further prepared by Pärt's setting of the psalm to this point. Ex. 24*b* shows the first four bars, choir parts only.

Each new verse is heralded by the timpani, expounding the same long–short rhythm, adding an extra beat each time; verse 1 therefore has a single [♩], verse 2 [♩ ♩] , verse 3 [♩ ♩], and so forth. (This system of rhythmic enumeration will be put to more extended use in the later *Litany*.)

The texture is strongly coloured by the two electric guitars, especially by the slow, high arpeggios picked out by the treble guitar, reflecting the M-voice movement of the bass guitar. The trumpet also plays a highlighting role, restricted at first to a single *a″* at the beginning of each of the first four verses (marking the words 'Tuba mirum' with a high A); it then joins in duet (as a T-voice) with the trombone. In the last verse (the reprise of 'Dies irae') both these instruments rise to a higher octave, with memorable effect, taking the trumpet to high *c‴*, before the final crescendo and allargando brings this section of the work to a shuddering halt.

In externals, this setting of the *Dies irae* does not differ hugely from its earlier appearance as *Calix*, but in almost every detail there are small—and sometimes not so small—changes, whereby the later version in every respect refines and reinforces the initial musical idea. Most important of all are the presence of a 'proper' T-voice for each

M-voice (as opposed to the simple repetition of the A minor triad) and the use of the reversed trochaic rhythm rather than an unvarying long–short throughout. The deployment of the instruments is also more subtle and more expansive in the later version; in particular, the organ's single metrical function is now replaced by three (one for the pedals and one for each manual).

Section 3

The thread of the interrupted psalm is picked up again by the solo bass, singing the first half of verse 4 quite alone, with C as pitch centre, and supported in the second half by a *pp* C drone. The method of M-voice construction is different from this point in the work on, and constitutes an important refinement of the tintinnabuli technique.

As observed above, the stressed syllable is used to determine a pitch change in the M-voice when it is otherwise reciting on a monotone. The M-voices are now restored to stepwise motion, beginning in the normal way from a pitch centre and proceeding from it syllabically by step. However, on the stressed syllable of each word the melodic direction changes. The syllable itself is prolonged by having two pitches, the second of which anticipates the pitch of the next syllable. Words of one syllable simply repeat the last pitch of the preceding word.

In Ex. 24c (i) a 'basic' M-voice version of part of the verse 4 text is given, followed (ii) by Pärt's actual version in this new manner (including rests), as sung by the solo bass. Although the pitch centre is now C, 'Ut' is on D♭ because the previous phrase had ended on that pitch; 'iustificeris' changes direction on the stressed fifth syllable, leaving an E♮ which is repeated for 'in'; 'sermonibus' would normally rise to C, but changes direction on the stressed second syllable. (Note that the number of crotchet rests is determined by the length of each word from its stressed syllable on; doubled after a punctuation point.)

Whereas in the *Stabat Mater* each of the three triadic pitches were used as M-voice pitch centres, Pärt now uses each pitch of the diatonic scale in turn, rising just over an octave, then descending quite quickly during the last three verses to a low G. This is shown in Ex. 24d, which gives the main pitch areas for the entire work; it also details (in parentheses) the symmetrically arranged number of singers in each verse, and shows the placing of the four instrumental interludes which divide up section 3.

Ex. 24c

157

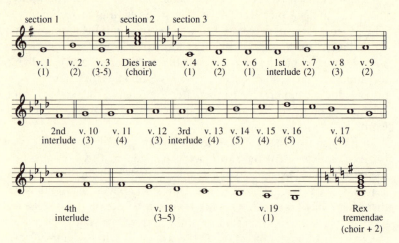

Note also how the regular sequence of three psalm verses and an interlude (or *Dies irae* after the first three verses) changes pace at verse 15; at this point the next interlude might be anticipated, but its appearance is delayed as the pitch centre scale moves on up to D♭ and then begins a more rapid descent.

Interludes

Throughout the first half of the *Miserere* psalm the instrumental contribution is extremely laconic; the end of each verse and sometimes words or phrases within a verse are marked by a brief response (based on the last word, from its stressed syllable to the end), but very often this is just a single note. In verses 9, 12, and 13, the responses during the verse are more persistent, but it is only at verse 16, after a splendid brass response, that the full interactive power of the soloists and instruments begins to be felt.

There are, however, four occasions on which the short response is replaced by a longer instrumental interlude. Each of these is based directly on the text of the previous verse, and, in effect, the music just sung is now played. There are no breaks between 'words' (though the same punctuation and overall phrasing is observed), and the melodic lines are inverted and duplicated at the sixth. The expressive continuity of line and the fuller texture create a strong contrast to the more halting exposition of the psalm text, thus providing a sense of temporary release.

In the first interlude (modelled on verse 6) the trombone projects a principal melody, and is accompanied by woodwind and guitars with frequent rests corresponding to anacruses in the text. The second interlude (based on verse 9) has three phrases, and features paired M-voices in contrary motion; an opening duet between clarinet and bass clarinet is answered by a setting of the second half of the verse for full wind, brass, and guitars; the same text model is then reused for a quieter concluding phrase. It is perhaps remarkable that a prose text should produce such a satisfying melodic shape—although in describing the composer's methodical procedures, it is easy to overlook the inventive imagination that foresees these possibilities and knows how to capture them in memorable music.

The third interlude conceals its texted, M-voice origins in verse 12 very effectively indeed inside a toccata-like organ figuration, joined gradually by the four woodwind instruments, plus tambourine and triangle, so that the total effect is quite dance-like, reminding us of the musical origin of the psalms. After the first half of the text's structure has been repeated five times, the second half of the structure comes into use (played just once); the organ is replaced by trumpet and trombone, and the music becomes more emphatic, leading directly into the resonant declamations of verse 13.

The fourth interlude is more reflective in mood, befitting the text of verse 17 which it echoes. The opening oboe solo ('sacrificium') is answered by the trombone ('cor contritum'). This opens on to verse 18, a delicious piece of writing in which the gentle friction of semi-tones and tones held over from the vocal line leaves a single pitch suspended in the air. This occurs four times, leading to a highly evocative setting of the word 'Jerusalem' at 'build thou the walls of Jerusalem'; and musical lines span outwards in both directions, coming to rest on a widely distributed C major dominant seventh, with the addition of F and A♭ (the ever present T-triad of F minor). The solo bass then sings the last verse.

The pitch centres shown in Ex. 24d are based on the lowest-sounding M-voice; at various points there is a second M-voice generally singing or playing a parallel sixth above the first. Also varying from verse to verse, other soloists sing T-voices generally in superior 1st position, though 2nd position also occurs. The T-triad throughout section 3 is that of F minor, which also provides the scale articulated by the M-voice pitch centres (as in Ex. 24d); however, the scale actually sung (and played) by the M-voices frequently employs E and B naturals, thus endowing the melodic lines with the added expressive potential of two augmented seconds. The combination of this melodic

mixture and the use of seven different M-voice pitch centres generates a harmonic texture that is immediately richer in dissonances than
anything in the tintinnabuli style hitherto. But the word 'dissonance'
must be used with caution. The harmony still results from the meshing together of triad and scale; as the scale used here creates four
minor seconds (diatonic major and minor scales normally have just
two), and as several of the M-voice pitch centres emphasize pitches
outside the triad, there is clearly a degree of tension in the music that
is not present, for example, in the *Stabat Mater*. Nevertheless, these
tensions do not operate functionally, except in the broadest sense.

The melodic scale that Pärt uses in this section actually incorporates the E minor triad, as Ex. 24*e* demonstrates. This scale therefore
links the main portion of the psalm to the opening verses and also to
the closing 'Rex tremendae'; the E minor tonality also creates a more
distant bridge to the A minor of the *Dies irae*, which none the less
stands properly apart from the main body of the psalm. The chord at
the end of verse 3 consists of *E, f♯′, b′,* and *c″,* which leads readily
enough into the ensuing A minor. The final chord of the *Dies irae*
consists primarily (E is also present) of a grinding B and C semitone
in several octaves. These are the pitches which the bass then sings at
the beginning of verse 4, and only gradually does the sense of a C pitch
centre establish itself.

At the end of the psalm it is again the bass who sings, unaccompanied, and his last word, 'vitulos', drops away from a low G pitch
centre to bottom E, providing the gentlest of motions into the closing
E minor.

Section 4

The direction and mood of the first seven verses of the *Dies irae* are
completely reversed in this final section. Beginning low in the basses
(see Ex. 24*f*), a rising scale treads slowly upwards in crotchets with
the inexorable confidence of a walking bass; the tenors accompany this
with a 2nd position superior T-voice. Above them, but at half the
speed, the female voices sing the same pattern, except that the altos
provide a 1st position inferior T-voice to the sopranos' scales. Sop-

Ex. 24*e*

Ex. 24f

rano and alto soloists add individual notes to this process (drawn from a mostly unheard M-voice sequence a third above the choir's scales). There are also individual notes from bass guitar, tam-tam, and (E) bell. The organist's left hand holds a chord of E minor (second inversion), while the pedals double the crotchet walking bass; meanwhile the right hand plays a descending minim scale (with T-voice), which crosses underneath the sustained chord (the T-voice stops) and continues on down to a low C. The choir and soloists meanwhile have stopped singing, though it is as if their sound has merely disappeared into ever higher regions. The bell sounds again, and the organ chord is left on its own.

The dramatic contrast between the two sections from the *Dies irae* was already envisioned in *Calix*. In a sense, the *Miserere* is simply the fulfilment of that earlier work, the psalm providing a meaningful context for the terrors of the *Dies irae*, and then at length creating a more personal preparation for the transformative vision of the final section. Even so, the greater proportion of the work receives its impetus from what many Churchmen have called 'the psalm of psalms', a prayerful song of penitence and humility on which Pärt provides his own commentary, both musically and by juxtaposition with the medieval sequence.

9

SHORTER WORKS AND *LITANY*

Introduction

IN earlier chapters the discussion of individual works followed approximately their chronological order of composition, as this usefully portrayed the evolution of Pärt's musical language. By the time he arrived in the West, Pärt had consolidated the tintinnabuli style, so each new work appeared as a fresh manifestation of this strongly centred vision. Each work has a very specific identity, certainly, often using tintinnabuli principles in a manner unique to that work, but to discuss this later music in chronological order would imply that there has continued to be a strong linear development far more than is really the case. I make this observation in a qualified manner, because in certain respects the tintinnabuli style has grown, but this is less a case of development from one point to the next, and more one of expansion of a central concept. I do not mean to imply that Pärt has stood still, but rather that he has moved around 'within' tintinnabuli, stretching certain elements in different ways perhaps, but always able to return (one feels) to the basic tintinnabuli language at a moment's notice.

Of course, the possibility always exists that future works may bring about a stylistic metamorphosis that may yet make into precursors works which at present seem self-contained. (I find that the need, or at least the potential, for such a move is suggested by *Litany*). Meanwhile, in this chapter I have chosen to group the works according to language or genre, the larger works of the period having already been discussed in the previous two chapters. This was in part so that they might not appear to overwhelm the shorter works, though clearly with Pärt the size of a work has nothing to do with its relative musical value. I none the less conclude with the most recent work, *Litany*, which received its première as this book was nearing completion.

Works in German

In choosing Latin texts for all his early tintinnabuli vocal pieces, Pärt had enjoyed the advantage of a language whose hieratic qualities were conveniently linked to the musical styles which had so recently influenced him in forming his new technique. Furthermore, the inflected nature of the language provides a rich variety in the length of words, and this, in Pärt's initial syllabic approach, proved to be an invaluable tool for creating an array of interesting musical phrases. With its greater frequency of monosyllables, English would have served him much more poorly in this respect, and although German certainly has its measure of polysyllables, these do not predominate in the kinds of texts to which Pärt is drawn. Having settled in the West, it was not altogether surprising that he should consider settings of texts in the contemporary vernacular, and living in Germany this was naturally enough the first language he approached. But we shall see that the respective idiosyncrasies of the German and English languages encouraged him in new methods of melodic invention which in turn fertilized his treatment of Latin. However, it is important to stress the word 'encouraged', as it seems likely that such innovations as did occur would probably have developed anyway in response to an eventual need for a greater variety of melodic types.

Pärt's first essay in setting German came in response to a commission from the German musicologist Diether de la Motte, who in 1984 asked ten composers for a setting of *Es sang vor langen Jahren*, a poem by the German Romantic poet Clemens Brentano (1778–1842). Pärt's setting is for alto voice with the accompaniment of violin and viola, and is subtitled *Motette für de la Motte*. The words are not 'religious', though in their fusion of human love and spiritual purity they are far from worldly. Pärt divides the poem in half, beginning each half with an expanding melodic arc, and ending it in a series of (A minor) triadic melodies—the ending being an almost exact musical repeat of comparable lines in the first part. The melodic arc simply adds a pitch in turn above and below the voice's E pitch centre, but fills in the intervening spaces or not as the words require. Furthermore, some words are treated more as passing syllables than the separate entities they had been in earlier compositions (see Ex. 25), partly to balance the metric demands of the poetic line, but mostly, one feels, to achieve a satisfying musical balance while adhering closely to the general logic of the melodic system. The melodic and triadic writing for both voice and strings is altogether reminiscent of the *Stabat Mater*, which was completed the following year.

Also in 1984 Pärt composed another German work: *Ein Wallfahrtslied* for baritone and string quartet. This song of pilgrimage is in fact a setting of the German text of Psalm 121: 'I will lift up mine eyes

Es sang vor lang - en Jahr - en wohl auch die Nach - ti - gall.

unto the hills'. The singer recites the text on a monotone (first *e*, then *b* in the middle section, returning at the end to *e* again), and it is this simplest manner of text articulation which will come to play such an important role in subsequent text settings. In this work the voice calmly confides its thoughts, anchored securely to its two pitches, but surrounded by an ocean of instability softly floating by in a mysterious, chromatic string texture. This shifts gradually away from E minor and back again by semitonal increments that never jar or assert any sense of troubled dissonance.

Reading the chronological list of works for the years 1985–8, it is possible to detect a slackening of creative output after the *Stabat Mater*[1] and to see it pick up again during 1988, leading to the richly productive years 1989–90. The first work to indicate the strength of this resurgence is the setting of the great 'O' antiphons for Advent, which were then followed by no less than eight choral works over the next two years.

The *Seven Magnificat Antiphons* might well have been composed in Latin—Pärt must surely have been attracted to the reverse acrostic formed by the opening texts in that language (the German and English are also given here for ease of reference):

O Sapientiae	O Weisheit	O Wisdom
O Adonai	O Adonai	O Adonai
O Radix Jesse	O Spross aus Israels Wurzel	O Root of Jesse
O Clavis David	O Schlüssel Davids	O Key of David
O Oriens	O Morgenstern	O Morning Star
O Rex Gentium	O König aller Völkern	O King of all
O Emmanuel	O Immanuel	O Emanuel

Ero cras: tomorrow I shall be with you. The acrostic pin-points the theme of these texts with their joyful promise of immanence after long waiting, expectation, and patience. That Pärt chose or agreed to set these texts in German suggests his readiness to stretch the expressive potential of tintinnabuli, for by presenting such words in the vernacu-

---

[1] A similar gap can be found at the very beginning of the decade, though this is hardly surprising, given the upheaval attendant upon any emigration.

lar language of his audience,[2] he could hardly avoid a more overt representation of the text than had been customary for him. This is achieved not through word-painting or isolated quasi-dramatic gestures, but by emphasizing details of mood and elements of contrast between the seven sections taken as a whole. Liturgically the texts function, one each, as antiphons to the Magnificat at Vespers on the seven evenings preceding Christmas Eve, but Pärt combines them into a single 'concert' work in seven sections. Each section is conceived as a separate musical entity, but related in a balanced overall scheme of tonal contrast, vocal scoring, and the general pacing of tempo and dynamic level. Each of the seven is a lucid realization of the general mood of its text, and has the appearance of expressive flexibility; yet everything in this work draws upon the closely regulated operation of tintinnabuli principles, handled with extreme but hidden virtuosity.

The overall conception of the work reveals careful tonal organization (see Ex. 26a). These tonalities together make up a chain of thirds with A at the centre, and this particular cluster of pitches is actually sounded in the work's opening moments (see the words 'O Weisheit' in Ex. 26b). Nos. 1, 4, and 7 in A major or minor use the full choir and broadly similar musical material (especially 1 and 7). Nos. 2 and 3, using the two minor keys closest to A in the chain of thirds, take the male and female voices in turn, and contrast the upper and lower voices within each group. In nos. 5 and 6, using the two minor keys furthest from A in the chain of thirds, we find combinations of two different modes (E major and minor) in 5, and of three different speeds in 6.

What will engage our attention here is the varied quality of M-voice which Pärt creates, using principally a mixture of the melodic mode technique already described and a style of recitation in which stressed syllables determine changes of pitch. An example of the latter occurs right at the opening of the work (see Ex. 26b) where the T-voices essentially recite the text on C♯ and E, moving a step up or down (alternately) for the main stressed syllable of each word (this is most

Ex. 26a

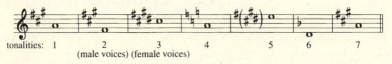

tonalities: 1   2   3   4   5   6   7
(male voices) (female voices)

[2] The work was commissioned by R.I.A.S., the Radio Chamber Choir in Berlin.

apparent in the example shown at the word 'her*vor*gegangen'); but as before, there is no change of pitch for monosyllabic words, regardless of their 'status'. Similarly, the sopranos and basses interject their open A–E interval on every other word, also regardless of relative importance.

The melodic principle changes slightly in no. 2. There is still the element of recitation, but this now arises purely from the frequency of monosyllables in the text. Meanwhile, for words of more than one syllable, the number of syllables directly determines the number of pitches each word uses (as in earlier tintinnabuli): however, these pitches are disposed so that the stressed syllable will always be the one furthest from the pitch centre (operating still above and below the pitch centre in strict alternation). In Ex. 26c the four syllables of 'Adon*ai*' take the four pitches from F♯ to B; but in order to provide the

stressed syllable with the highest of these, the word begins on G♯ (so as to approach the B by step), and the F♯ is heard only at the end of the word.

The concluding repeat of 'O Adonai' inverts the shape of the opening, taking the basses down to a low C♯; these dark colourings are beautifully apt for the words and blend readily into the low alto range at the beginning of no. 3. Here the same M-voice principles obtain, except that the pitch centres rise through the triad (and the pauses between phrases steadily diminish) to impel the music upwards towards the loud, high outburst of sound in no. 4. The C♯ minor tonality of no. 3 is given added edge by raising the pitch before tonic and dominant by a semitone (thus B♯ and F✗); the interval at the end of each phrase (on two occasions a semitone—see the end of Ex. 26d) is then held as a drone under the next phrase, the chromatic intervals duly intensifying the yearning and expectation expressed by the text.

In no. 4 the melodic principle again changes slightly to incorporate a descending A minor scale. The pitch moves a step downward after each stressed syllable (see Ex. 26e). The text has four main phrases, and at the beginning of each one the music recommences its descent from a high A. But the fourth phrase is heard three times, beginning first on A, then E, and finally C, the music gradually sinking lower and lower. The last syllable of all ('Tod*es*') does not resolve downwards as might be anticipated, but instead leads to the glistening mixture of E major and minor with which Pärt evokes the image of the Morning Star in no. 5. The use of E major for the T-voice and E minor for the M-voice recalls the Turba in *Passio*, though with very different results. The M-voice technique is conventional enough (but with each stressed syllable having two pitches, the second of which it shares with the following syllable), but now the T-voice technique has changed: the soprano T-voice moves in 1st position inferior to the alto M-voice, *except* for stressed syllables, for the duration if which it moves to 1st position superior (though with the exception of monosyllabic words like 'Glanz'). The tenor and bass parts mirror this motion, the lower basses also adding drone pitches to alternate phrases. The T-voice melodic line created by this new process is distinctly smoother than usual, and is especially appropriate for the words of this antiphon. (See Ex. 26*f*.)

No. 6 restores the more conventional relationship between T- and M-voices, the stressed syllables guiding the M-voice as in no. 4. But in this piece the sopranos sing the text once in a steady 3/2, while the male voices sing it twice at double the speed. The altos meanwhile recite the text in steady crotchets on a monotone, which gains considerable force as the music makes a single, relentless crescendo (see Ex. 26*g*).

Ex. 26*d*

This ends abruptly, to be followed in no. 7 by a quiet, tender setting of the words 'O Immanuel' that gradually rises in pitch and dynamic. The soprano part simply moves slowly up the A major triad, but is accompanied (on alternate beats) by a series of triads that move chromatically up the scale just beyond an octave: in this process (a similar version of which Pärt will return to in *The Beatitudes*) any two adjacent chords always retain one pitch in common, while the other two pitches change. (See Ex. 26*h*.) This chromatic crescendo leads back to a repeat of the text with music similar to the work's opening (but with all voices singing all the time). The piece then concludes with a third rendition of the 'O Immanuel' text, even closer to the opening music, but now sung very softly; where earlier the soprano and bass interjections came every other word, they now alternate (in octave Es) every two words.

Ex. 26g

Ex. 26h

The whole work is of only moderate length (about 15 minutes), but is so richly detailed in its response to language, and offers a glimpse of so many technical subtleties, that it repays close attention, and opens up an array of possibilities which the composer proceeds to explore over the next few years.

Because of the variable scoring that attends many of Pärt's shorter instrumental works,[3] a concise list according to instrumentation would categorize many of them too rigidly. For example, organists can learn that there are four[4] works for solo organ: *Trivium*, *Pari Intervallo*, *Annum per annum*, and *Mein Weg*. But only the latter two are conceived completely idiomatically for the instrument. *Trivium* belongs to the first group of tintinnabuli pieces, and although it uses pedals and has the appearance of a 'real' organ work (and to my knowledge has only ever been performed on the organ), its musical essence is none the less abstract, and could perfectly well be realized, say, by strings or any other appropriate group of instruments.[5] *Pari Intervallo* actually began life as a work for four wind instruments (in D minor); an organ version was subsequently made (transposed to E♭ minor), and it is in this form that the work has become familiar; potentially, however, the scoring remains open.

Trivium presents a single melodic line in three different tintinnabuli contexts. In the first section, the M-voice is in the middle register with an alternating 2nd position T-voice, both set above a pedal D. The second section has a much fuller sound: a second M-voice has been added, moving a parallel sixth below the original; 1st and 2nd position T-pitches have been applied to each M-voice in turn; M-pitches outside the D minor triad are doubled at the octave; and the pedal D is sustained, but now an octave lower than in the first section. In the final section the sound gives the impression of having emptied, as the pedal D stops, and we hear simply the clear melodic line and an alternating T-voice.

The title of this little piece can be read as a literal description of its tripartite structure—trivium originally meant a place where three roads met—though it is possible to read more into it (as is true of many of Pärt's titles). We hear three 'voices' (the two hands and the pedals); there are indeed three sections of which the middle one has a sense of harmonic congestion; and of course there is the sound of the triad throughout. We cannot help also recalling the seven medieval liberal arts, divided into four sciences of number (the quadrivium: arithmetic, music, geometry, astronomy) and three arts of the word

---

[3] The implications of this will be discussed in Ch. 10.

[4] Another is in process of composition, as of October 1995.

[5] This is my perception only, and does not have the composer's authority!

(the trivium: grammar, rhetoric, dialectic), though admittedly it strains credulity to find any significance for this in the music!

The title of *Pari Intervallo* describes its musical material much more specifically: a pair of M-voices moving in strict parallel throughout, mostly by step, with the infilling of two T-voices. It is in fact the upper M-voice which in effect leads the way, shadowed two octaves and a third lower by the second M-voice. There are six phrases of 12 bars each (one new M-pitch per bar), and each phrase begins on one of the triadic pitches, moving first up the triad, then back down to rest on the tonic, the strict parallel between the two voices being relinquished at the end, just as it had taken three bars to establish at the beginning. This bald description does little to account for the sombre beauty of the piece, which immediately envelops the listener. It was composed in 1976 'in memoriam' for a friend who had died, and is a superb example of the elegiac mode that also permeates *Cantus* and the more recent *Silouan's Song*.

Annum per annum takes its title from the thought of the mass being celebrated daily year after year in the cathedral for whose ninehundredth anniversary (Speier in south-west Germany) it was commissioned; the work is dedicated to St Cecilia as the patron saint of sacred music. An introduction and coda surround five movements, each carrying a letter title symbolizing the sections of the ordinary of the mass—thus K G C S A. The introduction consists of an open D–A fifth spread across several octaves, sustained in the right hand, and pulsated in a single rhythmic [♩ ♪] motif by left hand and pedals, repeated many times as the dynamic fades from an opening *ff* down to literally nothing; the organist is even instructed to switch off the instrument's motor so that the sound fully disappears—though the effectiveness of doing so naturally varies greatly from organ to organ. There then follows a set of five movements in which an isorhythmic cantus firmus with sequentially changing pitch sequences (themselves reminiscent of *Modus/Sarah*) is played in the left hand and pedals, while the right hand presents a series of variations based on a similar melodic line. These variations develop in dextrous complexity and harmonic resonance until the last (A-gnus) movement, in which the melodic material is heard at its simplest. Each of the five sections has the same length, having eight phrases of 13 beats (3 + 3 + 3 + 4), although the A-gnus is extended by two phrases. Half-way through the work (the middle of the C-redo) the mode switches from D minor to major. In the work's coda the opening idea is presented in reverse,

but with a D major triad sustained throughout, ending in a reverberant *fff*.

The title of *Mein Weg hat Gipfel und Wellentäler* is taken from a
poem in the *Livre des questions* by Edmond Jabès which describes
the moments of splendour and the moments of tribulation that attend
the spiritual path, likening them to the cresting waves and answering troughs in a deep ocean swell. The music captures this image to
perfection with three layers of melodic-triadic activity, each mirroring
the other, but moving at three different speeds: the highest voice has
quavers, the middle has crotchets, the lower (pedal) part has minims.
Each voice traces the same outline of rising and falling phrases, which
start out small and then grow increasingly larger in both directions. In
each layer the same note-values are relentlessly reiterated, creating a
mood of obdurate insistence, which duly reinforces the poem's sense
of effort and endurance. These characteristics are reinforced by the
music's E-Phrygian modality, to which is added the conflict of G♯ in
the M-voices against G♮ in the T-voices.

Instrumental Works: Chamber Music

Only three pieces will be discussed in this section, although several
others must at least be referred to under the putative label 'chamber
music', if only to remind the reader that they are mentioned elsewhere. The first of these is the exquisite *Spiegel im Spiegel* (mirror in
the mirror) for violin[6] and piano, which was the last work that Pärt
completed before leaving Estonia. Rooted in F major by the piano, the
violin takes A as its pitch centre, and constructs an additive melodic
sequence around it. (This is shown in Ex. 27*a*; note the alternation of
M-mode pairs.) The piano imitates this motion, cradling it in a gentle
arpeggio figure that sounds the violin's M-pitch (but an octave higher)
preceded by two other pitches: the sixth below the M-pitch (moving
in parallel) and the T-pitch that lies between them closest to the M-
pitch. Ex. 27*b* shows a schematic reduction of the violin and piano
parts at the beginning (the arpeggio accompanying the violin's A pitch
is in fact played six times, and each of the other pitches twice). The
additive melodic process continues until nine pitches are in use in
both directions (including the violin's low *g*). The effect is of a gesture
gradually tilting the M-pitch and the stable triad that accompanies it,
first one way, then the other.

Shortly after arriving in the West, Pärt composed the new version

---

[6] The string part can also be played down an octave by cello.

of *Fratres* for violin and piano (commissioned for the 1980 Salzburg Festival). In the next few years he composed various works for just a handful of instruments with voice or voices in various combinations. These include the *Wallfahrtslied* for baritone and string quartet and *Es sang vor langen Jahren* for alto voice with violin and viola, which have been mentioned above. The principal chamber work of the early 1980s was undoubtedly the *Stabat Mater* for string trio and three voices, which was discussed in Chapter 8.

As Pärt's reputation began to grow, fixed ensembles such as orchestras and string quartets began to look more closely at his music. The Kronos Quartet, for example, fostered a version of *Fratres* that has now joined the several other versions in the catalogue, helping to maintain that work as one of Pärt's most often performed titles. Similarly, *Summa* has now been made available in purely instrumental versions, including one for string quartet (but with two violas instead of two violins). The only work originally conceived for the quartet medium, since the early work of his student days, is the tiny, almost evanescent *Psalom* (psalm), in which nine varied statements of a single melodic idea are brushed into being, each one vanishing in turn into silence.

There remains only one 'chamber' work to mention: Adagio—an arrangement for piano trio of the slow movement from Mozart's piano sonata K. 280. This was composed in memory of the violinist Oleg Kagan, and presents an engaging if minimal commentary on the original work, together with some occasional murmurs of complaint. Only the sparse opening and the whispered conclusion give any suggestion of tintinnabuli practice.

Instrumental Works: Music for Strings

The tintinnabuli style has produced no works for full orchestra except *Litany* and, if we stretch the concept of orchestra, *Miserere*; but nothing without voices. There are, however, a number of works for string orchestra, which are to be reckoned among Pärt's finest. His predilection for this medium can perhaps be explained by the string timbre's ready blend, allowing the music to retain its dramatic anonymity without loss of expressive intensity. The list of such works includes *Cantus* and *Tabula Rasa*, while *Fratres* and *Summa* have also now been published in string orchestral versions; in addition, both the Te Deum and the *Berlin Mass* feature choral textures accompanied by strings. Several of these works call for an additional instrument, such as the bell in *Cantus* and the prepared piano in *Tabula Rasa* and the Te Deum, and their role is always highly significant in the overall texture. In more recent years Pärt has added two more works for string orchestra to his œuvre, *Festina Lente* and *Silouan's Song*.

The idea of hurrying slowly expressed by the title *Festina Lente* will appear anything but puzzling to advocates of Pärt's music, who will probably be aware of his often long gestational pauses between periods of more overt creativity. Such pauses characterized the discovery of the tintinnabuli style itself, and have continued to occur. Indeed, Pärt has often alarmingly announced that he might not compose any more music—only to do so with splendid and inevitable assurance! *Festina Lente* illustrates this idea from a different perspective. Using the now familiar technique of metric canon, it presents a single melodic line simultaneously at three different speeds (in the proportion 4:2:1), the impetuous tendencies of the swifter highest voice being constantly steadied by the lower voices.

The melodic line, a steady alternation of short–long/long–short, is itself compounded of melodic and triadic elements, with frequent leaps of a minor sixth. It is heard four times at the fastest tempo (played by the first and second violins), while the middle voice (violas) plays the melody twice, and the lowest voice (cello and double basses) plays it once; in the process there are some variations in detail, especially in the way in which each part in turn fragments towards the end. The middle (viola) voice is heard throughout without a tintinnabuli part, and, as in *Cantus*, this gives it a more subjective role. The higher voice begins similarly, but by the end of its first melodic exposition has begun to subdivide into both M- and T-voices, the latter increasing in activity as the work proceeds. The lowest M-voice is accompanied right from the beginning by a 1st position T-voice, which is heard two octaves above (played by violins 3 and 4), though at the point where a T-voice is added to the highest voice, it too subdivides into further degrees of tintinnabular activity (third and fourth violins separately, while the cellos mix tintinnabuli pitches in a line that still mostly follows the resolute progress of the M-voice basses). After the music has faded into four bars of silence, there follows a brief coda at reduced speed, in which the highest and lowest voices exchange their previous tempos, and all three levels, violas included, now feature both M- and T-voices. (There is also an ad lib harp part which doubles various parts of the string texture as a colouristic device.)

Silouan's Song will be described only briefly; but in the rapt concentration of its four pages of score is embedded some of Pärt's most heart-rending music. Its unusual eloquence arises not as the result of an abstract musical design, but from the fact that the M-voice is derived directly, syllabically, from a written text. This text is drawn from the writings of the Staretz[7] Silouan (1866–1938), a Russian monk who lived much of his life in the Russian monastery of St Panteleimon on Mt Athos. The words begin (in translation): 'My soul yearns after the Lord and I seek Him in tears.' Pärt appears[8] to have adopted a technique similar to that used in the *Seven Magnificat Antiphons*, in which the stressed syllable of each word determines the pitch change; polysyllabic words therefore produce reiterated pitches such as those heard at several places in *Silouan's Song* (e.g. bars 40–4; see Ex. 28). The basic texture of the work consists of two M-voices in contrary motion (their pitch centre being C in the key of F minor), each accompanied by 1st position T-voices (at first one, later two). With sensitive and subtle variation of scoring, Pärt takes a remarkably simple idea, and fashions from it one of his most beautiful works.

This is perhaps the place to comment on a more specific instance

Ex. 28

[7] 'Staretz': an elder, a monk whose experience of spiritual matters endows him with the wisdom and insight necessary to be a guide to others. Staretz Silouan was placed in the canon of saints by the Ecumenical Patriarchate of the Orthodox Church in 1988.

[8] 'appears', because I do not have access to the Russian original.

of the influence of Russian Orthodoxy on Pärt's life and work. During the last years of Silouan's life, the monk Sakharov (later Archimandrite Sophrony) worked as his assistant, and later wrote an account of his life and teachings.

In his foreword to the writings of Staretz Silouan, Sophrony makes the following observation which can, I think, illuminate for us the kind of ideal which has inspired Pärt aesthetically.

The Staretz, who was almost illiterate, writes of what was given him to behold. Often his language is like that of the psalms, which is natural since it springs from unceasing prayer. The rhythm is slow, as is characteristic of profound prayer. Again and again he returns to the same theme—that God and all that is of heaven are made known only through the Holy Spirit; the Saviour loves mankind with infinite love, and this love is communicated only through the Holy Spirit. The Holy Spirit is the Spirit of peace, of compassion, of love for enemies.

Only a few thoughts engage the Staretz' soul, his mind, but ontologically these thoughts are most profound. They are the measure of all that exists. Whoever in the depths of his being is inspired by such thinking beholds the whole world as it were through a mysterious spiritual prism.[9]

The reader should not imagine that some kind of hagiographic implication lurks behind my association of this passage with Pärt. We must not falsely confuse the man with the music. The passage is given because it exemplifies a particular mode of spiritual intensity and 'holy poverty' which seem to be at one with the vision embraced by Pärt in his tintinnabuli music. As Sophrony elsewhere recognizes, such material is destined for a very narrow circle of people who share an interest in Christian asceticism. Pärt's gift to us is to render such a densely concentrated sensibility in musical form so that it can leap beyond its specific context to touch us without the need of this or that language, and beyond the conventions of formal religion too.

In another of Silouan's writings, *Adam's Lament*, we encounter almost the same words that preface *Silouan's Song*, put now into the mouth of Adam: 'My soul wearies for the Lord, and I seek Him in tears. How should I not seek Him?' Unlike much of today's new tonal and 'minimalist' music, Pärt's style cannot be described as purely Edenic. It carries an oppressive weight upon its shoulders, and is written, if anything, from a post-Edenic position. The music proposes

---

[9] Sophrony, pp. 263–4.

178

a vision of perfection, certainly; it also encompasses a radiant sense of compassion and quiet glory. But in doing so, it is not ignorant of evil. Obliquely perhaps, but none the less profoundly, it recognizes the bitter waste of human failure, the anxiety and loneliness of our condition. But rather than explore these as 'subjects', the music concentrates instead on the notion of healing, by seeking out the seeds of transformation which are lodged in each one of us.

One of the most ancient conventions for expressing this exile is the story of Adam and Eve's banishment from the Garden of Eden, the eternal life history of each one of us and our loss of innocence. This state is powerfully expressed in the opening of *Adam's Lament*, and will serve to conclude this brief excursus:

Adam, father of all mankind, in paradise knew the sweetness of the love of God; and so when for his sin he was driven forth from the garden of Eden, and was widowed of the love of God, he suffered grievously and lamented with a mighty moan. And the whole desert rang with his lamentations.[10]

Works in Church Slavonic

To an outsider, the most impressive aural feature of a Russian Orthodox service is the sense of being surrounded by a flow of sound, a continuity that fills the space of the church. Beginnings and endings seem to merge together as different kinds of utterance overlap, yet all is totally without haste or insistence. The fabric of this sound is immensely varied, and ranges from recitation by a solo priest to full-blown choral responses (in a generally static harmonic idiom); but the musical aspect never overrides the verbal: it consists in 'a series of gradations of the musical phenomenon in intimate connection with the word'.[11]

Many different stylistic periods are represented in the repertoire of this music, of course; yet it is the nationalist style of the late nineteenth century that most familiarly represents the 'Russian' sound. This aesthetic might seem the antithesis of Pärt's cool intensity, but it is possible to imagine that we hear an echo of that sound world in tintinnabuli. Certainly it is possible to transpose the concept of an interpenetrative flow of sound into an overall vision of Pärt's musical style. Similarly, listening to the very different three-part

---

[10] Ibid., p. 448.
[11] Gardner, p. 24.

heterophony of early Russian polyphony, one can also detect the same diatonic clusters that occur in tintinnabuli, though here they arise from a purely linear practice. Technically, these fanciful connections may be somewhat illusory, but if one's ear is to be trusted, then in two of the three Church Slavonic works, the sense of kinship becomes quite apparent; the fact that it is not apparent in the third work only serves to strengthen our perception of Pärt's awareness of the idiom and his ability to borrow from it or even allude to it, or not, at will. For the same reason we can dismiss the notion that it is simply the language that creates this suggestion of recognition.[12]

In the first of Pärt's Russian works, the *Two Slavonic Psalms*, the tintinnabuli technique functions normally, but a slightly new idea controls the melodic system. The first psalm is in A minor, and there are two M-voices each employing two pitch centres in strict rotation; the upper M-voice uses A and C as pitch centres (using modes 1 and 2 respectively), changing from one to the other at the beginning of each word; this is mirrored a sixth lower by the 2nd M-voice, alternating C and E. Two T-voices are sounding, though they are in fact the same line doubled at the octave, creating a 1st position inferior to the upper M-voice and 2nd position inferior to the lower M-voice.

The tempo of the music is quite quick, and the complete text (Psalm 117, which has only two verses of two phrases each) is sung five times in succession. During the second and fourth times, a threefold Alleluia is sung between each of the phrases. These Alleluias begin on a chord of C major before shifting back to A minor—just enough harmonic colour to provoke thoughts of Russianness! Although this psalm calls for five voices,[13] it never uses more than four of them simultaneously and, given the octave doubling of the T-voice (and with the exception of one chord only in the Alleluias), there are only three independent parts at any time. The vocal scoring is symmetrically balanced, the phrases between the Alleluias providing the clearest contrast between high and low ranges.

The same music is used for the Gloria in both psalms, and extends the melodic idea just described, so that now each phrase (rather than each word) begins on a succession of triadic notes, and from there moves by step up the natural minor scale on E. The words are then

---

[12] Church Slavonic is an older Russified form of the Slavonic language, which became fixed in the 16th to 17th centuries (through the medium of print); there are some differences in pronunciation from modern Russian, the earlier form being, as one might expect, more phonetic.

[13] SATB and countertenor.

repeated with the music descending and now curling round a succession of slow Amens (also sounding the E minor triad). The effect is quite magical.

The second psalm (Psalm 131) is given a German subtitle: *Kindliche Ergebung* (filial submission). It is sung by the three lower voices, and once again the two M-voices are made by alternating two triadic pitches in each of them (for each word, as in the first psalm, but now in the key of E minor). The single T-voice lies between them, in 1st position superior to the lower part. The tempo is slow, and the close vocal texture gives an added richness to the sound which, again, it is hard not to associate with Russian choral singing (see Ex. 29).

This association is openly evident in the later Russian piece, a setting of *Bogoroditse Dyevo*, which was commissioned by the choir of King's College, Cambridge, and first performed at their annual carol service in 1990—though the text is in fact that of a dismissal hymn normally sung towards the end of Vespers during an Orthodox Vigil (a combination of Vespers and Matins). Here we find few significant traces of tintinnabuli technique at all, beyond the frequent incidence of parallel thirds. The harmonic qualities seem entirely indebted to the traditions of Russian choral music, as do the opening monotonal recitations of the text, which are answered chordally. There is then a brief flirtation with the relative minor, followed by an exultant fortissimo with the voices resonantly spaced in thirds around a central repeated A (upper and lower voices in contrary motion). The whole text is then repeated, recited on a tonic second inversion; there is a final ritardando, and the music resolves in a perfect cadence. A joyful work—quite as unexpected in the Pärt canon as the earlier *Solfeggio* had been.

Standing apart from these two works is Pärt's other setting of Church Slavonic, which carries the German title, *Nun eile ich zu euch*. The text of this work is taken from the Canon of Repentance, and both mood and technique are redolent of what by now we might refer to as the classic tintinnabuli style. The key is D minor, and only this triad is used for the T-voice; there are no chromatic pitches (though the tenor uses E♭ when necessary to avoid augmented fourths). The M-

Ex. 29
♩ = 88

Ghos-po-di   ñe vozh-ñe-ses-ya sert-sye mo-ye,   ni-zhe vozh-ñe-sos-tse-ya o-chee mo-ye.

181

voices are derived syllabically from the text using the four melodic modes in their basic manner, though deployed with judicious variety and fixing on A and F as the pitch centres for the S/A pair of voices (which thus sometimes move in parallel thirds) and A and E for the T/B pair (sometimes producing parallel fourths). A slow, regular tempo is established at the outset which does not waver; nor does the opening rhythmic pattern of steady minims for the M-voice, answered on the off-beats by the T-voice in detached crotchets.[14]

The text is divided into four parts, and is sung almost throughout in an alternation of two and three voices (a change in the number occurs at the beginning of each verbal phrase). One voice dominates each section in turn; the alto and tenor are present in different capacities throughout, joined in alternate sections by the bass or soprano. Just three separate phrases form the exception to this, at the beginning of sections 3 and 4, and for the concluding 'Amen', where all four voices are heard together.[15] Both this work and the *Two Slavonic Psalms* were initially intended to be sung by a consort of solo voices; however they can also (and perhaps most successfully) be sung chorally.

Works in English

As *Litany* will be discussed separately below, only one work chiefly concerns us in this section, a setting of *The Beatitudes* which Pärt completed in 1990. Again, although initially sung by solo voices, the work is probably more successfully rendered by (small) choir.[16]

For some time in the late 1980s Pärt had looked for an English text to set; for a while he considered the medieval miracle plays, but ultimately settled on this shorter text (from Matt. 5: 3–12). Faced with a language dominated by short words, Pärt now opted for a more sustained manner of recitation in which only stressed syllables are offset from the pitch centre (a step alternately in either direction) and using a pattern of chromatic shifts quite rare in tintinnabuli music,

---

[14] It is the singers' task to create a sense of line from these crotchets: see Ch. 10 on performance practice.

[15] It now seems likely that Pärt will undertake further settings of Church Slavonic texts, and that *Nun eile ich* will become the first in a series of related works, joined recently by *Memento mori* (1995).

[16] The initial sketches had a fifth (bass) voice singing the low pedal notes, which was replaced by organ in the final version; after the work's première in 1990, it was further revised for publication in 1991.

[A - (men)]

though not without precedent (the last of the *Seven Magnificat Anti-phons*, for example).

Each verse except the last begins with a stressed syllable, '*Bless*-ed', and so each makes the same initial gesture, like a psalm intonation rising to the *tenor*, or main note of recitation (Ex. 30*a* shows the first verse). The harmonic pattern of the first half of the work is shown in Ex. 30*b*, where the reader can observe that the triads alternate major and minor, their roots descending alternately by a major and minor third, but with the larger drop of a fourth after the third chord and then after every six chords. A series of organ pedal notes underpins this progression, rising by semitones through the fifth from D♭ (C♯) to

G#. The regularity of the progression is halted and turned around during the sung 'Amen'; the voices fall silent, and the organ then traces its way back through the harmonic sequence in a pattern of quintuplet arpeggios in each hand, back to the opening F minor harmony. Beneath this toccata-like texture is another series of long pedal notes, which now descend in whole tones down to C. The F minor arpeggios then rise up through an octave, bringing the piece to a rather inconclusive ending.

In another English setting (*And One of the Pharisees*, for three voices, text from Luke 7) the use of both chordal and solo recitation is even more markedly similar to chant techniques of liturgical recitation.[17] The concept is taken up again in Pärt's next English piece, *Litany* (see below).

Berlin Mass, *Magnificat, and Shorter Latin Works*

De Profundis was the first new composition written after Pärt's emigration, and belongs more with the Estonian tintinnabuli works, with their unwavering adherence to a simple unfolding of material in basic tintinnabuli manner, than to the relatively more intricate manner of the later Latin works. It is scored for male voices (TTBB), organ, and percussion (bass drum, E bell, and tam-tam)—the percussion is marked 'ad lib', though much would be lost by its omission. The organ provides a relentless walking bass beneath alternate phrases, while the voices declaim the text in steady minim beats throughout. The voices are heard at first singly, then in pairs, in threes, and finally all four together. As the words of the psalm (Vulgate no. 129) almost insist, the music begins low in the bass, answered in the next phrase by a tenor at the other extreme (see Ex. 31), before moving more into the middle registers.

Ex. 31

17 Pärt has only recently decided to publish this work, written *c*.1989.

The whole work articulates a single dynamic arch, gradually rising upwards in pitch and dynamic towards the point where the four voices first come together, creating a sustained, rather than a sudden, climax. The voices here maintain their forte dynamic over two phrases, but the organ pedal (in accordance with the overall design) is absent from the second of these, and the music has already been tilted quite naturally back down towards piano again.

After *De Profundis*, Pärt's next Latin setting was the Magnificat for mixed choir, one of the happiest meetings of tintinnabuli technique and words of a non-penitential character. The music perfectly expresses the uplifted, tender joy of the Virgin Mother, but readily encompasses the text's other imagery without any sense of 'setting the words'. Thus the music has the feel of spontaneous lyricism, though this little masterpiece is anything but spontaneous in its construction, and displays the tintinnabuli technique at its most supple and refined.

The underlying pattern of the work is one of a series of responses between 'verse' and 'tutti', if we interpret these terms somewhat broadly. The 'verse' element is represented by a two-voice texture (a solo soprano reciting the text solely on C, joined by different single vocal lines in turn), and the 'tutti' is a three-part texture (different portions of the choir, sometimes doubled at the octave to suggest six parts). The opening of the work is shown in Ex. 32*a*. In the 'tutti' sections we find the M-voice consistently in the lowest part with two superior T-voices (1st and 2nd positions, naturally, though the former is sometimes transposed an octave higher to open up the texture). The M-voice construction uses a slightly revised version of the method already encountered in *Seven Magnificat Antiphons* (see above, Ex. 26*c*), whereby the number of syllables determines the notes to be used, but the stressed syllable takes the note furthest from the pitch centre and is approached by step. Here, the stressed syllable is alternately the pitch centre and, in the next word, the note furthest away from it. Thus, Ex. 32*b* ('verse') shows the pitches that would have been yielded by Pärt's original method, alternating modes 1 and 2; these can be compared with the actual version composed (shown in Ex. 32*a*).

The processes used by Pärt in the 'verse' sections are less easy to determine, and indeed he seems to have allowed himself an unusual degree of freedom here. The work's opening shows the stressed syllable causing a change of melodic direction; the words could be rendered as in the Ex. 32*b* 'tutti', and although the word 'mea' is a

Ex. 32a

Ex. 32b

problem, this model easily (though loosely) translates into the actual composed version (Ex. 32a). This solution does not hold for other verse sections, however, although the stressed syllables do frequently coincide with a change of melodic direction. More generally, we can discern the faint outline of scales behind these melodic shapes, frequently curving away at a stressed syllable, but always (in every verse section) positioned so as to arrive on C at or towards the end of the section (in other words, coming into unison with or an octave away from the solo soprano's repeated c''). The choral 'tutti' always resolves this into a clear F minor.

A moment of word-painting occurs at 'dispersit superbos' when the T-voices are displaced by a beat's rest before the stressed syllable, 'dispersed'; though, as the same approach is taken for a later passage ('et divites dimisit'), the idea quickly assumes a purely musical identity.

Only twice does the work briefly reach forte, and conspicuously *not* at points where the text speaks of power or putting down the mighty. The second of these fortes incorporates the words 'puerum suum', where the choir breaks into a genuine six-part texture, the lower three voices being mirrored by the upper three. Soon after this point a quiet sustained *g* is set up in the altos, which is added to the solo soprano *c″* for the last verse. The choir then repeats the opening words very softly, adding a T-voice in 3rd position (= 1st position transposed) and joined by the soloist for the very last word.

The *Berlin Mass* was composed for the 'German Catholic Days' held in Berlin in May 1990. The première took place as part of a church service in what was then still, though only just, East Berlin. At this point the work was scored for four solo voices and organ, but it was later (1992) revised for chorus and string orchestra. (The published score retains the option to use solo voices, but a choir seems vastly preferable.) The work includes a setting of the Pentecost sequence *Veni Sancte Spiritus*, preceded by two Alleluia verses. Though optional, these provide a very useful contrast to the mass texts, coming conveniently between the word-laden Gloria and Credo; and it would be a pity to omit these in concert performances.

Apart from the use of scale patterns, there has been little incidence of motivic structure in the tintinnabuli music, especially in works derived from a text. In the *Berlin Mass*, although the text plays as strong a role as ever, the frequency with which we encounter the rising and falling four-note pattern, hitherto described as modes 1 and 2, leads us to consider them as the prevailing motifs of this work. Although this 'motif' is expanded and contracted according to the syllabic structure of the text at any point, it nevertheless seems to have exerted a strong influence over the initial formulation of each movement's specific system. In the very opening Kyrie we hear the four-note motif descending from the pitch centre, which is then answered (in the same voice) beginning an octave higher, thus completing an octave scale, whose reappearance here is more than fortuitous. (See Ex. 33*a*.)

Ex. 33*a*

Ky - ri - e   e - le - i - son.

Of course, the tintinnabuli process itself is responsible for the particular four notes, but we notice that the M-voice construction now gives an additional pitch to each main stressed syllable, so that each word has one more pitch allotted to it than there are syllables (previously, the second pitch was simply 'borrowed' from the next syllable).

After 'Kyrie' has been sung alone, the 'eleison' is given an alternating T-voice; the strings then answer this opening statement with a G drone and the motif inverted (but five pitches, echoing the last word). Three voices sing the next 'Kyrie', reversing the melodic direction, and 'eleison' is sung by all four. The reader will probably by now be accustomed to the fact that the simplicity of the material and the baldness of my description of it can give no hint of the mysterious beauty of the resulting sound.

In the Gloria only the first and last words in each phrase receive an extra pitch, and the resulting disposition of three- and four-syllable words ensures the frequent occurrence of the four-note motif. The M-voices are created by the alternation of modes 2 and 4 or 1 and 3, with string interjections frequently doubling the voices, providing quaver arpeggio figures, and always echoing the last phrase after a full stop.

The Alleluia verses begin with a luminous choral 'Alleluia' introducing the chant-like melody of the solo verses, both elements drawing strongly on the four-note motif. This acts as an introduction to the Pentecost sequence *Veni Sancte Spiritus*, which is sung by different single voices in turn, over an octave E drone. (The upper strings add short responses, following the punctuation: a two-note T-motif at commas and a longer three-note echo at the end of each line.) The vocal line consists, in fact, of a single melodic idea whose construction also neatly confirms the significance of the four-note motif in the mass as a whole. It is heard in its originating form only once (at the very end of the sequence, where the choir sings 'Amen', the strings answer with the next melodic segment, and the choir ends with 'Alleluia'); though the final note is not sounded for reasons that will be explained below. (See Ex. 33*b*.)

The melody is built out of the four-note motif, ascending and then descending from G, with the simple addition of tintinnabuli pitches. There are 22 pitches, but as each verse contains only 21 syllables, there is always one pitch left over, which becomes the first pitch of the next verse. There are 10 verses in all, plus a concluding Amen and Alleluia—in effect, an eleventh verse. The asterisk above the central B in Ex. 33*b* shows the starting-point for verse 1. The C before it becomes the starting-point of verse 2, and so on back through the sequence of eleven pitches to the 'start'. As is so often the case with Pärt's ingenious constructions, we are left at the end of a system which is about to start again with the next pitch, E. Ex. 33*c* shows verse 1 and the beginning of verse 2 (the vocal part, in bass clef in the score, is here put in treble clef for ease of comparison with Ex. 33*b*). The prevailing 3/4 metre is nicely varied at certain points, ostensibly to reflect shifting emphases in the text.

The setting of the Credo in this work, though the mood is much more buoyant, shows striking similarities to *Summa* in the steady rise and fall of its scalar melodies and the seemingly random disposition of the text across the musical phrases, so that one pair of voices will often end or pick up again in the middle of a word, while the other pair simply continues. Yet there is, of course, nothing random in the composition at all, and in fact both pairs of voices (S/A and T/B) are in a leap-frog canon at the octave throughout, and again as in *Summa*, a sequentially varied melody comprised of seven- and nine-pitch units is revolved through a process in which two pitches in turn are ex-

Ex. 33*b*

Ex. 33*c*

* = octave lower

189

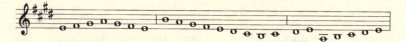

tracted and moved to the end of the melody until the exact opening sequence of pitches is reproduced, culminating in the final 'Amen'. The melody sets out the four-note motif already proposed as the basis of the mass, which here provides the model for a series of phrases rising first a fourth and fifth above the central pitch E, then dipping down below it, also by a fourth and then a fifth. Omitting some tintinnabuli passing notes, the basic pattern is as shown in Ex. 33*d*.

I use the word 'leap-frog' to describe the canonic activity, as each pair of voices in turn leads the canon for two phrases before dropping out for two phrases; the other pair meanwhile catches up, and then moves ahead to lead the canon in its turn, when the first pair re-enters, now a phrase behind.[18] The canon is a purely musical one, as the text is declaimed homophonically throughout. In each pair of voices (S/A, T/B), the lower part has the M-voice, while the upper part provides a T-voice in 2nd position superior. The frequent string interjections trace the same melodic outline, but with each two- or three-note unit in contrary motion to the voices.

The Sanctus is sung by the lower three voices only, and the strings here play a much more integrated role than in the other movements. While alto and bass move in parallel sixths (M-voices in alternating modal pairs, with pitch centres C♯ and E respectively), and the tenor sings a T-voice (1st position alternating) to the alto, it is the first violins which provide a transposed T-voice to the bass line. The double basses and cellos meanwhile play an M-voice in detached dotted quavers, moving in contrary motion to the altos.

The Agnus Dei also uses a canonic process, though only fully in the last of its three short sections. In the first two sections, the vocal lines are fashioned out of a simple descending scale, each note alternating with the appropriate T-pitches. Soprano and tenor thus imitate each other at a distance of four beats in the first Agnus and at the interval of a fourth. In the second Agnus, the voices exchange parts, and the distance closes to two beats. The strings have thus far provided upper tintinnabuli pitches (based only on the scalar pitches in the first voice),

[18] Somewhat reminiscent of medieval *Stimmtausch*, or voice exchange, except that here the voices do actually stop singing.

maintaining a tonality of C♯ minor. Now for the third section they settle on an open E–B fifth, while the voices sing in two pairs in direct canon at the unison, just one beat apart. Instead of scales, they revolve one tone above and below a B pitch centre integrated with T-pitches into a single set of four vocal lines, one in each pair in contrary motion to the other.

The disposition of tonalities in the *Berlin Mass* supports the normal grouping of the mass movements in a practical, liturgical sense. Thus the opening G minor for Kyrie and Gloria sets those two movements apart from the rest of the mass. The Credo's E major attaches it to the C♯ minor of the Sanctus and Agnus (resolved to E major at the end), which also function as a pair. In concert performance, this tonal gap is bridged, of course, by the G major of the first Alleluia verse, which shifts to B minor and then, for the second Alleluia verse to E minor, where it remains for *Veni Sancte Spiritus*.

The two motets *Beatus Petronius* and *Statuit ei Dominus* were both written in 1990 for the six-hundredth jubilee of the basilica of San Petronio in Bologna, and may be considered as a pair, though they can be performed separately. Pärt took the presence in the church of two organs as his starting-point, and composed for two organs and two choirs in antiphonal style. The two motets are contrasted in dynamic range and also in the manner of M-voice construction.

Beatus Petronius is reflective in mood, and presents the phrases of the text in choir 1 (in which the T-voices are broken up by rests), answered in choir 2 by the repeated invocation 'Beatus Petronius' (all voices sustained). Only at the end, with the organs now silent, do both choirs exchange new text, as a repeated g in the basses pulls the music into silence.

The M-voice in this work is created by the now familiar process of taking the one-pitch-per-syllable model and allotting the pitch furthest from the pitch centre to the stressed syllable, which is approached by step. Pärt also now fuses the M- and T-voice elements into one line to create an accompanying figure in the organ such as that shown in Ex. 34, where the T-voice element is alternately the second and first note in each pair of two.

Statuit ei Dominus has an architectural solidity befitting its text, in which choral declamation, one choir echoing the other over strong continuous pedal Ds, follows a descending sequence of M-voice pitch centres down over an octave to the concluding, repeated 'Alleluias'. This is offset, uniquely in Pärt's *œuvre*, by the use of a Gregorian melody at the beginning and in the middle; this is not directly quoted

in Pärt's music, though its contours must have pointed to the essential pattern of movement down through the D minor triad after an initial rising declamation.

Litany—*Prayers of St John Chrysostom for Each Hour of Day and Night*

A monastery may be set apart from the temporal flow of ordinary events, yet the passage of time is none the less acutely observed, traditionally with bells marking the hours and summoning the fraternity to prayer at the appropriate time of day or night. Similarly, the year's cyclic processes are marked out and ritually observed according to the liturgical calendar, duly hallowed by force of repetition. This measuring of time within timelessness (like the bells rung at sea to mark the track of time, where space stretches endlessly to the horizon's circle) provides the regulated motion, the matrix, in which the seed of the spiritual life can blossom. The macrorhythmic elements are not hard to discern: the turning of a single year in its changing seasons, the 12 months, the alternation of night and day, and the division of these into 12 hours each.

The words of Pärt's *Litany* are attributed to St John Chrysostom (*c*.347–407), and are comprised, as the work's subtitle tells us, of prayers for each hour of the day and night: 24 in all, therefore, none of them longer than a phrase or so, some just a few words, each one opening with the invocation 'O Lord'. Pärt's setting does not specify which half is day and which night, but duly observes the enumeration of the hours, reflecting it directly in the musical setting, while the work's overall structure divides naturally into two halves of 12 prayers each. (The first half further subdivides into eight and four, and the four into two.)

Pärt employs a full orchestra—for the first time since Symphony

No. 3—together with a mixed chorus and solo quartet (alto, two tenors, and bass). Broadly speaking, each prayer is set in the same way, and has four basic elements: an introduction incorporating some numerical reference to the 'hour'; the invocation 'O Lord', sung; the words of the prayer, sung (recited); and a concluding instrumental response. The way in which these elements are articulated, and their length and relative complexity, vary considerably across the work, but conform to a general process linking them together in one way or another with comparable elements in each of the work's other sections.

In both halves of the work there is a gradual buildup of texture from small beginnings towards a loudest point, from which the intensity quite quickly dissipates. The music starts with a high b''' in the strings, descending slowly through the harmonic scale of E minor, which is soon (though not immediately) confirmed as the tonality for the first half of the piece. The predominant rhythmic element here consists of steady dotted minims, occasionally broken up into gently rocking crotchet patterns. Only gradually does the music assemble its forces, but after section 9, which is suddenly vigorously rhythmic, a climax occurs in the tenth section, where an eight-part choral tutti declaims the text on the triads of E minor and B minor simultaneously. Then, without any change of harmony, the choir moves down in range, and makes a substantial diminuendo, leading into the last two sections of restored quiet. This is followed by a subtle shift into the new tonality of C♯ minor for the work's second half. This part of the work is characterized by a greater sense of motion and overall activity as the underlying dotted minim pulse is now dominated by the rhythmic motif [♩ ♩] or its reverse [♩ ♩]; also, throughout this half of the work, there is a steadier growth towards the final tutti in section 24, which then resolves into a quiet conclusion. At the very end the choral basses are singing a low C♯, and the sense of closure is complete. However, it cannot be merely fortuitous that the next pitch down, B, will eventually emerge high in the strings to set the litany of 24 hours in motion once again. The opening of the work is shown in Ex. 35a.

The psalmodic concept of antiphonal recitation, already familiar from earlier tintinnabuli compositions, is strongly present in this work. It owes nothing to specific chant models, of course, though it is permeated with the idiomatic manner of liturgical recitative especially appropriate to prayer, with its reiterative pitch centres relieved only by melodic punctuation. In Ex. 35a the alto part is a regular M-voice (using modes 3 and 4) following the text in the normal manner, and

indeed throughout the whole work the four modes are used consistently and conventionally for melodic construction (without any special treatment of stressed syllables). Where Pärt does depart from his
own conventions, however, is in the freedom with which he mixes
them together without any apparent system (other than an intuitive
sense of balance). All four modes are in use quite frequently, though
overall modes 1 and 3 (those moving above the pitch centre) are
encountered slightly more often than modes 4 and 2. Ultimately it is
the nature of the English language, with its strings of monosyllables,
that so strongly reinforces the impression of psalmodic recitation
encountered in this work. Had Pärt chosen to set the text in its original
Greek, we can only surmise how different the result would have
been.[19]

Litany is built entirely on two principles: melodic construction
derived from the text, as just discussed, and the enumeration of the
hours either in repeated rhythms or scales. Each hour's prayer is
numerically announced in the music, though at times this is less
obvious to the ear than at others. In the first half of the work Pärt
primarily uses scales for this purpose. The first four sections begin
with a descending scale (distributed across three octaves) in which the
pitches are sustained to form a cluster; in effect, these scales are
formed by the tintinnabuli triad of E minor filled in with passing

---

[19] For this very reason, none of Pärt's works can be sung in any language but the one which
the composer himself has used.

notes, and moving one step lower in the arpeggio for the beginning of each section. A different soloist in turn then sings the words of each prayer (their pitch centres also of course articulating the E minor triad), against which the choir sustains a single pitch in section 1, two pitches in section 2, and so on. It is thus the opening out of the triad in the choir that 'enumerates' the first four hours.

In sections 5–8, pizzicato scales in contrary motion give out the number of the hour (a 5-note scale for the fifth hour, and so on); and section 5 also has five bells, as if to announce this change in the manner of articulation. Section 9 provides new impetus too, with a change to duple patterns of crotchets and a delightfully intricate use of two sets of scales simultaneously, as shown in Ex. 35*b* (the slurs are merely to aid identification; all notes are accented and distributed across various string and wind instruments).

The scale introducing section 10 has a similarly dynamic force, while sections 11 and 12 bring a return of the opening string scale clusters (ascending from the depths in 11 and returning to them in 12). At the end of section 12 'Amen' is sung twice, quite simply, using mode 3 on the fifth of the triad. However Pärt brings about a magical change of harmony at this point: the cellos and double basses play a low E♭ (D♯) which acts as a melodic and harmonic lever to release the open fifth C♯–G♯. The choir sings the second 'Amen', still using mode 3 but on the fifth of the new triad of C♯ minor. (The double bass D♯–C♯ could even be understood as the 'Amen' on C♯ in 3rd position.) This is shown in reduced form in Ex. 35*c*. This enharmonic shift is similar in effect to the bass soloist's move at the end of the third section of the *Miserere*, where a semitone drop initiates that work's final section in E minor.

Ex. 35*b*

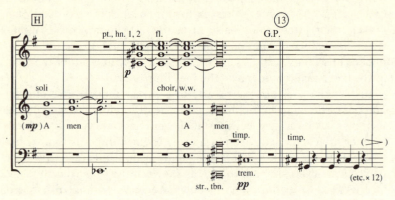

The timpani motif at figure 13 (played 12 times) marks the beginning of the second half of the work, sections 13–24. Time is in effect now flowing in both directions at once: the hours are marked in reverse by the timpani before every odd-numbered section (thus the motif will be heard 10 times before section 15, and so on down to two times before section 23), while the even-numbered sections are introduced by a growing descending scale (from two to eventually 12 pitches before the tonic) in the woodwind.

In the first four sections of the work the invocation 'O Lord' is sung first by the soloist, then echoed by the choir, who then sustain their pitches while the soloist sings the text of the prayer. Thereafter (sections 5–12) the choir has the invocation, and the soloists respond with the prayer. The soloists are heard one at a time in sections 1–4, then in pairs (sections 5–8), and then three at a time in the last four sections, with the exception of the climactic section 10, where all four are heard together for the first time. The number of chorus parts similarly expands from one to eight (in section 10), reducing to two for the last two sections. From section 5 on, the words of the prayer are followed by an instrumental response, which is built directly on the text setting just heard. In section 10 the choir also repeats the text of the prayer.

In the second half of the work, the initial vocal roles are reversed. The solo quartet sings the invocation, but now in the triple rhythm (see Ex. 35d) which had hitherto been confined to the instrumental passages. The choir sings the text of the prayers, answered instrumentally as before, but the process is now extended as the prayer is repeated by three of the soloists. Throughout this half of the work we hear at first only one or two parts of the choir in turn; in sections 22 and 23 this increases to three parts, and then finally in the last section the choir reaches its full strength, where it is joined by the orchestral tutti and solo quartet. Just as the beginning of section 9 (see Ex. 35*b*) announced the impending climax of that section, so in section 23 the prevailing triple rhythm is interrupted by a rhetorical duple rhythm (see Ex. 35*e*), and the gesture is immediately echoed in the orchestra, and then used to punctuate the texture at various points. The words at this point are certainly suited to such treatment: 'shelter me from certain men, from demons and passions, and from any other unbecoming thing'. In the last section the text 'for blessed art Thou unto the ages' similarly cues the return of the long sustained pitches heard at the opening, which now, naturally enough, draw the work to its close. The word 'ages' is sustained by the choir while the orchestra plays its response to the text; a strong tutti 'Amen' is then likewise sustained 'unto the ages'. A quieter mood of supplication is then restored as the soloists repeat the words of the prayer, the bass at half the speed of the others, remaining on C♯ throughout. The orchestra meanwhile recalls the descending scale clusters of the opening, but now played as a sequence of thirds which are lowered down to the final C♯ octaves (and the third, E) with which the work ends.

Ex. 35*d*

O Lord, O Lord

Ex. 35*e*

shel - ter me from cer - tain men,

Mention has been made of a certain similarity between the move to C♯ for the 'Amen' at the end of the first half and the beginning of the last section of the *Miserere*.[20] This was previously the only tintinnabuli work with a sense of orchestral sonority other than strings; beyond that we must look to the Third Symphony for a fully orchestral texture, and there are moments in *Litany* which seem, perhaps inevitably, to recall aspects of both these works. In all the tintinnabuli vocal works the main role of instruments was responsorial, either punctuating the text with echoes or providing a longer interlude; in either case, the musical material would typically repeat the melodic substance created by the text just sung. This function was clarified by the fact that only a single principal sonority (essentially strings or wind) stood in contrast to the voices. The frequent presence of an obbligato instrument—percussion, for example, or prepared piano—did not disturb this balance, and indeed assisted in the articulation of the work's discrete sonorous layers. While this approach is used in *Litany* too (having in mind the percussion's highly significant role), the presence of both string and wind sections allows Pärt to use each of them as further contrasted elements in a largely antiphonal manner—as one might expect—but he also integrates them into a mixed orchestral palette that is richer than any tintinnabuli score hitherto.

This is a new development, certainly, but it also presents a considerable challenge to the tintinnabuli style in its purest form, the essence of which rests not upon specific instrumental colours (still less on orchestral hybrids), but rather on an abstract musical design, a pattern of pitches and rhythms, which could be 'realized' in various ways. Of course many works, even from the late 1970s, had perfectly specific scorings, but these always employed a single sonority, with or without voices, so that one could quite readily envisage its abstract core; other works like *Passio* were essentially chamber music formations adapted to a larger context. While there is certainly no wash of orchestral colour in *Litany*, its integrated use of the whole orchestra creates problems of which the conductor must be aware: the mixture of instrumental hues tends to mute, slightly, the incisive triadic *Klang* which distinguishes the tintinnabuli style, overriding it with local orchestral effects. Despite its apparently normal orchestral garb, this work, like all the tintinnabuli works, requires an appropriate acoustic environment if it is to 'sound' with all its inner fullness.

[20] One is reminded also of the expressive use of a shift to C♯ minor in the Third Symphony; see Ex. 9c in Ch. 4.

10

PERFORMANCE PRACTICE

THIS chapter is addressed primarily to performers of Pärt's music, though as I subscribe to the view that the most profound commentary on or analysis of any piece of music ultimately resides in a good performance of it, its raison d'être is hardly a minor one. But of course the kind of language in which we seek to discuss the nuances of performance is even more hopelessly inexact than that employed for the more theoretical aspects of music. Accordingly, the chapter is a short one, and I have allowed myself a greater licence for what is, inevitably, personal opinion rather than verifiable fact.

Silence

The use of silence in Pärt's music has been commented upon often enough, generally as contributing to a perception of the music's spiritual nature; there are however some practical aspects to these silences which performers of the music cannot ignore.

Music is a negation of silence, but depends upon it for differentiation from the surrounding world of sound. Very often, Pärt uses silence as a creative element within the music, and in doing so requires the performer to realize this in different ways. This is not unique to Pärt, of course, but so many of his works incorporate such frequent and sometimes extensive silences that they become thematic in effect and must be treated accordingly; that is to say, the silence must be 'played'. To the question 'How do you play a silence?' I would answer naturally enough, 'By linking it to the surrounding sounds'. In other words, silence becomes musically creative by the way it is approached and ended. Inevitably, the attitude of the performers is crucial in this regard—but not as a sanctimonious pose. The musicians must mentally attend to the continuity of the work through the silence, as well as in the way they approach and leave it. The sounds may stop either abruptly or slowly with a *diminuendo al niente*; these are the extremes, but between them lies an infinite range of possibilities, ways of lifting the music out of sound into silence, perhaps only for a second or two, sometimes for longer. In the opening of *Tabula Rasa*, for example, the music gives the effect of disappearing upwards out of hearing and then returning; for a few moments we cannot hear the music, though we have perhaps the impression that it continues just out of range before it turns round and re-enters. The end of the work achieves a comparable effect, but in the opposite direction, the music dropping below the threshold of audibility, just as in listening to a bell, we cannot tell precisely where the sound stops.

Works such as *Arbos* and *Passio* begin with a massive, sudden gesture that tears a space in silence and pours music into it. Other works, such as the Te Deum and *Stabat Mater*, begin almost imperceptibly, seeping into our consciousness like ink into blotting paper, but then miraculously draining away again, leaving the page blank.

In the *Miserere* the words of the psalm are delivered one by one, surrounded by silence and brief instrumental echoes. As these silences are so numerous and short, they are incorporated into the rise and fall of the musical phrase, even while they threaten to break it up into fragments. After each silence the musician picks up the sound almost at the point where it stopped, depending on the length of the silence and the general direction of the music. If it has been necessary to fade the dynamic slightly before the silence, then normally the music will recommence at the quieter level. The rises and falls in the music are more emphatic in the *Miserere* than in *Passio*, although the latter also has its dynamic contours. But *Passio*, especially the part of the Evangelist, is like a long procession; in watching it, we participate, but our involvement is not necessarily equally intense at all points. This is not to suggest that the music is in any way diluted or attenuated; it is to argue for a different manner of listening, to acknowledge that Pärt has created a different kind of musical event than in his other large-scale works.

In a work such as *Nun eile ich* we find the problem of a melodic line broken up by rests (in the T-voices) presented in a more straightforward manner, though as this continues throughout the piece, it is crucial that the singers realize that they should not sing these syllables staccato, or even legato, but with equal weight. This can be done by following the disposition of lighter and stronger syllables and their place within the overall contours of the verbal phrase. Thus the words of the text will be reconnected 'naturally' across the rests. (This is also a work which benefits enormously from being sung in a suitably resonant acoustic.)

From time to time Pärt has agreed to participate in a public forum, usually in the form of a panel discussion. But at the University of Oregon in the summer of 1994 (during preparations for the première of *Litany*), he met with a group of student composers, and responded for over an hour to their questions. Some of the questions bore directly on his own approach to composition, and the most significant of his (translated) responses are summarized here.

A composition comes as a single gesture which is already, in essence, music. The path to this is hard; you descend to the lowest spiritual plane, the bottom of the world, not knowing what will be found. The only thing you know is that you don't know anything. If this gesture, like a seed, takes root, it must be cultivated with extreme care so that it may grow; meanwhile you are oscillating between heaven and earth. The compositional task is to find the appropriate system for the gesture. It is one's capacity for suffering that gives the energy to create.

At a more superficial level, he was asked how this approach is squared with the funding of work by the modern commissioning process? Pärt likened composing to the arduous task of rowing a small sailing boat across the ocean. When a commission comes along, it is like a wind filling the boat's sails. *Litany*, for example, was written in response to a commission, and composed in a comparatively short time (when plans for a yet larger work had, perhaps temporarily, to be shelved); but Pärt had been deeply acquainted with the text for some 20 years, and had long wished to find some 'musical resolution' for it. In a sense, then, he had been rowing this particular boat for a very long time indeed.

For larger compositions especially, Pärt creates a visual map of the work's form which he pins up on the wall of his study. This consists of the text, cut up into separate verses, with pitch indications and other musical data and the use of different colours to depict the voices and orchestration. The result, much more than a mere sketch, encapsulates the entire work at the point where the initial gesture has found its appropriate system.

Although Pärt has a keyboard at hand to try out sound combinations, he does not normally compose 'at the piano' in the sense of discovering musical ideas with his fingers. In 1989, during the composition of the *Miserere*, I travelled to Berlin to discuss the work with him. He showed me the work's physical portrait—the illustrated scheme—and proceeded to recreate portions of it at the piano, playing

not like a pianist, but rather like a sculptor, hewing vocal and instrumental sound out of this most unlikely box of wires and hammers.
Somehow this allowed me to hear the final work perfectly clearly—
and I was reminded of Pärt learning as a child to create his own
universe of sounds on the broken grand piano in his home.

Voices and Instruments

In the first flush of tintinnabulation, from 1976-1978, Pärt showed a
clear bias towards instrumental works, although very often a precise
scoring was not specified. This was a deliberate policy, and mirrors
the situation in Renaissance polyphony, where any suitable consort of
instruments, ranges permitting, can usually make perfect sense of a
given piece of music (and to a certain extent, this is true of baroque
music as well). This does not mean that performers and composers
were indifferent to the instrumentation—quite the contrary; but the
music was designed so that it could function in different ways without
losing its essential qualities, though once an instrumentation was
chosen, the timbres and idiomatic playing styles would be fully integrated into the performance. The nature of this responsibility towards
such 'open' material, the obligation it imposes to become involved in
the creative process, and of course the flexibility of the music (its
'willingness' to be useful) are all part of the attraction that early music
holds for modern performers, and in many of Pärt's earlier
tintinnabuli pieces the same criteria hold true.

But certain other practical considerations also weighed in favour
of instrumental production. Pärt had in any case been primarily an
instrumental composer in his earlier years, and the influence of his
main teacher, Eller, lay in the same direction. Estonia has an eminent
and active choral tradition, with huge summer choral festivals
every four years. But, as in most countries, the musical traditions
embraced by the largely amateur choral world are often not those
of the symphonic world, which is predominantly inhabited by profes-
sionals; and it seems fair to comment that until quite recently 'serious'
composers reserved their more 'serious' efforts for the orchestra.[1] If
this situation is now changing, in some countries at least, it is largely
thanks to the post-World War II proliferation of small professional
choirs and the accordingly growing number of skilled ensemble singers, particularly those adept at both contemporary and early vocal

[1] In Estonia, Veljo Tormis is a notable exception to this.

music. This non-operatic vocal tradition, with its concomitant potential for finer tuning, a technique that values flexibility above volume, and a more 'objective' singing style (which at its best achieves a kind of intense anonymity), has been especially useful to many of those contemporary composers who have been influenced by early music, and who are therefore happy to encounter singers whose stylistic experience draws upon the same sources.

Hortus Musicus, who premièred the first tintinnabuli works, has far more instrumentalists among its personnel than singers, a fact which may also have encouraged Pärt to continue his instrumental focus, for a while at least. Another important factor must have been the political problem of trying to arrange for performances of sacred texts in a country that did not officially condone them. We have seen how Pärt at first sought to avoid this issue by using vowels (*An den Wassern*) or giving his setting of the Credo the neutral title *Summa*. But he quite quickly moved on to more overtly religious titles and texts (*Missa Sillabica* and *Cantate Domino*). Once he had emigrated to the West, the balance tipped strongly in the opposite direction. Since 1980 more than three-quarters of his works have been vocal: of these a handful are for a cappella choir, while the remainder use various instrumental combinations. In practice the instrumental parts have sometimes been condensed into a single organ part, for which sensitive and creative use of registration is extremely important. (I have fond memories of the composer indicating the kind of organ timbre he wanted by pointing out a specific seam of colour in somebody's sweater.)

Playing the Notes

It is generally very easy to sing or play the right notes in a Pärt composition, but equally, it is generally very hard to sustain the right balance of intensity and, for want of a better word, objectivity. In this laconic world of sound, so often derived from words, yet always reaching beyond them to touch what they mean but cannot say, the phrasing of each line in the music is of crucial importance, as is the right balance between the different voices, especially between each T-voice and its M-voice. The performers must be committed to the music; they cannot simply turn up and play the notes. And apart from anything else, this requires the contribution of a certain amount of time.

A useful clue to the appropriate phrasing of tintinnabuli music can be found in the singing of plainchant, not least (though not limited to) the way in which phrases begin and end. Such music requires a full attentiveness from the singer, but must never be distorted by subjective mannerisms or the interjection of wilful expression.

In the balance between M- and T-voices, it is the M-voice which generally leads and can be allowed a slight prominence. In the exordium and conclusio of *Passio*, for instance, the falling and later rising scale needs to stand forward slightly from the triadic parts, though of course not crudely so. Elsewhere (in the Evangelist parts, for example) a more equal balance should obtain.

In the vocal music particularly it can be difficult to render the T-voice as smoothly as may be required (especially when it is in alternating position). Again we can find in the Turba chorus of *Passio* numerous instances when sudden, brief high pitches need to be squared with the verbal declamation. It is often not the highest note that is most important, and extra emphasis will need to be given to the appropriate syllable, especially if it occurs on a particularly low pitch. At the same time, care is needed to ensure that the result is not 'lumpy'.

This highlights one of the lingering problems that emerges from the application of the tintinnabuli technique to choral music. The compositional rationale often gives rise to a situation where high and low voices (soprano/alto, tenor/bass) must function together in the same range, which means that they will be in different relative vocal registers. Extra care is then needed to ensure a proper balance, and sometimes the answer may simply be to redistribute the singers.[2]

Another possible source of lumpiness arises from the frequent occurrence of longer notes in the middle of a phrase. (The Magnificat is full of such moments.) These longer notes can easily go 'dead' (so that you almost hear the singers counting), and then as the end of the note approaches there is a slight push as the voices lurch towards the next pitch. The singer, player, or conductor must find ways of keeping the tone of such notes alive without mitigating against the music's essential stillness.

Great importance must be attached to accurate tuning. A clear harmonic ringing is the music's very essence. Needless to say, no

---

[2] For many choirs the vocal range of the bass part in the Gloria of the *Berlin Mass* will be problematic, as it frequently rises to *f′* and twice even to *g′*. To divide the tenors is not a luxury that all choirs can utilize, though timbrally it can be the perfect answer in this instance, as the tenor part frequently dips down to the lower d which the basses only briefly touch on.

music benefits from bad intonation, but the triadic intoning which forms the basis of tintinnabuli music naturally requires the purest of intervals. This also calls for minimal pitch variation from vibrato, to allow for maximum impact of the intonation. Vibrato is a less acute problem for instrumentalists[3] than it is for singers, either in ensembles or choirs. But we perhaps need to make a distinction between the small 'natural' vibrato inherent in most voices and the applied vibrato of many trained singers. The fact remains that the music sounds (rings) best when it is perfectly tuned.

Much of Pärt's music is slow. In all instances the performer's task is to allow the music its appropriate *gravitas* (where it is as if each note contains a specific density of massive proportion), but to balance this with the need for fluency and motion. I recall a workshop rehearsal which Pärt attended, at which I was preparing a student choir for a performance of his *De Profundis*. The composer assisted at the piano by supplying the pedal notes (of what is an organ part). Although the tempo was already slow he played these notes very firmly and— always more slowly. In fact, no matter how slowly I took the piece, the pedal notes would always come a little later, and a little heavier! I do not imagine for a moment that Pärt intended any tempo other than that marked (crotchet = 108), but this is an indication of the way in which some of Pärt's works require great weight to be poured into them. Similarly, I have found it beneficial to rehearse other Pärt works at an exaggeratedly slow tempo, partly to infuse into the singers an understanding of the music's inner nature, partly to bring out an awareness of pitch and harmony and the constant local readjustments which each singer must make. It is perhaps no coincidence that I have borrowed these techniques from my experience with early music.

Finally, with regard to barlines, it will be obvious to conductors of the vocal works that the irregular barring reflects purely and simply the number of syllables in each word; it follows that the music's phrasing is irregular, and follows the ebb and flow of the text itself, rather than any fixed metrical scheme. This is a compositional convention that Pärt has followed since the earliest texted tintinnabuli works. In all such cases the barlines do not indicate any kind of stress or emphasis. This is relatively easy for singers to comprehend, as they have the text to guide them (and it is something that singers of Renaissance music are—or should be—accustomed to dealing with).

---

[3] They may listen to the inspired playing of Gidon Kremer and Tatjana Grindenko on the *Tabula Rasa* CD for beautifully tuned playing that generally does not eschew vibrato, but does, at times, dispense with it, with very eloquent results overall.

However, problems can arise for instrumentalists, who have nothing in front of them to differentiate one note from the next in this respect. With small ensembles it may be expedient actually to write in the text, or at least to mark the stressed syllables. The purpose will be not so much to accent these notes as to lighten others. The result should be that every singer and player knows the direction of the phrase at any given moment. With larger ensembles, however, it may be necessary to consider rebarring the music.[4] This issue carries over into those instrumental interludes, of varying lengths, which are in fact also based on the text, and which play a significant and sometimes relatively independent role in larger works such as *Passio*, the *Miserere*, and Te Deum. The conductor will have to decide whether to allow a 'natural' musical phrasing to emerge or to seek information from the relevant portion of text.

In Conclusion

Performers of Pärt's tintinnabuli works stand a good chance of experiencing something not so very common these days, but which used to be an essential ingredient of musical life in earlier times: the excitement of presenting new music to a wide audience and discovering that the lines of communication are completely and appreciatively open. Of course, Pärt is not the only composer of whom this can be said. But he is undoubtedly one of the leading exponents of what I have called 'abstract tonality', and it is thanks to him and to composers like him that the world of 'art' music has been rejuvenated in recent years and occasionally even enjoys popular esteem. Nor has it escaped people's attention that this flush of success has coincided with a surge of interest in chant and early music. This pattern of events should not be dismissed as mere fashion, as it clearly answers a strong need in many people—a spiritual as well as a musical need, and one that goes far beyond nostalgia. The composer's present celebrity may well subside in due course, but this will do little to counter the profound shift in musical sensibility that he has helped liberate. Thanks to Pärt and others, the future of music has been redefined.

Pärt does not provide music for all occasions. He addresses himself almost exclusively to texts having to do with prayer and ritual—even the dramatic story of the Passion is presented as a kind of frieze—and the instrumental works share unmistakably in the same general mood.

---

[4] The Credo of the *Berlin Mass* could be a case in point.

Similarly, what might be called the 'specific density' of his music is so considerable, that a little often goes a long way. Rarely has such acute feeling been wrung from so few notes. But if this description presents a somewhat downcast or introverted image, then something is missing from the picture.

On numerous occasions in his essays, the poet W. H. Auden admonishes us against making superficial connections between an artist and his art. One feels obliged to agree with him, yet not quite. Just as the sound of the poet's voice illuminates his work in a unique manner, so the rhythm (of speech, of movement) of a composer is strongly inflected in his music. This may result in little more than affirmation of what we have already discerned, but sometimes a personal encounter with an artist may bring to our attention some aspect of his art that might otherwise be overlooked. I have refrained from giving a close account of Pärt's life, and although I have alluded occasionally to certain personal memories, these have been kept to a minimum. I feel duty-bound, however, to mention Pärt's delightful sense of humour, which is in danger of being lost beneath a public persona so resolutely connected to the mysterious intensity of his music. A sense of play, of delight in innocence, is not so remote from Pärt as might be imagined. It is true that any overt touches of humour in his music are extremely intermittent, mostly occurring in the earlier, pre-tintinnabuli works. But a sense of humour, in the broadest sense, can be detected in the uplifted exaltation that irradiates the best of his music, and helps bring about a balance between light and dark, so that what might otherwise be sheer heaviness of soul is transformed from an earthbound into a spiritual lightness of being.

LIST OF WORKS* BY ARVO PÄRT

1958	Sonatine Op. 1 No. 1	piano
	Partita Op. 2	piano
1959	Sonatine Op. 1 No. 2	piano
	Meie Aed (*Our Garden*) Op. 3	cantata for children's choir and orchestra
1960	*Nekrolog* Op. 5	orchestra
1963	*Perpetuum Mobile* Op. 10	orchestra
	Symphony No. 1 'Polyphonic'	orchestra
1964	*Diagrams* Op. 11	piano
	Musica Sillabica Op. 12	12 instruments
	Quintettino	fl. ob. cl. hn. bn.
	Solfeggio	S.A.T.B. choir
	Collage sur B-A-C-H	orchestra
1966	*Pro et Contra*	concerto for cello and orchestra
	Symphony No. 2	orchestra
1968	*Credo*	piano, choir, and orchestra
1971	Symphony No. 3	orchestra
1976	*Modus*: see *Sarah Was Ninety Years Old* 1983/90	
	Für Alina (*Aliinale*)	piano
	Trivium	organ
	Pari Intervallo	for instrumental ensemble version for keyboard 1980
	An den Wassern zu Babel sassen wir und weinten (Psalm 137) [= *In Spe* 1976]	(original) version for S.A.T.B. and instruments (picc., ob., cl., bn., hn., vn., va., vc., d.b.) version for S.A.T.B. and organ
	Wenn Bach Bienen gezüchtet hätte (*If Bach had been a Bee-keeper*)	
1977	*Arbos*	chamber ensemble
	Cantate Domino	S.A.T.B. choir and

* This list contains only those works currently recognised by the composer as part of his canon.

		instrumental ensemble or organ
	Fratres	for instrumental ensemble version for chamber ensemble 1978 version for violin and piano 1980 (and numerous subsequent versions)
	Missa Sillabica	S.A.T.B. choir and instrumental ensemble or organ
	Variations (on the recovery of Arinushka)	piano
	Tabula Rasa	double concerto for two violins, string orchestra, and prepared piano
	Cantus in memoriam Benjamin Britten	string orchestra and bell
	Summa	
1978	*Spiegel im Spiegel*	vn. (or vc.) and piano
1980	*De Profundis*	male voice choir, organ, and percussion
	Annum per Annum	organ
1982	*Passio Domini Nostri Jesu Christi Secundum Johannem*	for T. and B. soli, S.A.T.B. quartet, S.A.T.B. chorus, org., ob., bn., vn., vc.
1983	*Sarah was Ninety Years Old* (revised version of *Modus* 1976) (further revised for 1990 recording)	
1984	*Ein Wallfahrtslied*	solo baritone (or tenor) and string quartet
	Es sang vor langen Jahren ('*Motet für de la Motte*')	solo alto, vn., and va.
	Te Deum (1984–5, revised 1986, and further modified for the 1993 recording)	
	Two Slavonic Psalms (Psalms 117 and 131)	S. A. Ct. T. B.
1985	*Stabat Mater*	S.A.T. soli; vn., va., vc.
1988	*Festina Lente*	string orchestra and harp
	Seven Magnificat Antiphons	S.A.T.B. choir
1989	*Miserere*	S.A.T.T.B. soli, choir, organ,

		and 10 instruments
	Magnificat	S.A.T.B. choir
	Nun eile ich zu euch (aus dem Busskanon)	S.A.T.B. soli or choir
	Mein Weg hat Gipfel und Wellentäler	organ
1990	*The Beatitudes*	S.A.T.B. soli or choir and organ
	Berlin Mass	S.A.T.B. soli or choir and organ
		version for choir and string orchestra 1991–2
	Beatus Petronius	2 choirs (S.A.T.B.) and organ
	Statuit ei Dominus	2 choirs (S.A.T.B.) and organ
1991	*Silouan's Song* 'My soul yearns after the Lord'	string orchestra
1992	*Bogoroditse Dyevo*	S.A.T.B. choir
	Adagio (Mozart arr. AP)	piano trio
1992	*And One of the Pharisees*	A.T.B. soli or choir
	Trisagion	string orchestra
1993	*Psalom* (revised version of work composed in 1986)	string quartet
1994	*Litany-Prayers of St John Chrysostom for Each Hour of the Day and the Night*	A.T.T.B. soli, choir, and orchestra
1995	*Memento Mori*	S.A.T.B. choir
1996	I am the True Vine	S.A.T.B. choir

BIBLIOGRAPHY

APEL, WILLI, *Gregorian Chant* (Bloomington, Ind., 1958).

ARMENGAUD, JEAN-PIERRE, *Entretiens avec Denisov* (Paris, 1993).

BATTCOCK, GREGORY, (ed.), *Minimal Art—A Critical Anthology* (New York, 1968).

BRADSHAW, SUSAN, 'Arvo Paart', *Contact*, 26 (1983).

BRUMFIELD, WILLIAM, and VELIMIROVIC, MILOS M. (eds.), *Christianity and the Arts in Russia* (Cambridge, 1991).

BUTLER, DOM CUTHBERT, *Western Mysticism*, 3rd edn. with 'Afterthoughts' and a new Foreword by Prof. David Knowles (London, 1967).

COOMARASWAMY, ANANDA K., *The Transformation of Nature in Art* (Cambridge, Mass., 1934; New York, 1956).

CRAIG-MARTIN, MICHAEL *et al.*, *Minimalism* (Liverpool, 1989).

ELSTE, MARTIN, 'An Interview with Arvo Pärt', *Fanfare*, 11/4 (Mar./Apr. 1988).

EVDOKIMOV, PAUL, *The Art of the Icon: A Theology of Beauty* (Redondo Beach, Calif., 1990).

FISCHER, KURT VON, *Essays in Musicology* (New York, 1989; originally published in German in 1973).

GARDNER, JOHANN VON, *Russian Church Singing*—Vol. 1: *Orthodox Worship and Hymnography*, trans. Vladimir Morosan (New York, 1980).

GERSON-KIWI, EDITH, *Migrations and Mutations of the Music in East and West* (Tel Aviv, 1980).

HAJDU, PETER, *Finno-Ugrian Languages and Peoples*, trans. and ed. G. F. Cushing (London, 1975).

HAPPOLD, F. C., *Mysticism* (London, 1973).

IBISH, YUSUF, and MARCULESCU, ILIANA, *Contemplation and Action in World Religions* (Houston, Tex., 1978).

JOHNSTON, RON, *Bell-ringing* (London, 1986).

LEVIN, NORA, *The Jews in the Soviet Union since 1917* (2 vols., New York, 1988).

LIEVEN, ANATOL, *The Baltic Revolution* (New Haven and London, 1993).

MCCARTHY, JAMIE, 'An Interview with Arvo Pärt', *Musical Times*, 130/1753 (Mar. 1989).

MELTZER, FRANÇOISE, and TRACY, DAVID (guest eds.), *Critical Inquiry*, 20/4 (Summer 1994).

MERRIAM, ALAN P., *Ethnomusicology of the Flathead Indians* (New York, 1967).

MERTENS, WIM, *American Minimal Music* (London and New York, 1983).

MEYENDORFF, JOHN, *A Study of Gregory Palamas*, 2nd edn. (Leighton Buzzard, 1974).

——, *Christ in Eastern Christian Thought* (New York, 1975).

MILOJKOVIC-DJURIC, JELENA, *Aspects of Soviet Culture: Voices of Glasnost, 1960–1990*, East European Monographs no. 307 (New York, 1991).

OLT, HARRY, *Modern Estonian Composers* (Tallinn, 1972).

OUSPENSKY, LEONID, *Theology of the Icon* (2 vols.) (New York, 1992).

PALAMAS, GREGORY, *The Triads*, ed. J. Meyendorff (New York, 1983).

PALMER, G. E. H. *The Philokalia*, compiled by St Nikodemus of the Holy Mountain and St Makarios of Corinth; trans. G. E. H. Palmer, Philip Sherrard, and Kallistos Ware (3 vols., London and Boston, 1979).

PRICE, PERCIVAL, *Bells and Man* (Oxford, 1983).

RAUN, TOIVO U., *Estonia and the Estonians* (Stanford, Calif., 1987).

REICH, STEVE, *Writings* (Halifax, Nova Scotia, and New York, 1974).

SCHWARZ, BORIS, *Music and Musical Life in Soviet Russia 1917–81*, enlarged edn. (Bloomington, Ind., 1983).

SOPHRONY, ARCHIMANDRITE, *Saint Silouan, The Athonite* (Maldon, Essex, 1991).

STRICKLAND, EDWARD, *Minimalism: Origins* (Bloomington, Ind., 1993).

TAAGEPERA, REIN, and MISIUNAS, ROMUALD J., *The Baltic States, Years of Dependence, 1940–1990*, rev. edn. (Berkeley and Los Angeles, 1993).

TARKOVSKY, ANDREY, *Sculpting in Time* (London 1986/9).

UEDA, MAKOTO, *Matsuo Basho* (New York, 1982).

VAITMAA, MERIKE, 'Arvo Pärt', in H. Tauk (ed.), *Kuus Eesti Tänase Muusika Loojat* (*Six Estonian Contemporary Composers*) (Tallinn, 1970).

——, 'The Vocal Compositions of Arvo Pärt', paper presented at the XXIV Baltic Musicologists' Conference, Viljandi 1990 (English version in manuscript kindly made available to me by the author).

WAESBERGHE, J. SMITS VAN, *Cymbala (Bells in the Middle Ages)*, Musicological Studies and Documents No. 1 (Rome, 1951).

WILLIAMS, EDWARD V., *The Bells of Russia* (Princeton, 1985).

ZASLAVSKY, VICTOR, and BRYM, ROBERT J., *Soviet-Jewish Emigration and Soviet Nationality Policy* (London, 1983).

ZHDANOV, ANDREI, *Essays on Literature, Philosophy and Music* (New York, 1950).

DISCOGRAPHY

The core tintinnabuli works are documented in the series of recordings made under the composer's supervision by ECM Records (New Series). Of these, Tabula Rasa serves as an important historical document, bringing together tapes made before and soon after Pärt's emigration—superb performances which served as the catalyst for the subsequent efflorescence of Pärt's music.

Neeme Järvi, who championed Pärt's work during the earlier years, has brought out two invaluable recordings largely devoted to the serial/collage works. There are still some works from this period that await a first CD recording, however. Although I have enjoyed the advantage of hearing Estonian Radio tapes of all the serial and even the student neoclassical works (and similarly, performances by Hortus Musicus of the early tintinnabuli works), sadly, none of these is currently available in any commercial format (and is probably unlikely to be).

Discographies quickly become out of date, and we can be sure that recordings of Pärt's music will proliferate over the next few years. Therefore I have decided to give a principal list of those seven current recordings solely devoted to Pärt which together provide an authoritative introduction to his music. This is then followed by a secondary list of selected recordings which include music by Pärt and other Estonian composers.

Principal Recordings of Music by Arvo Pärt

Tabula Rasa   *Fratres* (violin and piano) / *Cantus* / *Fratres* (for strings) / *Tabula Rasa*
Gidon Kremer and Tatjana Grindenko, violins; Keith Jarrett, piano, Alfred Schnittke, prepared piano; Staatsorchester Stuttgart, Dennis Russell Davies, conductor; 12 cellists of the Berlin Philharmonic Orchestra; Lithuanian Chamber Orchestra, Saulus Sondeckis, conductor
ECM New Series 1275 (1984)

Arbos   *Arbos / An den Wassern zu Babel sassen wir und weinten / Pari Intervallo / De Profundis / Es sang vor langen Jahren / Summa* (for 4 voices) / *Stabat Mater*
The Hilliard Ensemble, Paul Hillier, director; Gidon Kremer, Vladimir Mendelsson, Thomas Demenga;

	Brass Ensemble of the Staatsorchester Stuttgart, Dennis Russell Davies, conductor
	ECM New Series 1325 (1987)
Passio	*Passio Domini Nostri Jesu Christi Secundum Joannem*
	The Hilliard Ensemble, The Western Wind Chamber Choir, Paul Hillier, conductor
	ECM New Series 1370 (1988)
Symphonies	*Pro et Contra / Perpetuum Mobile / Symphony No. 1 / Symphony No. 2 / Symphony No. 3*
	Bamberg Symphony Orchestra, with Frans Helmerson, cello, Neeme Järvi, conductor
	BIS-CD-434 (1989)
Miserere	*Miserere / Festina Lente / Sarah Was Ninety Years Old*
	The Hilliard Ensemble, The Western Wind Chamber Choir and Instrumental Ensemble, Paul Hillier, conductor; Orchester der Beethovenhalle Bonn, Dennis Russell Davies, conductor
	ECM New Series 1430 (1991)
Collage	*Collage sur B-A-C-H / Summa* (for strings) / *Wenn Bach Bienen Gezüchtet Hätte / Fratres* (for strings and percussion) / *Symphony No. 2 / Festina Lente / Credo*
	Philharmonia Orchestra and Chorus, with Boris Berman, piano Neeme Järvi, conductor
	Chandos CHAN 9134 (1993)
Te Deum	*Te Deum / Silouan's Song / Magnificat / Berlin Mass*
	Estonian Philharmonic Chamber Choir; Tallinn Chamber Orchestra, Tõnu Kaljuste, conductor
	ECM New Series 1505 (1993)
	Litany ECM New Series (1996)
De Profundis	*De Profundis / Solfège / Missa Sillabica / Summa* (choral version) / *Magnificat / Cantate Domino / Seven Magnificat Antiphons / And one of the Pharisees / The Beatitudes*
	The Theatre of Voices, Paul Hillier, conductor
	Harmonia Mundi USA HM 7182 (1996)

Other Recordings with Music by Pärt

Music from Estonia, 2 vols. (published separately)

> Volume 1: works by Heino Eller (1887–1970) and Kaljo Raid (b.1922)
>
> Volume 2: works by Heino Eller, Arvo Pärt, Artur Lemba (1885–1963), Rudolf Tobias (1873–1918), and Veljo Tormis (b. 1930)
>
> The Scottish National Orchestra, Neeme Järvi, conductor
>
> Chandos CHAN 1235 (1987) and CHAN 8656 (1989)

Trivium	*Trivium / Mein Weg hat Gipfel und Wellentäler / Annum per Annum / Pari Intervallo* with works by Peter Maxwell Davies and Philip Glass Christopher Bowers-Broadbent, organ ECM New Series (1992)
Ikos	*Magnificat / The Beatitudes* with works by Górecki and Tavener and Gregorian chant Choir of King's College, Cambridge, Stephen Cleobury, conductor Chandos CDC 5 55096 2 (1994)
Annum Per Annum	*Annum per Annum / Pari Intervallo / Mein Weg hat Gipfel und Wellentäler / Trivium* with works by Cage and Scelsi Christoph Maria Moosmann, organ New Albion Records NAO74CD (1995)
Fratres	*Fratres* (6 versions) / *Summa / Festina Lente* I Fiamminghi, Rudolf Werthen, conductor Telarc CD 80387 (1995)
Piano Works	*Aliinale (für Alina) / Variations* with works by Górecki and Ustvolskaya David Arden, piano Koch 3 7301 2H1 (1995)

Recordings of Music by Other Composers

Bells in Russia [Glocken in Russland]
'Original recordings from famous churches and cloisters' (including two from Estonia).
Christophorus CD 74 553 (1988)
Russian Orthodox Church Music: there are now many recordings of this repertoire generally available, though admirers of Pärt's music may find the following performances directed by Anatoly Gridenko to be of special interest:
Chants Orthodoxes . . . Harmonia Mundi France LDC 288003 (1991)
Russian Medieval Chant Opus 111 OPS 30-120 (1994)
Forgotten Peoples by Veljo Tormis
Estonian Philharmonic Chamber Choir, Tõnu Kaljuste, conductor
ECM New Series 1459/60 (1992)
Symphonies Nos. 1–3 by Lepo Sumera (b. 1950)
Malmö Symphony Orchestra; Paavo Järvi, conductor
BIS-CD-660 (1994)
BIS Records have also recorded the complete symphonies and numerous other works by the Estonian composer Eduard Tubin (1905–82), who lived in Sweden after 1944.

INDEX

Certain musical terms which have special significance in Pärt's music are not listed in the index, but are discussed in Chapter 6. These include: *mode, M-voice, pitch-centre, tintinnabuli, T-voice.*

218